Mary Jones and Matthew Parkin

Cambridge International AS & A Level

Biology

Practical Teacher's Guide

CAMBRIDGE
UNIVERSITY PRESS

CAMBRIDGE
UNIVERSITY PRESS

University Printing House, Cambridge CB2 8BS, United Kingdom

One Liberty Plaza, 20th Floor, New York, NY 10006, USA

477 Williamstown Road, Port Melbourne, VIC 3207, Australia

314–321, 3rd Floor, Plot 3, Splendor Forum, Jasola District Centre, New Delhi–110025, India

79 Anson Road, #06–04/06, Singapore 079906

Cambridge University Press is part of the University of Cambridge.

It furthers the University's mission by disseminating knowledge in the pursuit of education, learning and research at the highest international levels of excellence.

www.cambridge.org
Information on this title: www.cambridge.org/9781108524865

First published 2018

20 19 18 17 16 15 14 13 12 11 10 9 8 7 6 5 4 3

Printed in Great Britain by CPI Group (UK) Ltd, Croydon CR0 4YY

A catalogue record for this publication is available from the British Library

ISBN 978-1-108-52486-5 Paperback

Cambridge University Press has no responsibility for the persistence or accuracy of URLs for external or third-party internet websites referred to in this publication, and does not guarantee that any content on such websites is, or will remain, accurate or appropriate. Information regarding prices, travel timetables, and other factual information given in this work is correct at the time of first printing but Cambridge University Press does not guarantee the accuracy of such information thereafter.

All examination-style questions, sample mark schemes, solutions and/or comments that appear in this book were written by the author. In examination, the way marks would be awarded to answers like these may be different.

....

Acknowledgements

Thanks to the following for permission to reproduce images:

Cover Colin Varndell/ SCIENCE PHOTO LIBRARY; Inside Fig 1.3 koosen/Getty Images; Fig 3.9 Goldfinch4ever/Getty Images

Introduction   **v**

Safety   **vi**

AS Practical Skills   **vii**

A Level Practical Skills   **xi**

1 Microscopy   1.1   Making a temporary slide and drawing cells   2
                              1.2   Measuring cells, using an eyepiece graticule and stage micrometer   4
                              1.3   Comparing animal cells and plant cells   6

2 Biological molecules   2.1   The biochemical tests used to identify different biological molecules   9
                              2.2   The semi-quantitative Benedict's test and serial dilutions   12
                              2.3   Using a semi-quantitative iodine test to compare the starch content of
                                    bananas   14

3 Enzymes   3.1   The time-course of an enzyme-catalysed reaction   17
                              3.2   The effect of substrate concentration on the rate of an
                                    enzyme-catalysed reaction   22
                              3.3   The effect of enzyme concentration on the rate of an enzyme-
                                    catalysed reaction   25
                              3.4   The effect of temperature on the rate of an enzyme-catalysed reaction   29
                              3.5   Immobilising urease   32
                              3.6   Investigating the effect of an inhibitor on the action of bromelain   34

**4 Cell membranes and
   transport**   4.1   The effect of salt solutions on eggs   37
                              4.2   Measuring the rate of osmosis using an osmometer   39
                              4.3   The effect of surface area : volume ratio on the rate of diffusion   43
                              4.4   The effect of temperature or concentration gradient on the rate of
                                    diffusion   45
                              4.5   Estimating the water potential of potato tuber cells   48
                              4.6   Estimating the solute potential of onion epidermis cells   50
                              4.7   Determining water potential using density   53
                              4.8   The effect of temperature on membrane permeability   55

**5 Cell division and
   nucleic acids**   5.1   Making a root tip squash   57
                              5.2   Investigating mitosis using prepared slides   59

6 Plant transport   6.1   Drawing low-power plan diagrams of prepared sections of stems
                                    and roots   61
                              6.2   Drawing high-power diagrams of cells and tissues   63
                              6.3   Estimating the rate of water loss through the stomata of a leaf   66
                              6.4   Using a potometer   69

iii

| | 6.5 | Investigating the effect of one factor on the rate of transpiration | 71 |
| | 6.6 | Drawing sections and identifying the tissues of a typical leaf and a xerophytic leaf | 75 |

7 Mammalian transport and gas exchange

	7.1	Identifying and drawing blood cells	77
	7.2	Observing and drawing the structure of the heart	79
	7.3	Observing and drawing the different structures of arteries, veins and capillaries	81
	7.4	Observing and drawing the structure of the respiratory system and its tissues	84

8 Energy and respiration

	8.1	Using a simple respirometer to calculate the respiratory quotient of germinating seeds	89
	8.2	The effect of temperature on the rate of respiration of an invertebrate	93
	8.3	The effect of glucose concentration on the respiration rate of yeast using a redox indicator	98
	8.4	The ability of yeast to use different sugars during fermentation	101

9 Photosynthesis

	9.1	Identification and separation of photosynthetic pigments using paper chromatography	104
	9.2	Effect of light intensity on the rate of photosynthesis	107
	9.3	Gas exchange in a water plant	111
	9.4	The effect of light wavelength on the light dependent reaction (Hill reaction)	113
	9.5	The effect of carbon dioxide concentration on rate of photosynthesis	118

10 Homeostasis and coordination

	10.1	The structure of the kidney	122
	10.2	Analysis of urine	126
	10.3	The role of gibberellic acid in the germination of barley seeds	129
	10.4	The effect of light wavelength on phototropism in wheat seedlings	133
	10.5	Investigating human reflexes	137

11 Inheritance, selection and evolution

	11.1	Studying stages of meiosis in an anther	140
	11.2	Modelling the effects of selection pressure on allele frequency	141
	11.3	Measuring and comparing continuous variation in two sets of leaves	145
	11.4	Investigating tongue-rolling	148
	11.5	Modelling the Hardy–Weinberg equations	149
	11.6	The effects of selective breeding in *Brassica oleracea*	151
	11.7	Comparing vitamin C content in two cultivars of *Brassica oleracea*	152

12 Ecology

	12.1	Using frame quadrats to assess abundance of organisms	155
	12.2	Using frame quadrats to compare biodiversity in two habitats	157
	12.3	Using a transect to investigate distribution and abundance of species	159
	12.4	Investigating a possible correlation between species distribution and an abiotic factor	161
	12.5	Estimating the population size of a small, mobile invertebrate	164

Practical work is an essential part of any advanced Biology course. For Cambridge International AS & A Level Biology, Paper 3 and Paper 5 focus on the assessment of practical skills. In addition, first hand knowledge of specific practical work is required by several learning objectives in the syllabus content, which is assessed on the theory papers.

The practical investigations in the workbook have been carefully chosen to:

- meet the requirements of all the learning objectives that require learners to undertake specific practical activities

- provide progressive guidance and practise in the Assessment Objective 3 (AO3) skills.

The practical skills grid on the following pages summarises the practical skills that are assessed in Paper 3 (AS) and Paper 5 (A level). You can use this grid to search for practical investigations that involve a particular skill. The learning objectives and skills that are supported are also listed at the beginning of each practical investigation.

Practical work is time-consuming but it is an essential part of scientific study. You should expect to spend around one quarter of your teaching time on practical work. For learners, doing a hands-on practical themselves is infinitely more useful than learning about a technique in theory only. Nevertheless, you will probably not be able to do every one of the practical investigations in this workbook, and will need to make a selection of those that you feel are most useful for your learners, and for which you are able to supply equipment and materials.

Biology experiments are notoriously unreliable, in comparison with Chemistry and Physics. This is because we are often dealing with complex systems where we are unable to control all variables adequately, and where measurement techniques may be difficult or imprecise.

Learners do, naturally, want to get the 'right' results. However, this will not always happen, and you and they should not expect it to. The important learning experiences, when carrying out practical work, are the range of skills that are being used and developed – the **processes** of planning, carrying out, observing, recording, analysing and so on. Unexpected results (or even no results at all) should not be dismissed as showing that the experiment 'did not work'. Instead, learners should look back at what they have done, and search for possible reasons for the unexpected results that they have obtained. This in itself is a highly valuable activity, and can encourage the development of higher order thinking skills such as evaluation and analysis. We have provided a set of sample results for each practical investigation, which you can give to learners who have not managed to obtain a complete set of results themselves, so that they can continue to answer all of the questions.

The Practical Investigations in this book have not been designed to reflect the structure of examination questions. This is because these investigations are designed to help learners to **develop** skills, rather than be assessed on them. Learners should also be aware that there is guidance on tackling Paper 3 and Paper 5 in Chapters P1 and P2 of the Coursebook in this series. There are also numerous exercises in the workbook that will help them to develop and practise these skills.

The practical investigations in this resource have been split into various sections, to help you when planning and carrying out these investigations. Where appropriate, tips to support students who may struggle with some aspects of the practical work have been given. These are indicated by this symbol: 🔧. Ideas to challenge more advanced learners have also been included and are indicated by this symbol: ⚙.

Safety of learners, teachers and technicians is paramount when planning and carrying out biology investigations. Most biology investigations have a relatively low level of risk, but even so, potential risks should never be ignored.

It is the responsibility of the biology teacher to carry out a thorough risk assessment before each investigation, and to ensure that learners and technicians are not exposed to any unnecessary risks. This should meet the standards set out by your local authority or educational provider.

The table in the Safety section in the Practical Workbook summarises the main types of risk associated with biology investigations.

It is strongly recommended that you refer to the CLEAPSS website, http://science.cleapss.org.uk/ for information about the risks associated with each chemical that is used in your laboratory, and that you obtain copies of the CLEAPSS Hazcards for each one.

These tell you the type of hazard involved with each chemical, and advice for handling the chemical, and for dealing with spillages or contamination. This information should be available to learners as they work in the laboratory, so that everyone is aware of the risks and how to handle them.

You may also like to download the free Student Safety Sheets from the CLEAPPS website. These can be printed and provided to learners. Word versions are available, so that you can modify these if you wish to suit the particular circumstances in your laboratory.

Cambridge Assessment International Education also provides excellent advice about all aspects of designing and using science laboratories, including safety, in the document *Guide to Planning Practical Science*. You can find this document as a downloadable pdf on the cambridgeinternational.org website.

The following grids map the practical investigations from the workbook to the mark categories for Papers 3 and 5, as listed in the Cambridge International AS & A Level Biology syllabus.

The grids are designed to aid you when planning practical and theory lessons, to ensure learners develop the practical skills required as part of this course.

Manipulation of apparatus, measurement and observation: MMO

Chapter number:	1	2	3	4	5	6	7
Making decisions about measurements							
(a) identify independent and dependent variables			3.2	4.4		6.5	
(b) decide the range and interval of the independent variable and how to achieve this			3.2, 3.4	4.2, 4.4, 4.6		6.5	
(c) decide how to identify a biological molecule, and how to estimate its quantity		2.1, 2.2, 2.3					
(d) describe an appropriate control for an investigation		2.1				6.5	
(e) decide which variables to standardise, and how to do this			3.3, 3.4	4.2, 4.4		6.5	
(f) decide how to measure the dependent variable			3.4	4.2, 4.4		6.5	
(g) use a range of techniques to measure the dependent variable			3.2, 3.3, 3.4, 3.5, 3.6	4.7		6.3, 6.4	
(h) decide on the frequency of measurement of the dependent variable			3.1, 3.2, 3.4	4.2, 4.4		6.5	
(i) decide whether to replicate or repeat measurements			3.4	4.4, 4.7		6.5	
(j) decide on an appropriate number of significant figures for measurements			3.1, 3.3, 3.4, 3.6				
(k) decide how to measure an area using a grid						6.3	
(l) set up a microscope to view and observe specimens, in order to make plan diagrams or draw cells	1.1, 1.2, 1.3			4.6	5.1, 5.2	6.1, 6.2	
(m) draw and label diagrams to show distribution of tissues						6.1, 6.6	7.3, 7.4
(n) identify cells seen through the microscope and label their structures	1.1, 1.3				5.1	6.2, 6.6	7.1, 7.4
(o) stain and make a slide of cells	1.1, 1.3				5.1		
(p) calibrate and use an eyepiece graticule and stage micrometer	1.2, 1.3					6.3	
(q) estimate the number of cells or organelles in a whole slide or field of view using a sample or using a grid					5.2	6.2	

Chapter number:	1	2	3	4	5	6	7
Successfully collecting data and observations							
(a) follow instructions to collect results	1.1, 1.3	2.1, 2.2, 2.3	3.1, 3.2, 3.3, 3.5, 3.6	4.1, 4.2, 4.3, 4.5, 4.6, 4.7, 4.8	5.1, 5.2	6.3. 6.4	7.2, 7.4
(b) assess the risk of a procedure						6.5	
(c) take readings using a range of apparatus			3.1, 3.2, 3.4, 3.5	4.1		6.4, 6.5	
(d) measure using counting				4.6	5.2	6.3	
(e) use clear descriptions of qualitative results		2.1, 2.2, 2.3		4.1, 4.8		6.1, 6.2, 6.6	7.1, 7.2, 7.3, 7.4,
(f) make observations of the distribution of tissues in a specimen, and record as a plan diagram						6.1, 6.6	7.2, 7.3, 7.4
(g) draw cells in a specimen to show correct shapes, thicknesses of cell walls, relative sizes and observable cell contents	1.1, 1.3					6.2	7.1
(h) measure cells and tissue layers using a calibrated eyepiece graticule, scale bars and/or appropriate magnification	1.2, 1.3					6.1, 6.2	
(i) use sampling, a grid and/or tally counts to collect data about the number of cells or cell organelles in a specimen				4.6	5.2	6.3	
(j) observe similarities and differences between two specimens	1.3					6.6	

Presentation of data and observations: PDO

Chapter number:	1	2	3	4	5	6	7
Recording data and observations							
(a) record raw data in a fully ruled table		2.1	3.1, 3.2, 3.3, 3.4, 3.5, 3.6	4.2, 4.3, 4.7, 4.8	5.2	6.3	
(b) prepare a results table with headings for independent and dependent variable and units in headings		2.1	3.2, 3.4, 3.5, 3.6	4.2, 4.3, 4.4, 4.7, 4.8			
(c) record quantitative data to an appropriate number of significant figures			3.1, 3.2, 3.3, 3.4, 3.6	4.1, 4.2, 4.3, 4.4			
(d) record qualitative data using clear descriptions		2.1, 2.2, 2.3		4.1, 4.8		6.1, 6.2	7.2
(e) draw plan diagrams to record detailed shapes and positions of tissue layers seen on a microscope slide or micrograph						6.1, 6.6	7.3, 7.4
(f) draw diagrams to show detail of individual cells seen on a microscope slide or micrograph	1.1, 1.3	2.1			5.1	6.2	7.1

Chapter number:	1	2	3	4	5	6	7
Displaying calculations and reasoning							
(a) show all the steps in a calculation			3.1, 3.2	4.1		6.3, 6.4	
(b) show all steps in calculations involving the calibration of an eyepiece graticule, finding the actual size of a specimen and/or linear magnification	1.2, 1.3					6.3	
(c) show all steps in calculations involving finding a total number from a sample, finding a mean, and determining the simplest ratio	1.2, 1.3					6.3, 6.5	
Layout of data or observations							
(a) select whether to display data as a graph or chart							
(b) decide which variable to place on which axis			3.2, 3.3, 3.4	4.2, 4.4, 4.5, 4.6		6.5	
(c) select suitable scales for graph axes and label graph axes fully including units			3.1, 3.2, 3.3, 3.4	4.1, 4.2, 4.4, 4.5, 4.6		6.5	
(d) plot points accurately, either as a small cross or an encircled dot			3.1, 3.2, 3.3	4.1, 4.2, 4.4, 4.5, 4.6		6.5	
(e) connect points with a best-fit line, a smooth curve or a set of ruled straight lines to join the points			3.1, 3.2, 3.3, 3.4	4.1, 4.2, 4.4, 4.5, 4.6		6.5	
(f) plot bar charts accurately, using a thin ruled line for the bars				4.1	5.2		
(g) decide whether to separate the bars, or to join the bars on a bar chart					5.2		
(h) make unshaded drawings with finely drawn, unbroken lines that use most of the available space and show all relevant features	1.1, 1.3					6.1, 6.2, 6.6	
(i) organise comparative observations to show differences and/or similarities	1.3	2.2, 2.3				6.6	

Analysis, conclusions and evaluation: ACE

Chapter number:	1	2	3	4	5	6	7
Interpreting data or observations and identifying sources of error							
(a) use quantitative results or provided data to calculate an answer using the correct number of significant figures			3.1, 3.2	4.1, 4.2, 4.3, 4.5, 4.6	5.2		
(b) find an unknown value from a graph			3.1, 3.2	4.5, 4.6			
(c) estimate the concentration of an unknown solution from qualitative results		2.2, 2.3		4.7		2.2, 2.3	
(d) identify the contents of unknown solutions using biological molecule tests		2.1, 2.2, 2.3				2.1, 2.2, 2.3	
(e) identify and deal appropriately with anomalous results			3.1, 3.2, 3.3, 3.4	4.1, 4.4, 4.5, 4.6			

Chapter number:	1	2	3	4	5	6	7
(f) describe patterns and trends in results			3.1, 3.2, 3.3, 3.4, 3.6	4.1, 4.2, 4,3, 4.4, 4.5, 4.6, 4.7, 4.8			
(g) identify significant sources of error in an investigation, and determine whether these are systematic or random errors		2.2, 2.3	3.1, 3.2, 3.3, 3.6	4.1, 4.2, 4.4, 4.6		2.2, 2.3	
(h) calculate actual or percentage error				4.2			
(i) estimate and evaluate the effect of errors on the confidence with which conclusions may be made		2.2, 2.3	3.1	4.4, 4.5, 4.6, 4.7		2.2, 2.3	
(j) calculate correct answers, to the correct number of significant figures, relating to size and magnification of specimens	1.2						
(k) compare observable features of specimens, using micrographs and prepared microscope slides	1.1, 1.3						
Drawing conclusions							
(a) make conclusions		2.1, 2.2, 2.3	3.2, 3.3, 3.4	4.2, 4.4, 4.6, 4.7, 4.8		6.3, 6.5	7.2, 7.3
(b) make scientific explanations using knowledge and understanding		2.3	3.1, 3.2, 3.3, 3.4, 3.5, 3.6	4.1, 4.7, 4.8		6.3, 6.5	
(c) give scientific explanations of observations of specimens, calculated values, and adaptations of a specimen for a particular habitat		2.1, 2.2, 2.3				6.6	7.3, 7.4
Suggesting improvements or modifications to extend an investigation							
(a) suggest how to better standardise relevant variables to improve an investigation		2.3	3.2, 3.6	4.8		6.3	
(b) suggest how to use a different measurement method to improve an investigation		2.3	3.2, 3.3, 3.6	4.8			
(c) suggest how to use replicates to obtain more data and calculate a mean			3.2, 3.3, 3.6	4.8	5.2	6.5	
(d) suggest how to modify or extend an investigation to answer a new question		2.3	3.4	4.8			
(e) suggest improvements to a procedure that will increase the accuracy of observations, including using measurement methods with smaller intervals		2.3	3.2, 3.3, 3.4, 3.6	4.8		6.3	

Planning: P

Chapter number:	8	9	10	11	12
Defining the problem					
(a) express the aim of an experiment or investigation as a quantifiable, testable, falsifiable prediction or hypothesis	8.2		10.1, 10.5	11.4, 11.5, 11.7	12.4
(b) identify the independent variable(s)	8.2	9.1, 9.4, 9.5	10.1	11.4, 11.7	
(c) identify the dependent variable(s)	8.2	9.1, 9.4, 9.5	10.1	11.4, 11.7	
(d) where the dependent variable cannot be measured directly, identify a measurable feature or aspect in the investigation	8.2	9.3, 9.4		11.7	
(e) identify the **key** variables to be standardised	8.1, 8.2	9.1, 9.2, 9.4	10.1	11.4, 11.5, 11.7	
Methods					
(a) use information provided in a scenario to describe how to vary the independent variable with accuracy	8.2		10.1	11.4	
(b) use information provided in a scenario to describe how to measure the dependent variable, including measuring instruments to use and a suitable number of significant figures	8.1, 8.2	9.1, 9.2, 9.4	10.1	11.4, 11.7	
(c) describe appropriate methods for standardising each of the other key variables	8.2	9.1, 9.2	10.1	11.7	
(d) describe suitable volumes and concentrations of reagents, including how to prepare different concentrations in % (w / v) and / or mol dm^{-3}	8.3	9.5	10.2	11.7	
(e) describe how to make different concentrations of solution using serial dilution or proportional dilution	8.3	9.5	10.2		
(f) describe any appropriate control experiments	8.1, 8.2	9.3	10.1		
(g) describe, in a logical sequence, the steps involved in the procedure	8.2, 8.4	9.1, 9.2	10.1, 10.5	11.4, 11.5, 11.7	12.4
(h) describe how to ensure the quality of results by considering any anomalous results, and the spread of results by inspection	8.1, 8.2	9.2	10.3	11.7	
(i) describe how to use standard deviation, standard error or 95% confidence intervals to assess the quality of results			10.3	11.7	
(j) describe how to ensure the validity of results by considering success of measuring the dependent variable and the precision required	8.2	9.2	10.3	11.4, 11.7	
(k) assess the risks involved in a procedure, identify areas where accident or injury is most likely and most serious	8.2			11.4, 11.7	12.4
(l) describe suitable precautions to minimise risk	8.2			11.4, 11.7	12.4

Analysis, conclusions and evaluation: ACE

Chapter number:	8	9	10	11	12
Dealing with data					
(a) decide which calculations are necessary to draw conclusions, including error levels, confidence limits and statistical tests	8.2		10.3, 10.5	11.2, 11.4, 11.5, 11.7	12.4
(b) use tables and graphs to identify key points in quantitative data, including their variability	8.1, 8.2, 8.4	9.1, 9.2, 9.4	10.3, 10.4, 10.5	11.2, 11.3, 11.4, 11.7	
(c) sketch or draw suitable graphs, including confidence limit error bars, calculated using standard error	8.2	9.2, 9.4	10.4,	11.2, 11.3, 11.4, 11.7	12.3
(d) choose appropriate calculations to simplify or explain data	8.2	9.2	10.2, 10.3, 10.4, 10.5	11.4, 11.7	
(e) carry out calculations to compare data, including percentage, percentage gain or loss and rate of change	8.1, 8.2	9.2	10.2, 10.4, 10.5	11.2, 11.3, 11.7	
(f) calculate species diversity index					12.2
(g) carry out calculations to estimate population size					12.1
(h) use standard deviation or standard error, or graphs with standard error bars, to determine whether differences between mean values are likely to be statistically significant			10.3	11.3, 11.7	
(i) choose statistical tests appropriate to the type of data collected, and justify the choice				11.4, 11.7	12.4
(j) state a null hypothesis for a statistical test			10.5	11.3, 11.7	
(k) use the t-test appropriately			10.5	11.3, 11.7	
(l) use the chi-squared test appropriately					
(m) use Pearson's linear correlation appropriately					12.4
(n) use Spearman's rank correlation appropriately	8.2	9.2			12.4
(o) calculate the degrees of freedom for a data set				11.3, 11.7	
(p) use a probability table to determine the significance of a calculated value for the t-test and the chi-squared test			10.5	11.3, 11.7	
(q) recognise the different types of variable (qualitative: categoric or ordered and quantitative) and the different types of data presented					
Evaluation					
(a) identify anomalous values in given data and suggest how to deal with them	8.1, 8.2, 8.3	9.2	10.3, 10.5	11.2, 11.5	
(b) suggest possible explanations for anomalous readings	8.1, 8.2	9.2	10.3		
(c) assess whether provided data has been replicated sufficiently, and whether the range and interval of the independent variable were suitable	8.3, 8.4	9.2, 9.4			12.2
(d) explain why replicating data is important and the practical limits on replication	8.2	9.4	10.5	11.4, 11.7	12.1
(e) identify instances where more measurements need to be taken with an increased or decreased value of the independent variable to provide a wider range of values	8.2, 8.3	9.4			
(f) identify instances where more measurements need to be taken within the original range of the independent variable, to provide more detailed information	8.2	9.2, 9.4			

Chapter number:	8	9	10	11	12
(g) assess whether the method of measurement of the dependent variable is appropriate	8.1, 8.3	9.1, 9.5		11.4	
(h) assess the extent to which other variables have been effectively standardised	8.2	9.2		11.4	
(i) use evaluations to make informed judgements about how much confidence can be placed in conclusions	8.2	9.2, 9.3	10.3, 10.4, 10.5	11.4, 11.5, 11.7	12.1, 12.2
(j) use evaluations to make informed judgements about the validity of the investigation	8.3	9.2, 9.3	10.3, 10.5	11.4, 11.5	12.4
(k) use evaluations to make informed judgements about the extent to which the data can be trusted for testing the hypothesis		9.2	10.3, 10.5	11.5	12.4
Conclusions					
(a) make conclusions that include key points of the raw data, processed data, graphical representations and statistical test results	8.1, 8.2, 8.3, 8.4	9.2, 9.5	10.2, 10.4	11.2, 11.4, 11.5, 11.7	12.4
(b) quote relevant figures from raw or processed data	8.1, 8.2	9.2, 9.5	10.2, 10.3	11.5, 11.7	12.4
(c) decide whether a given hypothesis is fully supported or not supported by the experimental data	8.2			11.3, 11.5, 11.7	
(d) identify strengths and weaknesses of any support for or against the hypothesis	8.2	9.4		11.7	
(e) give detailed scientific explanations of the data and conclusions	8.1, 8.2, 8.3, 8.4	9.1, 9.2, 9.4	10.1, 10.2		12.3
(f) make further predictions and hypotheses, based on conclusions		9.1			12.4
(g) make relevant suggestions about how an experiment could be improved	8.2	9.3	10.4, 10.5	10.2, 11.4, 11.5, 11.7	12.2, 12.5

Chapter outline

This chapter relates to Chapter 1: Cell structure in the coursebook.

In this chapter, learners will complete practical investigations on:

■ 1.1 Making a temporary slide and drawing cells

■ 1.2 Measuring cells, using an eyepiece graticule and stage micrometer

■ 1.3 Comparing animal cells and plant cells

Practical investigation 1.1:
Making a temporary slide and drawing cells

Learning objective: 1.1(a)

Skills focus

The following skill areas are developed and practised (see the skills grids at the front of this guide):

MMO	Making decisions about measurements: (l), (m), (n), (o)
	Successfully collecting data and observations: (a), (g)
PDO	Recording data and observations: (f)
	Layout of data or observations: (h)

Duration

This practical is likely to take around 1 h. Learners who are not familiar with using a microscope may need a little longer.

Preparing for the investigation

- Most learners will have used a microscope before, but some may not. It is also likely that the microscopes available for them to use in the ASAL course are different from those used in previous courses. You may like to demonstrate the use of the microscopes before asking learners to explore their own.

- It is generally a good idea to allocate a particular microscope to each learner, or to a pair of learners, and for them to use the same microscope each time.

This can help them to become very familiar with it, and also encourages them to be responsible for taking good care of it. However, if learners will eventually be taking their practical examination in an unfamiliar laboratory using unfamiliar microscopes, you may prefer to ensure that each learner has experience using a different kind of microscope from time to time.

- For assessment of the learners' drawings in Part 2, you could provide a list of criteria and ask learners to exchange drawings with each other and assess the drawings against the list. See Table 1.1 for a sample assessment sheet. This encourages them to think hard about these criteria, and involves them more closely in their own learning than if you simply mark their drawings and provide feedback. Later, you can add your own assessments to their work.

- Note that this diagram is a high-power detail, showing individual cells and the structures within them. It is suggested that you do not introduce this term until later, when learners learn how to draw low-power plans that show tissues only, with no individual cells.

Equipment

Each learner or group will need:

- a light microscope, preferably a high quality A level-type microscope equipped with a ×10 eyepiece and at least two objective lenses

- a source of illumination (this could be built into the microscope, or a lamp, or bright light from a window)

- two or three microscope slides

- two or three coverslips

- a dropper pipette
- a mounted needle or seeker
- forceps (tweezers)
- sharp scissors or a blade (safety razor or scalpel)
- filter paper or paper towel
- tile

- some pieces cut from an onion bulb
- a medium-hard (HB) pencil
- a good quality eraser

Access to:

- iodine in potassium iodide solution

Feature of drawing	How well was this achieved?	Comment
takes up at least half of the space available		
drawn using a sharp pencil		
all lines are clear and single, with no overlaps and no gaps		
cell walls are shown as double lines		
proportions of different structures are correct		
there is no shading		
label lines are drawn with a ruler and touch what they are labelling		
labels are written clearly and do not overlap the drawing		

Table 1.1

Additional notes and advice

- You could either provide whole onion bulbs for learners to use, or you could cut sections from the layers in the bulbs and place these in beakers of water, ready for them to use.

- Microscopes should be the best quality that your school can afford. It is frustrating for learners to have to use microscopes that do not focus clearly. Ensure that microscopes are regularly serviced and checked.

Safety considerations

- Learners should have read the safety guidance section within the workbook before carrying out this investigation.

- Standard laboratory safety procedures should be followed always.

- Learners should be shown how to handle a sharp blade safely.

- Iodine in potassium iodide solution generally contains ethanol as a solvent and may therefore be flammable. Learners should wear eye protection and wash off any spills on their skin or clothes. (Unlike solid iodine, this solution does not produce iodine vapour.) Low hazard.

Carrying out the investigation

- It is unlikely that any major problems will occur. Learners may have difficulty in spreading out the epidermis in the drop of water without folding it, but with practice this is generally achieved by most.

- It is possible that the onion cells may contain starch grains; if so, these will stain dark blue when the iodine is added. However, starch grains are not always present, so learners should not be surprised if there are none.

- There is a strong tendency for many learners to be so focused on 'getting it right' that they may draw an idealised diagram of the epidermis, rather than drawing what they can see. It is important to emphasise that they are being asked to **observe carefully** and to **record their observations**. This exercise is all about developing these practical skills, not their recall of the structure of plant cells. If possible, move around and look at the learners' slides through their microscopes, and compare their drawings with what they can see.

  Learners who finish within the allocated time, and have made diagrams that you consider to be good quality, could be provided with a prepared slide of TS root and asked to draw three or four cortex cells.

3

Sample results

Method

Part 2

3

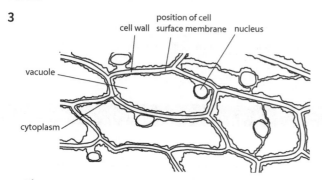

Figure 1.1

4 See Figure 1.1.

Part 3

3 It is possible that the onion cells may contain starch grains; if so, these will stain dark blue when the iodine is added. However, starch grains are not always present, so learners should not be surprised if there are none.

Practical investigation 1.2: Measuring cells, using an eyepiece graticule and stage micrometer

Learning objective: 1.1(b) and (c)

Skills focus

The following skill areas are developed and practised (see the skills grids at the front of this guide):

MMO	Making decisions about measurements: (l), (p) Successfully collecting data and observations: (a), (h)
PDO	Recording data and observations: (c)
	Displaying calculations and reasoning: (b)
ACE	Interpreting data or observations and identifying sources of error: (a), (j)

Duration

This practical is likely to take 1 h. You may like to extend this time to provide more practice in using a graticule and micrometer.

Preparing for the investigation

- Learners often become confused when using an eyepiece graticule and stage micrometer. It could be helpful to use Exercise 1.5, in the Cambridge AS & A level Biology workbook, *Using an eyepiece graticule and stage micrometer*, to practise this skill theoretically before doing this investigation. On the other hand, some learners may understand the procedures more easily when they are actually handling the graticule and micrometer themselves.

- Eyepiece graticules can be obtained relatively cheaply, but stage micrometers tend to be expensive. Cambridge Assessment International Education supply a low cost kit for you to make your own. You can download the publications list from the cambridgeinternational.org website. Click on the 'support for teachers' tab. This list also includes many different prepared slides.

- The instructions ask learners to make their first set of measurements using a prepared slide of a transverse section through a leaf. This ensures that they are looking at some clearly visible cells, and also may be more interesting for them than spending yet more time looking at onion epidermis cells. However, you (and they) may prefer to make the measurements using the onion epidermis cells first. Either sequence is fine.

- If learners always use the same microscope, then once they have calibrated a particular objective lens, they can use this calibration for all future measurements using that same objective lens and same eyepiece. Note, however, that a new calibration will be required for each of the objective lenses.

Equipment

Each learner or group will need:

- a microscope, with a graticule in the eyepiece

- prepared slide of section through a leaf

- onion epidermis slide from Practical investigation 1.1 (or a new one can be made)

Access to:

- a stage micrometer

Safety considerations

- Learners should have read the safety guidance section of the workbook before carrying out this investigation.

- Standard laboratory safety procedures should be followed always.

- There are no additional significant safety issues associated with this investigation.

Carrying out the investigation

Some learners may become confused about which scale they are looking at. Swivelling the eyepiece causes the eyepiece graticule scale to move but not the stage micrometer scale.

Learners can often carry out each step in the measurement and calibration when following instructions, but find it difficult to remember what to do when they need to think about this for themselves. Step-by-step instructions are provided for measuring the palisade cells, but not the onion epidermis cells. You could provide a 'help sheet' to take learners through, step-by-step, when measuring the onion epidermis cells. For some learners, it could be valuable to repeat this several times, measuring different types of cell each time.

Some learners may have difficulty converting mm to μm, or may forget to do so when calculating magnification. See *Exercise 1.1, Units for measuring small objects*, and *Exercise 1.2, Magnification calculations*, in the Cambridge AS & A level Biology workbook, for guidance and practise in doing this.

Sample results

Part 1

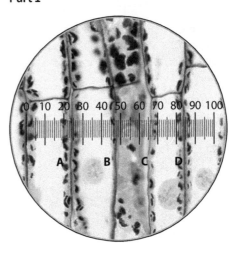

Answers to the workbook questions (using the sample results)

Part 1

5 Four palisade cells measure 84 graticule units.

Part 2

3 Alignments at 0,0 and 80, 0.24.

4 24 small divisions on the stage micrometer scale = 24 × 10 μm = 240 μm

This equals 80 divisions on the eyepiece graticule scale.

So 1 division on the eyepiece graticule scale = 240 ÷ 80 = 3 μm.

5 Using the answer to Part 1 Question 5, 84 graticule units = 3 × 84 μm = 252 μm.

6 This was the width of 4 cells, so the mean width of one cell is 252 ÷ 4 = 63 μm.

7 Sample value for the width of 6 onion epidermis cells = 156 graticule units.

8 156 graticule units = 156 × 3 = 468 μm

So the mean width of one onion epidermis cell = 468 ÷ 6 = 78 μm.

Part 3

1 The answer will depend on the learner's drawing.

2 The answer will depend on the width of the drawing measured in 1. Their calculation here should be:

magnification = size of drawing ÷ size of actual cell(s)

The answer should be given as a number with a **x** sign in front of it, and no units, for example, **×40**.

Practical investigation 1.3:
Comparing animal cells and plant cells

Learning objective: 1.1(a)

Skills focus

The following skills are developed and practised (see the skills grids at the front of this guide):

MMO   Making decisions about measurements: (l), (m), (n), (o), (p)
        Successfully collecting data and observations: (a), (g), (h), (j)

PDO   Recording data and observations: (c), (f)
        Displaying calculations and reasoning: (b)
        Layout of data or observations: (h), (i)

ACE   Interpreting data or observations and identifying sources of error: (a), (j), (k)

Duration

This practical is likely to take about 1 h.

Preparing for the investigation

- Learners should be quite confident using a microscope by now, and should also be beginning to build confidence in using an eyepiece graticule and stage micrometer to make measurements. They can now use these skills to compare the appearance of three types of cell.

- If learners move straight into this activity from Practical investigation 1.1 or 1.2, they will already have temporary slides of onion epidermis. If not, they will need to make a new slide.

Equipment

Each learner or group will need:

- a microscope, with a graticule in the eyepiece

- prepared slide of section through a leaf

- onion epidermis slide from Practical investigation 1.1 (or a new one can be made)

- clean microscope slides and cover slips

- dropper pipette

- iodine in potassium iodide solution

- methylene blue stain

- cotton bud or similar

Access to:

- a stage micrometer

Additional notes and advice

- Check local regulations about the use of human cheek cells. If this is not possible, then you can try scraping cells from the inner surface of a trachea from an animal such as a sheep (obtainable from a butcher).

- Cotton buds are compacted cotton wool attached to the end of a short plastic stick (Figure 1.3). They can generally be obtained from pharmacies or supermarkets, where they are sold for use with cosmetics or for baby bathing.

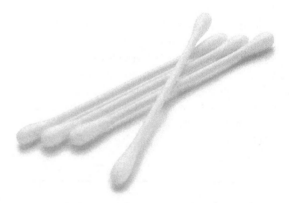

Figure 1.3

- Methylene blue stain can be bought from biological suppliers. It is very commonly used as a vital stain (i.e. one that is taken up by living cells) in temporary slides. If you have difficulty obtaining it from a biological supplier, you may be able to buy it from a shop selling fish for people to keep in ponds or tanks, where it is used as a treatment for fungal infections of fish. However, the concentration of the stain from this source may not be ideal for staining cells.

Safety considerations

- Learners should have read the safety guidance section within the workbook before carrying out this investigation.

- Standard laboratory safety procedures should be followed always.

- Ensure that cotton buds are placed into a container of disinfectant (e.g. Lysol) immediately after use. This prevents the unlikely event of pathogenic bacteria being transferred from the mouth of one learner to another.

- Make sure that learners understand that they should simply run the cotton bud gently over the inner surface of their cheek. They should **not** dig the bud into the skin. There will be loose cells on the cheek surface which will readily adhere to the cotton wool.

- Methylene blue is classed as harmful (it is a reducing agent, and has various uses in medicine). Learners should avoid getting it on their skin or clothes, and should wear eye protection. If it does stain fingers, however, it is very unlikely to cause any harm.

Carrying out the investigation

- When making the cheek cell mount, learners may be puzzled that they cannot see anything on the microscope slide when they have rubbed the cotton bud onto it. They should continue with adding the stain; in most cases, cells will then become visible.

- Learners may have difficulty in locating the stained cells on the slide. They should be reminded to begin with the lowest power objective lens, and search the slide systematically until they see something. They can then move onto a higher power lens to look for individual cells.

- Some learners may construct their comparison table using what they **know** about cells, rather than using what they can **observe and measure**. This will become obvious if they mention structures such as cell membranes or endoplasmic reticulum, which they will not be able to see.

  Some learners may need more support in constructing the comparison table. You could consider having a 'help sheet' available with an outline table for them to copy or complete, perhaps with one or two rows already filled in for them.

  Learners who require a challenge could work in a group to research the functions of these three types of cell, and consider how each is adapted to its functions.

Sample results

Part 1

5

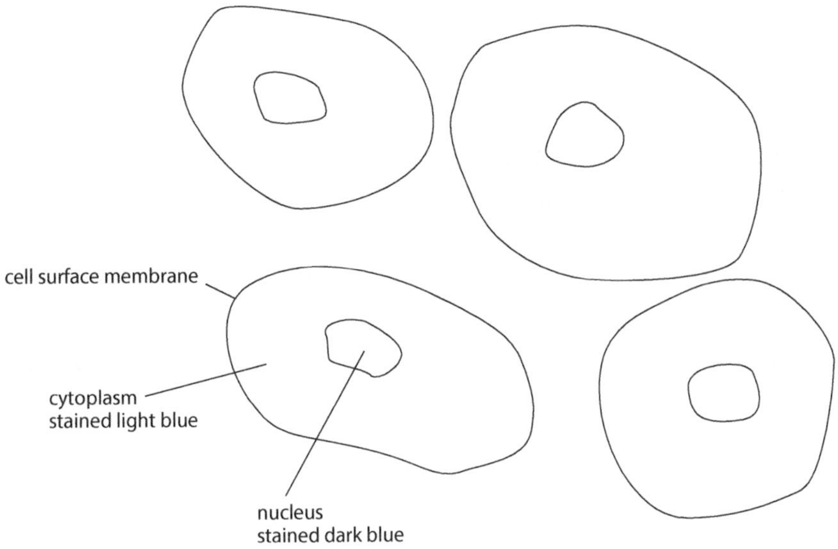

Figure 1.4

Answers to the workbook questions (using the sample results)

Part 1

6   Width of cheek cells in eyepiece graticule units: 14, 11, 13

Mean width of one cheek cell = 12.7 eyepiece graticule units

7   Using the same conversion factor as in Practical investigation 1.2, one division on the eyepiece graticule scale = 3 μm.

8   Therefore the mean width of one cheek cell = 38.1 μm.

9   Learners should measure each of the three cheek cells they have drawn along exactly the same positions as they made the measurements on the microscope slide. The measurement should be made in mm.

They should then calculate the mean width of the three cheek cells they have drawn, in mm.

The calculation is then:

$$\text{magnification of drawing} = \frac{\text{mean width of cheek cells in drawing in mm} \times 1000}{\text{mean width of cheek cells in answer to 9}}$$

The magnification should be given as a whole number, preceded by the × sign, and with no units.

Part 2

Answers will depend on the learner's observations and measurements. Some possible table entries are given in Table 1.2:

Feature	Onion cells	Palisade cells	Cheek cells
mean diameter / μm	78 μm	63 μm	38.1 μm
cell wall present	yes	yes	no
cytoplasm present	yes	yes	yes
chloroplasts present	no	yes	no
nucleus present	yes	yes	yes
position of nucleus	near the side of the cell	near the side of the cell	approximately central
shape of cell	approximately rectangular	approximately rectangular	approximately circular
large vacuole present	yes	yes	no
cell grouping	cells joined to one another	cells joined to one another	cells not joined

Table 1.2

This chapter relates to Chapter 2: Biological molecules in the coursebook.

In this chapter, learners will complete practical investigations on:

- 2.1 The biochemical tests used to identify different biological molecules
- 2.2 The semi-quantitative Benedict's test and serial dilutions
- 2.3 Using a semi-quantitative iodine test to compare the starch content of bananas

Practical investigation 2.1:
The biochemical tests used to identify different biological molecules

Learning objective: 2.1(a)

Skills focus

The following skill areas are developed and practised (see the skills grids at the front of this guide):

MMO	Making decisions about measurements: (c), (d)
	Successfully collecting data and observations: (a), (e)
PDO	Recording data and observations: (a), (b), (d)
ACE	Interpreting data or observations and identifying sources of error: (d)
	Drawing conclusions: (a)

Duration

The work should take approximately 1 h to complete but it could be split over two lessons if time is an issue.

Preparing for the investigation

- The practical work in this investigation is quite simple although learners will need to work through it methodically.

- Learners should know how to set up Bunsen burners safely. They will need to be shown how if they have not used them before.

- Most of the investigation is based upon observation and the recording of qualitative results.

- Learners should understand the main groups of biological molecules: carbohydrates (monosaccharides such as glucose, fructose, galactose; disaccharides such as sucrose, maltose and lactose and polysaccharides such as starch), proteins and lipids.

- Many test tubes are needed and learners should be encouraged to wash them out thoroughly between experiments. The emulsion test should be done last as it is difficult to remove all traces.

- The emulsion test for lipids should only be carried out at the end when all naked flames are extinguished.

Equipment

Each learner or group will need:

- minimum of 10 test tubes

- test-tube rack

- Bunsen burner, tripod, gauze and heat-proof tile (alternatively, whole class thermostatically controlled water baths may be used set to 85°C)

- test-tube holder

- glass beakers, 500 cm^3 and 50 cm^3

- pipette, 10 cm^3, and pipette filler (if pipettes are not available, small measuring cylinders or syringes may be used)

- Benedict's solution, 25 cm^3

- biuret solution, 25 cm^3

- iodine solution in a dropper bottle

- ethanol, 20 cm^3

- distilled water, 50 cm^3

- dilute hydrochloric acid (2M) in a dropper bottle

- sodium hydrogencarbonate (solid)

- spatula

- 20 cm³ 1% starch solution

- 20 cm³ 1% protein solution (albumin or casein)

- vegetable oil (any oil such as olive oil or sunflower oil. Avoid nut oils to reduce risk of allergic reactions)

- 20 cm³ 10% glucose

- 20 cm³ 10% fructose

- 20 cm³ 10% sucrose

- 20 cm³ 10% lactose

- 20 cm³ 10% maltose

- 20 cm³ 'unknown' solutions X, Y and Z

Additional notes and advice

Stock solutions

- Benedict's solution may be purchased ready made from suppliers. To make 1 dm⁻³, dissolve 170 g sodium citrate crystals and 100 g sodium carbonate crystals in 800 cm³ warm distilled water. In a separate beaker, dissolve 17.0 g copper(II) sulfate crystals in 200 cm³ cold distilled water. Mix both solutions whilst constantly stirring.

- Biuret solution may be purchased ready made from suppliers. If it is not available, separate solutions of sodium hydroxide and copper sulfate may be used. Sodium hydroxide concentrations of between 1 and 2 dm⁻³ should work and a 1% solution of copper(II) sulfate made in distilled water is then added. Biuret solution should not be stored for long periods in glass bottles.

- Iodine solution may be purchased ready made from suppliers. To make 100 cm³ iodine solution, grind 1 g iodine and 1 g potassium iodide in a mortar, gradually adding distilled water to dissolve the crystals. Pour the solution into a measuring cylinder and make up to 100 cm³ with distilled water.

- 2 mol dm⁻³ hydrochloric acid. Dilute 200 cm³ concentrated hydrochloric acid with 800 cm³ distilled water.

- 1% starch solution. To make 500 cm³, add 5 g soluble starch powder to approximately 300 cm³ distilled water in a beaker. Heat to boiling point until all the starch dissolves then make up the solution to 500 cm³ with cold distilled water. Store in refrigerator and use within two days.

- 1% protein solution. Either albumin or casein can be used. Slowly dissolve 1 g commercial albumin powder in 100 cm³ cold water (it will take time). Alternatively, use a 1 in 10 dilution of raw egg white. For a 1% casein solution, dissolve 1 g casein powder in 100 cm³ distilled water. Alternatively, powdered milk can be used but at slightly higher concentrations. Store in refrigerator.

- 1% glucose (and other sugars). To make 100 cm³, weigh out 1 g of sugar and make up to 100 cm³ with cold distilled water. Store in refrigerator for up to two weeks.

- Solution X: To make 100 cm³, weigh out 1 g glucose, 1 g albumin. Dissolve in 100 cm³ distilled water.

- Solution Y: To make 100 cm³, weigh out 1 g sucrose. Dissolve in 100 cm³ distilled water.

- Solution Z: To make 100 cm³, weigh out 1 g glucose, 1 g starch. Dissolve in 100 cm³ distilled water.

Safety considerations

- Learners should have read the safety section within the workbook before carrying out this investigation.

- Standard laboratory safety procedures should be followed always.

- Before carrying out the emulsion test all naked flames should be extinguished. This is extremely important as ethanol is highly flammable.

- When making up the solutions, special care should be taken with substances such as concentrated hydrochloric acid, sodium hydroxide and solid iodine.

- Eye protection should be worn always.

- Iodine solution should not be poured into natural water as it is harmful to aquatic organisms.

- If concentrated acids and alkalis are used when making up the solutions, extra care should be taken: high quality eye protection should be used and protective gloves.

- Some learners may be allergic to certain oils. Do not use oils such as groundnut / almond / peanut oil.

Carrying out the investigation

- It is important to trial the tests before the investigation to ensure that they give the correct results.

- If starch is kept for too long it can begin to break down, releasing glucose. It should be made up fresh and stored for only up to two days in the refrigerator.

- Biuret solution should not be kept for long periods in glass bottles as it will react with the glass and stop working.

- Test tubes should be rinsed out carefully but after reducing sugar tests there may be a residue that will not come off easily. It is advisable to have many other clean test tubes.

- Learners should be reminded that it is important to wash out pipettes thoroughly between different solutions.

- Sucrose can sometimes be contaminated with glucose and so give a positive reducing sugar test – it should be tested before the experiment.

- The reducing sugar test should have shown that sucrose did not cause Benedict's solution to change colour. To carry out a non-reducing sugar test, it is important that a negative result is obtained with the reducing sugar test before proceeding.

Help should be provided for any learners with physical disabilities in the laboratory when using boiling water baths. It is good practice to not sit down in the event of boiling water being spilled. Where this is not possible (for example, with learners who are in a wheelchair), alternative provisions such as thermostatically controlled water baths can be used.

Colour-blind learners may have difficulty discriminating between the colours of the Benedict's test. They may need another learner to read out colours.

Learners could be encouraged to trial food items that are available to identify the molecules – care should be taken to avoid risk of allergies.

As an extension activity, learners should try carrying out reducing sugar and non-reducing sugar tests on a mixture of glucose and sucrose solutions and comparing the results of the two tests.

Sample results

Biological molecule	Final colour of solution after biochemical test				
	Iodine	Biuret	Reducing sugar	Non-reducing sugar	Emulsion test
1% starch	blue / black				
1% protein		lilac / purple			
10% glucose	yellow / orange	blue	red / orange and cloudy		
10% fructose			red / orange and cloudy		
10% maltose			red / orange and cloudy		
10% lactose			red / orange and cloudy		
10% sucrose			blue and clear	red / orange and cloudy	
vegetable oil					white and cloudy
water	yellow / orange	blue	blue and clear	blue and clear	
ethanol					colourless

Table 2.1

Biological molecule	Final colour of solution after biochemical test			
	Iodine	Biuret	Reducing sugar	Non-reducing sugar
solution X	yellow / orange	lilac	red / orange and cloudy	red / orange and cloudy
solution Y	yellow / orange	blue	blue	red / orange and cloudy
solution Z	blue / black	blue	red / orange and cloudy	red / orange and cloudy

Table 2.2

11

Answers to the workbook questions (using the sample results)

a i Contents of unknown solution X: protein, reducing sugar (glucose), non-reducing sugar (sucrose) may or may not be present

Contents of unknown solution Y: non-reducing sugar (sucrose)

Contents of unknown solution Z: starch, non-reducing sugar (glucose), non-reducing sugar (sucrose) may or may not be present

ii X and Z both contain a reducing sugar which will give a positive result with both reducing sugar and non-reducing sugar tests. As the tests are qualitative, it is difficult to determine if there is extra precipitate or not.

b · Monosaccharides that are reducing sugars: glucose, fructose, galactose

· Disaccharides that are reducing sugars: lactose, maltose

· Disaccharides that are non-reducing sugars: sucrose

c To act as a control and show what a negative test looks like for comparison.

d The tests are qualitative as they do not give an indication of the number of molecules present.

e i Both reducing and non-reducing sugar tests use a Benedict's test. This means that glucose would react with both tests.

ii The non-reducing sugar tests hydrolyses the sucrose into glucose and fructose. These are both reducing sugars and then react with the Benedict's solution. When bound together in sucrose, neither the glucose nor fructose is able to donate electrons.

iii Carry out reducing sugar tests on both solutions. This will show which one solution is glucose as it will give a positive test. Then carry out a non-reducing sugar test on the other solution to confirm it is sucrose.

f The solution contains a mixture of both reducing and non-reducing sugars. If it contains both glucose and sucrose, for example, the reducing sugar test will generate a precipitate from just the free glucose. If a non-reducing sugar test is carried out, the sucrose is hydrolysed into glucose and fructose so that the solution now contains additional glucose and fructose. These will now react with Benedict's solution to produce additional precipitate.

Practical investigation 2.2:
The semi-quantitative Benedict's test and serial dilutions

Learning objective: 2.1(b), 2.2(d)

Skills focus

The following skill areas are developed and practised (see the skills grids at the front of this guide):

MMO	Making decisions about measurements: (c) Successfully collecting data and observations: (a), (e)
PDO	Recording data and observations: (a), (b), (d) Layout of data or observations: (i)
ACE	Interpreting data or observations and identifying sources of error: (c), (d) Drawing conclusions: (a) Interpreting data or observations and identifying sources of error: (g), (i)

Duration

The work should take approximately 1 h to complete.

Preparing for the investigation

· Learners should have carried out Practical Investigation 2.1 and so understand the reducing sugar test.

· Solutions should be tested before the investigation to ensure that they work correctly.

· Individual boiling water baths can be set up by learners but the experiment can also be carried out using thermostatically controlled water baths set at 85°C.

· Comparing colours is very subjective and this should be discussed as a source of error. It is worthwhile different groups of learners comparing what they decided the colours matched up to.

· This experiment is a useful way of introducing the ideas of quantitative and qualitative data. It is also an appropriate point to discuss the idea of uncertainty in the results as only an approximate concentration can be inferred.

Equipment

Each learner or group will need:

- nine test tubes
- test-rube rack
- Bunsen burner, tripod, gauze and heat-proof tile (alternatively, whole class thermostatically controlled water baths may be used set to 85°C)
- test-tube holder
- glass beakers, 500 cm³, 50 cm³
- pipette, 10 cm³ and 1 cm³ and pipette filler (if pipettes are not available, small measuring cylinders or syringes may be used)
- Benedict's solution, 100 cm³ (see Practical investigation 2.1)
- distilled water, 100 cm³
- 10% glucose solution, 50 cm³
- 'unknown' concentration of glucose, 20 cm³ (see Practical investigation 2.1). This should be 0.05% concentration.

Safety considerations

- Learners should have read the safety guidance section within the workbook before carrying out this investigation.
- Standard laboratory safety procedures should be followed always.
- There are no additional significant safety issues associated with this investigation.

Carrying out the investigation

- This should be quite a straightforward practical.
- Learners will often find the idea of serial dilutions difficult and will often ask for help.
- It is important that the tubes are mixed carefully for each dilution before removing 1 cm³.
- Learners may need to set up two water baths or share additional water baths.

  Colour-blind learners may have difficulty discriminating between the colours of the Benedict's test. Another learner may need to help them identify the colours.

  Learners could also be provided with a range of ready made fruit juice drinks and asked to estimate the sugar concentrations of each.

Sample results

Test-tube number	Glucose concentration / %	Colour of Benedict's solution
1	10	brick red
2	1	orange
3	0.1	yellow
4	0.01	green
5	0.001	pale green
6	0.0001	blue

Table 2.3

The colour of the unknown solution was green/yellow.

Answers to the workbook questions (using the sample results)

a   The concentration of glucose in the 'unknown' solution is approximately 0.1 / 0.01%. It may lie within a range of 0.1–0.5%. Learners' answers may vary here depending on how they saw the colours – it is very subjective.

b   A fully quantitative method would give an accurate, exact concentration of glucose. This method allows learners to approximate the amount of glucose without being certain of the exact concentration.

c   The exact concentration can only be judged to lie between 0.1% and 0.01% as there is no colour standard for 0.05%. There would also be too little difference in colour between standard concentrations that were made between 0.1 and 0.01%. The human eye would not be able to detect the differences.

d All the standard solutions and the test solution had a volume of $9\,cm^3$ to which $5\,cm^3$ Benedict's solution were added. If $1\,cm^3$ were not discarded, it would have had $10\,cm^3$ glucose which could affect the reaction.

e Control variables included:

- temperature of water bath: higher or lower temperatures may affect the reaction speed

- length of time in water bath: leaving the solutions longer may have resulted in more reaction. (Ideally, the length of time should be sufficient to ensure the reactions are complete)

- volume of glucose solution: more solution would result in more intense colour due to increase of glucose

- volume of Benedict's solution: different amounts would affect whether the reaction had gone to completion

- concentration of Benedict's solution: different amounts would affect whether the reaction had gone to completion.

f If the amount of Cu^{2+} runs out before all the glucose molecules have oxidised / donated electrons, it is not an accurate measure of glucose concentration. Theoretically, if more Benedict's solution were added, more precipitate would form. If insufficient, the glucose concentration would be estimated to be lower than it is.

g Tube 6 is a control. This shows the colour that Benedict's solution turns when heated. It could be argued that simply heating Benedict's solution causes it to change colour even without glucose.

h Alternative methods could be:

- filtering the solution to collect the precipitate. This would be dried and weighed. A calibration graph could be plotted of mass of precipitate against glucose concentration and used to determine glucose concentrations of other solutions.

- using a colorimeter to measure the red colour or blue colour or turbidity. A calibration graph could be plotted of absorbance against glucose concentration and used to determine glucose concentrations of other solutions.

i 10%, 5%, 2.5%, 1.25%, 0.625%, 0.3125%

Practical investigation 2.3:
Using a semi-quantitative iodine test to compare the starch content of bananas

Learning objective: 2.1(a)

Skills focus

The following skill areas are developed and practised (see the skills grids at the front of this guide):

MMO	Making decisions about measurements: (c) Successfully collecting data and observations: (a), (e)
PDO	Recording data and observations: (a), (b), (d) Layout of data or observations: (i)
ACE	Interpreting data or observations and identifying sources of error: (c), (d), (g), (i) Drawing conclusions: (a), (b) Suggesting improvements or modifications to extend an investigation: (a), (b), (c), (d), (e)

Duration

The work should take approximately 1 h to complete. It is easier to complete within the time period if learners work in pairs.

Preparing for the investigation

- Learners should understand how to make solutions of different concentrations from stocks by using proportional and serial dilutions. This practical asks learners to plan their own dilutions – these should be checked before they start the practical.

- The practical requires the sourcing of bananas that are as green as possible. If very green bananas are not available, plantains may be used. Ripe, yellow bananas are needed. Black, over-ripe bananas should be prepared in advance.

- Learners should understand that unripe bananas contain large quantities of starch which is then gradually converted to sucrose, glucose and fructose as the bananas ripen.

- The practical could be modified to compare different fruit and vegetables such as new or old potatoes, sweet potatoes, apples, etc.

Equipment

Each learner or group will need:

- nine test tubes
- test-tube racks
- iodine solution in a dropper bottle
- 1% starch solution, 50 cm³
- distilled water, 100 cm³
- pipettes, 10 cm³, 1 cm³, pipette filler (if pipettes are not available, small measuring cylinders or syringes may be used)
- pieces of banana flesh from green, yellow and black bananas
- knife or scalpel
- Bunsen burner, tripod, gauze, heat-proof tile (alternatively, whole class thermostatically controlled water baths may be used set to 85°C)
- test-tube holder
- glass beakers, 500 cm³ and 50 cm³
- spatula.

Safety considerations

- Learners should have read the safety guidance section within the workbook before carrying out this investigation.
- Standard laboratory safety procedures should be followed always.
- Iodine solution should not be flushed into natural water where it can harm aquatic organisms.

Carrying out the investigation

- Learners will need support in working out the dilutions. They should show these to the teacher before they start to make them.
- Learners may need support in determining the differences in colour intensity.

- The starch concentrations in the different bananas may be variable and, depending on the banana, may not yield the predicted differences.
- The banana extract may need diluting with distilled water if it is too concentrated. This should be discussed when determining the actual starch concentration.

Help should be provided for any learners with physical disabilities in the laboratory when using boiling water baths. It is good practice to not sit down in the event of boiling water being spilled. Where this is not possible (for example, with learners who are in a wheelchair), alternative provision such as thermostatically controlled water baths can be used.

Learners with dyspraxia may need support when cutting up the bananas pieces.

Learners with visual impairments may need support when comparing the colours of different solutions.

As extension work, other fruits and vegetables could be tested. Learners could also predict how the water potential of the banana would change as starch is converted to sucrose. They could plan a further experiment to estimate how water potential changes with ripeness of bananas.

Sample results

Test-tube number	Concentration of starch / %	Colour of iodine solution
1	1	black
2	0.1	dark blue
3	0.01	pale blue
4	0.001	very pale blue
5	0.0001	orange

Table 2.4

The colour of the iodine solution with each of the bananas was:

green: dark blue

yellow: pale blue–blue

black: orange–very pale blue

Answers to the workbook questions (using the sample results)

a The approximate starch concentrations may be very variable and will depend very much on the bananas the learners use.

For example:

- green (unripe): concentration: 1.0%; range: >1.0%

- yellow (ripe): concentration: 0.25%; range: 0.25–0.5%.

- black (over-ripe): concentration: 0.1%; range: 0.1–0.25%

b As bananas ripen, the starch is hydrolysed into glucose. Some of this is converted into other sugars such as fructose and sucrose.

c The estimated ranges of starch concentrations are very high so no differences would be detected when, for example, starch concentrations of 0.1 and 0.5% are tested. This could be improved by using a colorimeter to produce a calibration curve with known standards (this could be demonstrated to learners).

d Limitations:

- lack of sensitivity at low concentrations of starch

- difficult to detect differences in intensity of colour at higher concentrations of starch

- it is highly subjective due to use of human eye (lack of precision)

- the estimated ranges are very high and so inaccurate

- the banana extracts may not have solubilised all the starch

- sections of a banana may have different starch concentrations

- the investigation is unreliable as only one banana of each type was used.

Chapter outline

This chapter relates to Chapter 3: Enzymes in the coursebook.

In this chapter, learners will complete practical investigations on:

- 3.1 The time-course of an enzyme-catalysed reaction
- 3.2 The effect of substrate concentration on the rate of an enzyme-catalysed reaction
- 3.3 The effect of enzyme concentration on the rate of an enzyme-catalysed reaction
- 3.4 The effect of temperature on the rate of an enzyme-catalysed reaction
- 3.5 Immobilised urease
- 3.6 Investigating the effect of an inhibitor on the action of bromelain

Introduction

Enzyme experiments are an important part of any AS Biology course. They provide a very wide range of opportunities to access many of the skills that will be tested in practical exams, as well as helping learners to understand the facts and concepts covered in the learning objectives on this topic, which will be tested in theory exams.

There is a very large number of possible enzyme experiments that learners could be asked to do. We have selected six investigations in this chapter, for these reasons:

- This set of practical investigations enables learners to become familiar with several different enzymes – catalase, amylase, urease and protease.

- These enzymes are generally possible for any school to obtain, as all of them can be found in biological materials – they do not need to be bought in.

- This set of investigations gives learners experience of measuring rate of reaction by either measuring the disappearance of substrate (amylase and protease) or appearance of product (catalase and urease).

- It provides experience of several different techniques for measurement.

- It covers the learning objectives relating to enzyme investigations in Section 3.2 of the syllabus.

There are many other enzymes that you can use, such as lipase and lactase. You can also, if you wish, change the enzymes that are used for the investigations in this chapter. For example, you could use catalase in Practical investigation 3.3, instead of amylase. You could use lactase instead of urease in Practical investigation 3.5, and test for

its activity by allowing milk to flow over it and testing for glucose using glucose test strips.

Enzyme experiments, like all Biology experiments, have a well-deserved reputation for not always behaving in the way that you expect. As explained in the introduction to the Practical Workbook, it is very important to appreciate that getting the 'right' results is not the main point of the exercise – it is the **process** that is more important. Of course, learners will be more satisfied if their results are what they expect, but they should not feel that their experiment 'has not worked' if their results are unexpected. Such results provide good opportunities for looking critically at the experimental procedure, to identify possible reasons for the unexpected results obtained.

Practical investigation 3.1:
The time-course of an enzyme-catalysed reaction

Learning objective: 3.1(d)

Skills focus

The following skill areas are developed and practised (see the skills grids at the front of this guide):

MMO   Making decisions about measurements: (h), (j)
Successfully collecting data and observations: (a), (c)

PDO   Recording data and observations: (a), (c)
Displaying calculations and reasoning: (a)
Layout of data or observations: (c), (d), (e)

ACE   Interpreting data or observations and identifying
        sources of error: (a), (b), (e), (f), (g), (i)
        Drawing conclusions: (b)

Duration

The practical work will take about 1 h, depending on the familiarity of learners with the apparatus and techniques. The analysis and evaluation questions will take 45–60 min.

Preparing for the investigation

- Learners should know and understand the terms substrate, product and rate of reaction. They should understand how enzymes function, in terms of random collisions between substrate and the enzyme's active site.

- This experiment uses catalase extracted from celery stalks, and it is not possible to know the concentration or activity of the enzyme. Learners are therefore asked to do preliminary work themselves to determine appropriate volumes and concentrations of enzyme and substrate, and this is very valuable for them, helping them to think deeply about what they are doing and why, rather than simply following a set of instructions. However, if you are short of time, you could do this preliminary work yourself, and simply ask the learners to do the second part of the experiment, in which they measure the rate of oxygen production over time.

Equipment

Each learner or group will need:

- two or three stalks of celery

- about 20 cm³ of 10 volume hydrogen peroxide solution (this can generally be obtained cheaply from a local pharmacy)

- an electric blender

- a filter funnel and muslin (fine cloth that can be used for coarse filtering; using filter paper will take too long)

- two 250 cm³ beakers

- a large test tube, preferably a side-arm test tube

- a gas syringe

- tubing to make an airtight connection between the test tube and the gas syringe

- a timer (e.g. on a phone)

- a retort stand, boss and clamp

- an apparatus for measuring small volumes, for example two 5 cm³ or 10 cm³ syringes or two graduated pipettes.

Additional notes and advice

- Any biological material will contain catalase. If celery is not available, try other plant material, such as potato, carrot, apple or other fruit or vegetable. Animal tissues, such as liver, can also be used, but the catalase in these is often so active that it is very difficult to measure the rate of reaction.

- If you have 20 volume hydrogen peroxide rather than 10 volume, you can dilute it by 50%. Alternatively, learners could be provided with 20 volume hydrogen peroxide.

- If no electric blender is available, learners can grind pieces of celery stalk with water in a pestle and mortar. However, this is time-consuming, and only small quantities can be dealt with at a time.

- This method uses gas syringes to collect the gas evolved. This is by far the simplest and most reliable method of measuring the rate of oxygen formation. If you do not have gas syringes, you may be able to borrow them from the Chemistry department. If you have good quality 'ordinary' plastic syringes, you can try using these instead, but do make sure that they are gas-tight, and that the syringe barrel moves smoothly.

- If no suitable syringes are available, you could try one of the methods shown in Figure 3.1.

Safety considerations

- Learners should have read the safety guidance section within the workbook before carrying out this investigation.

- Standard laboratory safety procedures should be followed always.

- Learners should take care when using sharp blades to cut the celery stalks.

- Hydrogen peroxide 20 or 10 volume irritates eyes and skin. Safety glasses should be worn throughout. Hydrogen peroxide decomposes slowly even with no catalyst present, so oxygen gas may build up in a bottle. Store in a cool, dark place and take care when opening.

- If the gas is given off very quickly, the plunger in the gas syringe can shoot out of the syringe barrel with some force, and travel quite a distance. To avoid this, tie the plunger loosely to the barrel, so that if it does shoot out, it cannot travel far.

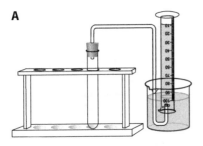

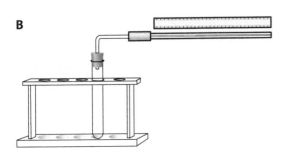

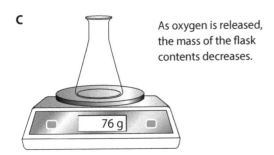

As oxygen is released, the mass of the flask contents decreases.

76 g

Figure 3.1

Carrying out the investigation

- It is strongly recommended that you encourage learners to make their own decisions when carrying out the preliminary work. This increases their engagement with the problems to be solved, and increases their understanding of the reaction and how they are measuring its rate. Only intervene when it is clear that learners cannot progress without your guidance.

- It is possible that their first attempts will result in a rate of production of oxygen that is too fast to measure. They can try diluting the enzyme extract, or diluting the hydrogen peroxide solution, or reducing the ratio of the volume of enzyme extract: volume of hydrogen peroxide solution. They may need several attempts before arriving at a concentration and volume of enzyme and substrate that produces a measurable rate. Encourage them to be systematic in their approach.

- If the rate of production of gas is too slow, they could try preparing a fresh enzyme extract using more celery and less water.

- The most common problem encountered while doing the experiment is that the apparatus is not airtight. Check all joints and ensure that suitable diameters of rubber tubing have been used to join the glassware. If problems persist, use petroleum jelly to seal suspect joins. Melted candle wax also works well, but can be difficult to clean off afterwards.

- After adding the enzyme extract to the hydrogen peroxide, it is impossible to completely place the bung back into the test tube immediately. This means that some gas will escape, and the measurement of volume will be too low. (This is a source of error that learners should identify and comment on as they answer question **h**.) The time delay is reduced if learners work in pairs or small groups.

Learners may find it difficult to work out what to do in the preliminary work, if the rate of reaction is too high or too low. Use questioning to help them to work this out for themselves, for example ask: *What do you think will happen to the rate of reaction if you decrease the concentration of the substrate?*

Some learners, especially those whose English language skills are not strong, may have difficulties in wording their answers to some of the questions, for example **b** and **e**. You could provide sentences with gaps for them to complete, and/or provide a list of words and phrases that they can use in their answers.

Question **g** is difficult. You could ask each group to discuss the question among themselves, and then ask each group to present their decisions to the rest of the class. Discuss their answers as a whole class, and then ask each learner to write down their individual answer in their own words.

A valuable additional exercise would be to provide learners with different methods of collecting the gas and measuring its volume. Some suggestions are shown in Figure 3.1. You could allocate different methods to different groups, and then discuss which apparatus provides the most reliable results and why. This will help learners to develop their understanding of making decisions about how to measure the dependent variable.

Ask learners to suggest how they could use this technique to compare the rates of activity of catalase taken from two different vegetables, or from celery stalks that have been kept in different conditions (e.g. in a fridge and in a warm kitchen). They can begin to think about the variables that they will try to keep the same. If time allows, they could carry out their investigation.

Common learner misconceptions

- The words 'catalase' and 'catalyse' are very similar, and it is worth spending a few moments pointing this out to learners, ensuring that they understand each term.

- When interpreting the graph, learners may not appreciate that the reaction has stopped when the oxygen volume no longer increases. They may read the graph as showing that oxygen continues to be given off, expecting the line to fall to 0 when no more is produced.

Sample results

Time / s	30	60	90	120	150	180	210	240	270	300	330	360	390	420	450	480	510
Volume of oxygen / cm³	2.0	5.5	7.5	9.5	11.5	13.0	14.5	16.0	17.0	18.5	19.5	20.5	21.0	21.0	21.5	22.0	22.5

Table 3.1

Answers to the workbook questions (using the sample results)

It is highly preferable that learners should use their own results when answering the questions. In this case, you will need to check their answers to questions **a, b, c, d, e** and **f** against their results.

The following answers relate to the sample results.

a

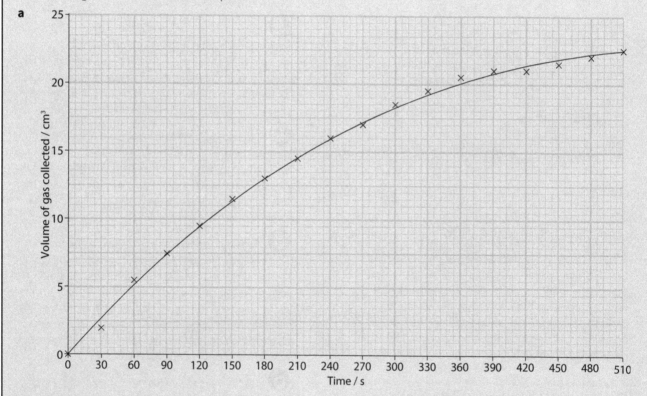

Figure 3.2

b The rate of reaction is rapid at first, and gradually becomes slower with time.

c At time 0, before the enzyme has begun to break down the hydrogen peroxide.

d The graph has not levelled off, so there is still some oxygen being released, meaning that there is still some substrate that has not been broken down even after 510 s.

e When the catalase is first added to the hydrogen peroxide, the concentration of substrate is highest. The frequency of collisions between the catalase molecules and the hydrogen peroxide molecules, and the rate of formation of enzyme–substrate complexes, is high. As time progresses, the concentration of substrate gradually decreases, as it is broken down by the enzyme. The frequency of collisions therefore also decreases. Eventually, there would be no substrate left, so the rate of reaction would become zero.

f

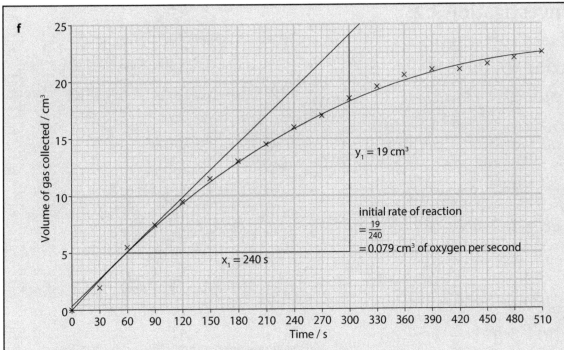

Figure 3.3

g As the reaction progresses, the concentration of substrate decreases. If we want to investigate the effect of substrate concentration on the rate of reaction, then substrate concentration is our independent variable, and we need to measure it and know what it is. We cannot do this if the substrate concentration is changing. We therefore need to measure the rate of reaction right at the start of the reaction, before the substrate concentration has decreased significantly. Only then can we be sure that the substrate concentration is the same for each experiment.

h **ii** A random error. Gas will escape from the test tube at the start of the reaction. After that, once the bung is in place, it will not escape. We therefore lose some gas at the start, so the total volume of gas collected is too low. However, once the bung is in place, all the gas is collected and the *change* in volume will be correct.

    iii A random error. Readings may be taken a little bit before or a little bit after the required time. This is

likely to produce points on the graph that do not lie neatly on a curve, because a point plotted at, say, 30 s actually belongs at 31 s.

iv A systematic error. If the scale is not quite correct, then each reading is likely to be 'out' by the same value each time. It could give readings that are either too high or too low, depending on what is wrong with the scale.

v A random error. It is a single error that takes place just once. The tangent should be drawn as close to the origin as possible, but this is difficult to do, and the curve is very steep (almost a straight line) here. Drawing the tangent in the wrong place or at the wrong angle will have a significant effect on the calculated value for the initial rate of reaction, which could be either too high (if the tangent is drawn at too vertical an angle) or too low (if the tangent is drawn sloping too much to the right).

Practical investigation 3.2:
The effect of substrate concentration on the rate of an enzyme-catalysed reaction

Learning objective: 3.2(a)

Skills focus

The following skill areas are developed and practised (see the skills grids at the front of this guide):

MMO	Making decisions about measurements: (a), (b), (g), (h) Successfully collecting data and observations: (a), (c)
PDO	Recording data and observations: (a), (b), (c) Displaying calculations and reasoning: (a) Layout of data or observations: (b), (c), (d), (e)
ACE	Interpreting data or observations and identifying sources of error: (a), (b), (e), (f), (g) Drawing conclusions: (a), (b) Suggesting improvements or modifications to extend an investigation: (a), (b), (c), (e)

Duration

The practical work will take between 60 and 90 min, partly depending on how quickly learners are able to determine how to make up the different concentrations of substrate, and to do this. The analysis and evaluation questions will take around 30 min.

Preparing for the investigation

- Learners should have carried out Practical investigation 3.1, so that they are familiar with the enzyme and the technique for measuring rate of reaction.

Equipment

Each learner or group will need:

- two or three large stalks of celery
- approximately 100 cm³ of 10 volume hydrogen peroxide solution
- an electric blender
- a filter funnel and muslin
- two 250 cm³ beakers
- five 100 cm³ beakers or other small containers
- method of labelling beakers, for example glass-marking pen
- a large test tube
- a gas syringe
- tubing to make an airtight connection between the test tube and the gas syringe
- a timer (e.g. on a phone)
- a retort stand, boss and clamp
- apparatus for measuring small volumes, e.g. two 5 cm³ or 10 cm³ syringes or two graduated pipettes.

Additional notes and advice

- See Practical investigation 3.1 for suggestions for alternative equipment.
- You may prefer to use 20 volume hydrogen peroxide, as this will give you a greater possible range of substrate concentrations.

Safety considerations

- Learners should have read the safety guidance section within the workbook before carrying out this investigation.
- Standard laboratory safety procedures should be followed always.
- Learners should take care when using sharp blades to cut the celery stalks.
- Hydrogen peroxide 20 volume or 10 volume irritates eyes and skin. Safety glasses should be worn throughout. Hydrogen peroxide decomposes slowly even with no catalyst present, so oxygen gas may build up in a bottle. Store in a cool, dark place and take care when opening.
- If the gas is given off very quickly, the plunger in the gas syringe can shoot out of the syringe barrel with some force, and travel quite a distance. To avoid this, it is important to tie the plunger loosely to the barrel, so that if it does shoot out, it cannot travel far.

Carrying out the investigation

- Please see the points described for Practical investigation 3.1.

- If learners begin with the lowest concentration of substrate, they may find that the reaction scarcely takes place at all, and may waste a lot of time watching their apparatus while no measurable quantity of gas is given off. It is therefore suggested that you encourage them to begin with the highest concentration and work systematically downwards.

Some learners may have difficulty in deciding how to make up the different concentrations of substrate. They need to become confident with doing this, as it is often expected in examination questions, so it is important to encourage them to try to work it out for themselves. If this fails, refer them to Figure P1.2 in the coursebook. If this is not available, prepare a handout showing Figure 3.4.

Learners who require a further challenge, and who have a set of results that has produced a suitable graph, could use their graph to calculate the Michaelis–Menten constant, K_m. There is guidance on how to do this in the Biology workbook.

Example of how the learners could prepare the different concentrations

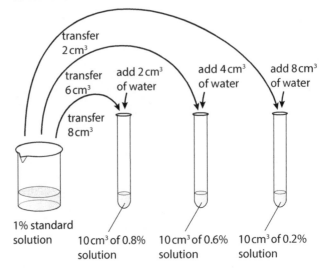

Figure 3.4

Sample results

Time / s	Volume of oxygen / cm³				
	100% substrate	80% substrate	60% substrate	40% substrate	20% substrate
0	0	0	0	0	0
30	2.0	3.0	2.0	1.0	0
60	5.5	4.5	4.0	2.0	0.5
90	7.5	6.5	6.0	3.5	0.5
120	9.5	8.0	8.0	5.0	1.0
150	11.5	10.0	9.5	6.0	1.0
180	13.0	11.0	11.0	7.0	1.5
210	14.5	12.5	12.0	8.0	2.0
240	16.0	13.5	13.0	8.5	2.0
270	17.0	15.0	13.5	9.0	2.5
300	18.5	16.0	14.0	10.0	3.0
330	19.5	16.5	14.5	10.5	3.0
360	20.5	17.0	15.0	10.5	3.5
390	21.0	17.5	15.0	11.0	3.5
420	21.0	18.0	15.5	11.0	4.0
450	21.5	18.5	15.5	11.5	4.0
480	22.0	18.5	16.0	11.5	4.5
510	22.5	19.0	16.0	12.0	4.5

Table 3.2

Answers to the workbook questions (using the sample results)

a

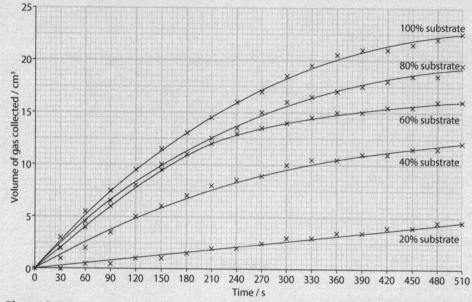

Figure 3.5

b The results given here are approximate; much depends on exactly where and how the tangent is drawn to the curves.

Substrate concentration as percentage of stock solution	Initial rate of reaction / cm³ oxygen s⁻¹
100	0.42
80	0.41
60	0.34
40	0.15
20	0.02

Table 3.3

c

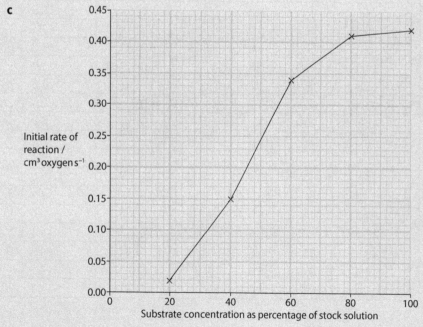

Figure 3.6

d In the raw results, the volume of oxygen produced after 30 s is greater for the 80% substrate concentration than for 100% substrate concentration.

e The greater the concentration of substrate, the greater the initial rate of reaction.

Some learners may find that their graph levels off at higher concentrations of substrate, in which case their conclusion should be:

The greater the concentration of substrate, the greater the initial rate of reaction. At very high substrate concentrations, however, a maximum rate of reaction is reached.

f The greater the concentration of substrate, the more hydrogen peroxide molecules are present in any given volume of the reacting mixture. This increases

the chance that a hydrogen peroxide molecule will collide with an active site of a catalase molecule. The more frequent these collisions, the faster the rate of reaction.

(Note that it is the **frequency** of collisions that is important, not the **number** of collisions.)

At very high concentrations of substrate, all active sites may be occupied all of the time, so that increasing the substrate concentration even more does not increase the rate of reaction.

g, h Any of the errors listed in question **h** in Practical investigation 3.1 can be included.

New sources of error include those involved in making up the dilutions of the hydrogen peroxide solutions, and keeping the control variables constant.

Practical investigation 3.3:
The effect of enzyme concentration on the rate of an enzyme-catalysed reaction

Learning objective: 3.2(a)

Skills focus

The following skill areas are developed and practised (see the skills grids at the front of this guide):

MMO   Making decisions about measurements: (e), (g), (j)
Successfully collecting data and observations: (a)

PDO   Recording data and observations: (a), (c)
Layout of data or observations: (b), (c), (d), (e)

ACE   Interpreting data or observations and identifying sources of error: (e), (f), (g)
Drawing conclusions: (a), (b)
Suggesting improvements or modifications to extend an investigation: (a), (c), (e)

Duration

The practical work will take between 60 and 75 min. The analysis and evaluation questions will take around 30 min.

Preparing for the investigation

- Learners will find it helpful to have done Practical investigations 3.1 and 3.2 before this one. They should know how to make up a range of concentrations by dilution, and be able to identify random and systematic errors.

- Amylase bought from educational suppliers is usually obtained from fungi or bacteria. There may be information with the amylase stating information such as its optimum temperature (which may be as high as 80°C). However, you should test the activity of the amylase yourself. Make up a 1% solution of amylase (that is, dissolve 1 g of amylase in a little cold water, and then make up to 100 cm³) and a 5% solution of soluble starch. Add 1 cm³ of amylase solution to 1 cm³ of starch solution, and mix thoroughly. Take samples every minute or so, checking for the continuing presence of starch. Ideally, you want all the starch to disappear within a time range between 5 and 15 min. If it disappears too quickly, try diluting the amylase solution. If too slowly, dilute the starch solution.

- The instructions do not suggest controlling pH. Ideally, this should be a control variable, and you could keep it constant by using a buffer solution that matches the optimum pH of the enzyme. However, in practice pH will not vary, so it may be better to bypass this step and simply use distilled water.

Equipment

Each learner or group will need:

- about 50 cm³ of a 1% solution of amylase (or the concentration you find works well)

- about 50 cm³ of a 5% solution of starch (or the concentration you find works well)

- two 250 cm³ beakers

- five 100 cm³ beakers or other small containers

- method of labelling beakers, for example, glass-marking pen

- at least 12 clean test tubes

- six glass rods

- a timer (e.g. on a phone)

- apparatus for measuring small volumes, for example, two 5 cm³ or 10 cm³ syringes or two graduated pipettes

- iodine in potassium iodide solution, with a dropper

- two white tiles, preferably with a series of hollows (a spotting tile or dimple tile)

- starch-free paper for cleaning the glass rods.

Access to:

- distilled water

- a thermostatically controlled water bath.

Additional notes and advice

- If you do not have a thermostatically controlled water bath, learners can make their own by filling a large beaker with water at room temperature. They can measure the temperature at intervals throughout their experiment, to check that it stays constant. In practice, it is not possible to hold the temperature absolutely constant, so this will become a significant source of error to discuss.

- If you cannot buy amylase, then learners could use their own saliva as a source. Saliva can be collected in a boiling tube.

Safety considerations

- Learners should have read the safety guidance section within the workbook before carrying out this investigation.

- Standard laboratory safety procedures should be followed always.

- Although all enzymes can produce allergic reactions in a small minority of learners, the concentration of amylase used in this investigation is unlikely to pose any significant risk.

Carrying out the investigation

- This is a notoriously unreliable experiment. Amylase can sometimes fail to digest the starch at all, or it may do it so quickly that you cannot measure any differences in rate between the different concentrations. It is essential that you trial the experiment before asking learners to do it, to try to find suitable concentrations of enzyme and substrate.

- The starch solution should be made up with soluble starch, but some schools have problems in obtaining soluble starch that reacts appropriately with iodine in potassium iodide solution. Check that the starch solution gives a strong positive result (a strong blue–black colour) when tested with the iodine solution.

- A very common source of problems is that learners contaminate one solution with another. They may fail to clean a glass rod that has been in contact with one solution before inserting it into another. This can be so significant that it can completely prevent any useful results being obtained at all. Cleaning with paper towel may not be sufficient, particularly if your supply of paper towels contain starch (test one with iodine in potassium iodide solution to find out). It is recommended that a different glass rod is used for testing each solution, and this is washed thoroughly in clean water after each test. If paper is used for drying or cleaning the glass rods, this must be entirely starch-free.

- It is very difficult, if not impossible, to decide exactly when the iodine solution no longer gives a positive result for starch. It can be helpful to have two reference iodine solution spots – one to which a drop of starch solution has been added, and one to which a drop of water has been added.

Some candidates may have difficulty in deciding how to make up the different concentrations of amylase. See the suggestions in this section in Practical investigation 3.2.

Some learners may have difficulty in understanding how the colour of the iodine solution can be interpreted in terms of the reaction. Try using questioning to help them to work this out for themselves. For example, if they get an orange–brown colour when adding a sample to the spot of iodine, you could ask: What does this colour mean? If you had done this test before you added the enzyme, what colour would you have got? Why? So where has the starch gone? How can we tell how long the starch took to disappear? If it disappeared quickly, what does that tell us about the rate of the reaction?

Learners who complete the investigation quickly and successfully, could be asked to suggest why adding iodine solution to the reacting mixture and watching for a colour change, rather than taking samples and adding to drops of iodine solution, might not be a good method to use. (The answer is that the presence of iodine molecules could affect the rate of the reaction.)

Common learner misconceptions

- The results of this practical investigation are less intuitive to understand than those involving catalase. For catalase, we can see the product and measure its volume. For amylase, there is no visible change when starch is hydrolysed to maltose. We begin with a colourless solution, and end with a colourless solution, with no gas being given off. The detection of disappearance of substrate (starch) involves an extra step that, for some learners, makes it difficult for them to understand exactly what is happening.

Sample results

Concentration of enzyme solution / percent	Time taken for starch to disappear / s
1.0	before the first test
0.8	60
0.6	120
0.4	120
0.2	180

Table 3.4

Answers to the workbook questions (using the sample results)

a

Concentration of enzyme solution / percent	Time taken for starch to disappear / s	Rate of reaction / 1000 ÷ time
1.0	before the first test	not measurable
0.8	60	16.7
0.6	120	8.3
0.4	120	8.3
0.2	180	5.6
0.0	did not disappear	0.0

Table 3.5

b

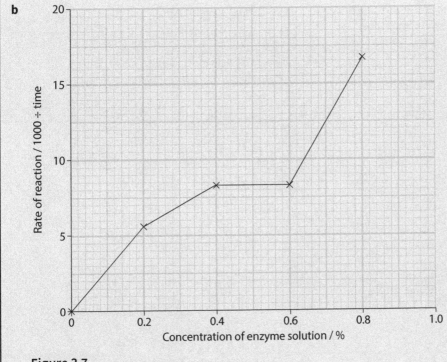

Figure 3.7

c The greater the enzyme concentration, the greater the rate of reaction. (Learners may find that at very high enzyme concentrations the rate of reaction does not increase any further as enzyme concentration increases.)

d The greater the concentration of enzyme, the greater the chance of a starch molecule colliding with an active site of an amylase molecule. The more frequent these collisions, the faster the rate of formation of enzyme–substrate complexes, and the faster the rate of reaction.

(Note that it is the **frequency** of collisions that is important, not the **number** of collisions.)

e Temperature, the concentration of substrate. Learners may also mention pH, even though this has not been controlled.

f, g Learners will probably 'reuse' sources of error from Practical investigations 3.1, 3.2 and 3.3. Take care that they select sources that are applicable to **this** investigation and that, where necessary, they reword them.

Possible answers include:

- Apparatus used for measuring volume may be inappropriate. For example, if a measuring cylinder or syringe was used, modify by using a graduated pipette.

- pH could fluctuate during the reaction; modify by add the same volume of the same buffer solution to each reacting mixture.

- Samples were taken at only 1-min intervals, so we cannot judge the time for the starch to disappear any more precisely than to the nearest minute (this can explain the same time being recorded for two different concentrations of amylase in the sample results); modify by taking samples more frequently.

- Judgement of the colour of the iodine solution; modify by comparing against a set of standards or a colour chart.

h Make sure that answers relate to *this* investigation, and do not suggest testing other enzymes or other variables.

- Do three repeats for each enzyme concentration, and calculate a mean value for the time taken for the starch to disappear. (Note: it is not enough just to do repeats; a mean must also be calculated.)

- Use a wider range of enzyme concentrations, and more intermediate values (that is, smaller intervals of the independent variable), to obtain more points on the graph and therefore a clearer picture of its shape.

i In this reaction, the product is maltose. There is no quick way of measuring its production – we would need to do a quantitative Benedict's test, which is time-consuming. It is much easier to measure the disappearance of starch, as this can be quickly and simply tested for using iodine in potassium iodide solution.

In the catalase reaction, the product is oxygen, which is a gas and is therefore given off from the reaction vessel and can be collected and measured easily. It would not be easy to measure the disappearance of the substrate, as there is no easy test for hydrogen peroxide.

Practical investigation 3.4:
The effect of temperature on the rate of an enzyme-catalysed reaction

Learning objective: 3.2(a)

Skills focus

The following skill areas are developed and practised (see the skills grids at the front of this guide):

MMO   Making decisions about measurements: (b), (e), (f), (g), (h), (i), (j)
Successfully collecting data and observations: (c)

PDO   Recording data and observations: (a), (b), (c)
Layout of data or observations: (b), (c), (d)

ACE   Interpreting data or observations and identifying sources of error: (e), (f)
Drawing conclusions: (a), (b)
Suggesting improvements or modifications to extend an investigation: (d), (e)

Duration

The practical work will take between 60 and 75 min. The analysis and evaluation questions will take around 30 min. Please see also the section *Carrying out the investigation*, for the possible effect of group size on the duration of the investigation.

Preparing for the investigation

- Learners will find it very helpful to have done Practical Investigations 3.1, 3.2 and 3.3 before this one. This will give them experience of the reaction and methods of measuring the rate of production of oxygen, and also how to use water baths to maintain a chosen temperature. They should know how to make up a range of concentrations by dilution, and be able to identify random and systematic errors.

- Learners are asked to suggest their own values for the independent variable, temperature. However, if you are using thermostatically-controlled water baths, they will not have a choice about this. You could involve the class in discussing the temperatures at which they would like the water baths to be set.

Equipment
Each learner or group will need:

- one or two stalks of celery

- about 100 cm³ of 10 volume hydrogen peroxide solution

- an electric blender or pestle and mortar

- a filter funnel and muslin (fine cloth that can be used for filtering)

- two 250 cm³ beakers

- five 100 cm³ beakers or other small containers

- method of labelling beakers, for example, glass marking pen

- a large test tube

- a gas syringe

- tubing to make an airtight connection between the test tube and the gas syringe

- a timer (e.g. on a phone)

- a retort stand, boss and clamp

- an apparatus for measuring small volumes, for example, two 5 cm³ or 10 cm³ syringes or two graduated pipettes.

Access to:

- distilled water

- several thermostatically-controlled water baths, and/or apparatus to make your own water baths using large beakers of water.

Additional notes and advice

- If you do not have thermostatically controlled water baths, learners can make their own. They should use a large beaker of water, and adjust the temperature by adding ice or hot water from a kettle. Temperatures above room temperature can be maintained by placing the beaker on a tripod and gauze above a heat source (Bunsen burner or spirit burner) and constantly adjusting the heat to try to maintain a constant temperature.

Safety considerations

- Learners should have read the safety guidance section within the workbook before carrying out this investigation.

- Standard laboratory safety procedures should be followed always.

- Learners should take care when using sharp blades to cut the celery stalks.

- Hydrogen peroxide 20 volume or 10 volume irritates eyes and skin. Safety glasses should be worn throughout. Hydrogen peroxide decomposes slowly even with no catalyst present, so oxygen gas may build up in a bottle. Store in a cool, dark place and take care when opening.

- If the gas is given off very quickly, the plunger in the gas syringe can shoot out of the syringe barrel with some force, and travel quite a distance. To avoid this, it is important to tie the plunger loosely to the barrel, so that if it does shoot out, it cannot travel far.

- Some of the water baths will need to be at quite high temperatures, for example 80°C. If learners are using beakers on tripods as water baths, they should make sure that these are standing well back from the edge of the bench.

Carrying out the investigation

- Please see the issues described for Practical investigation 3.1.

- If you do not have thermostatically-controlled water baths, it can be difficult for learners to maintain the temperature they want in their water baths. There is no easy solution to this; they should discuss it as a significant source of experimental error.

- If many groups are sharing the same thermostatically-controlled water baths, a careless learner in one group may disrupt another group's apparatus. All groups should also label their apparatus using a waterproof marker, to avoid confusion.

- If learners are working in pairs, they may need to work with one temperature at a time rather than trying to run the experiments for each temperature simultaneously. This means that a longer time will be needed to carry out the investigation. If they are in larger groups, they may be able to organise themselves so that different members of the group work on different temperatures, but there is then a risk that different individuals will do something slightly different that may affect their results (in other words, they are introducing an uncontrolled variable).

This is the first task in this book in which learners are asked to plan part of their method. They are greatly helped by having used the technique before, but still may feel insecure in deciding on the temperatures to use (Steps 1 and 2). Use questioning to help them with this, for example ask: What is the highest temperature you can get using a water bath? What is the lowest temperature you can get? What do you think the optimum temperature of the enzyme might be? So which five/six temperatures will you investigate?

They may also need help in deciding their control variables (Step 5). Again, use questioning to support them. Ask: What is your independent variable in this investigation? What other variables do you know about, that affect the rate of an enzyme-catalysed reaction? So which other variables do you need to try to keep constant?

Learners who complete the investigation quickly and successfully could carry out their suggested method for investigating the effect of pH on the activity of catalase (see question **e**). This would be a useful activity, as it provides an opportunity to become familiar with the use of buffer solutions.

Common learner misconceptions

- Learners may expect the catalase to have an optimum temperature of 37°C. This is unlikely to be the optimum temperature for an enzyme extracted from a plant; their optimum temperatures are often significantly lower than this.

Sample results

The volume of oxygen was collected after 2 min.

Temperature / °C	Volume of oxygen collected at 120 s / cm³
0	0.5
20	12.5
40	10.5
60	6.5
80	1.0

Table 3.6

Answers to the workbook questions (using the sample results)

a

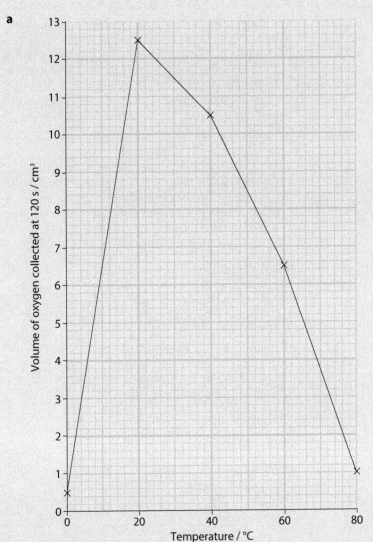

Figure 3.8

31

b The conclusion should be a concise statement relating temperature to rate of reaction. For example, for the sample results, the conclusion could be:

Increasing temperature from 0 to 20°C causes an increase in the rate of reaction. The optimum temperature for this enzyme lies somewhere between 0 and 40°C. Increasing the temperature above 40°C causes a decrease in the rate of reaction.

Notice that, although the maximum volume of oxygen was collected at 20°C, we do not know if more would have been collected at a temperature below this or above it. We cannot determine the optimum temperature of the enzymes, only say that it lies somewhere between 0 and 40°C.

c As temperature increases from 0 to 20°C, the kinetic energy of the catalase molecules and hydrogen peroxide molecules increases. This increases the frequency of collisions of hydrogen peroxide molecules with the active site of catalase, and therefore increases the rate of reaction.

Above 40°C, the high temperatures cause breakage of hydrogen bonds within the catalase molecule, disrupting the shape of the active site and making it less likely that hydrogen peroxide can bind with it. At the highest temperatures, all the catalase molecules are denatured, so no hydrogen peroxide can bind and no reaction takes place.

d The learners' results will have given them a range of temperatures between which the optimum temperature must lie. They could do further experiments using temperatures within this range. For the sample results, temperatures of 5, 10, 15, 25, 30 and 35°C could be trialled.

e A range of buffer solutions should be made up, using at least five values – for example, pH 2, 4, 6, 8 and 10. Temperature should be kept constant by standing the tube containing the hydrogen peroxide and catalase in a water bath at a temperature close to the optimum for the enzyme. Concentration and volume of enzyme and substrate should be kept constant, as the learners have just done in their investigation into the effect of temperature.

Practical investigation 3.5:
Immobilising urease

Learning objective: 3.2(d)

Skills focus

The following skill areas are developed and practised (see the skills grids at the front of this guide):

MMO — Making decisions about measurements: (g)
Successfully collecting data and observations: (a), (c)
PDO — Recording data and observations: (a), (b)
ACE — Drawing conclusions: (b)

Duration

The practical work will take between 40 and 45 min. The analysis and evaluation questions will take around 30 min.

Preparing for the investigation

- Check the activity of the urease, to ensure that it does produce sufficient ammonia to give a measurable change in pH when added to urea. A 0.6% solution of urease is suggested below, but you may need to use a more or less concentrated solution.

- The sodium alginate solution should be made up beforehand. Follow any instructions with the sodium alginate powder to dissolve it. It may need warming, and will need stirring. It can take some time to dissolve; if you have a magnetic stirrer and a hot plate this will help considerably. The solution will be quite jelly-like, but must be sufficiently liquid to be able to be picked up in a dropper pipette; dilute it with water if necessary.

- Learners may like to know that urease breaks down urea to ammonia and carbon dioxide:

$$CO(NH_2)_2 + H_2O \longrightarrow 2NH_3 + CO_2$$

Ammonia dissolves in water to produce ammonium hydroxide, which is a strong alkali. Although carbon dioxide dissolves to produce a weak acid, the overall effect is an increase in alkalinity – that is, an increase in pH.

Equipment

Each learner or group will need:

- about 50 cm³ of 0.6% urease solution

- about 100 cm³ of 2% urea solution

- a 20 cm³ syringe barrel, with a short length of rubber tubing attached to its nozzle

- a clamp to hold the tubing closed

- a retort stand, boss and clamp to support the syringe barrel

- a small piece of muslin

- a tea strainer

- several glass beakers (small or medium size)

- about 80 cm³ of 3% sodium alginate solution (this can often be obtained more cheaply from suppliers of cooking ingredients than from educational suppliers)

- about 100 cm³ of 3% calcium chloride solution

- a timer (e.g. on a phone)

- an apparatus for measuring small volumes, e.g. two 5 cm³ or 10 cm³ syringes or two graduated pipettes

- a pH meter and probe

- a dropper pipette with a fine nozzle.

Additional notes and advice

- If you cannot buy urease, you can extract it from dried soya beans. Soak the beans in water overnight and then liquidise them in an electric blender (or use a pestle and mortar). Filter; the enzyme will be present in the filtrate. Fresh soya beans can also be used. If you use beans, test the extract to determine an appropriate concentration to use in this experiment.

- A tea strainer is a small piece of kitchen equipment used to strain drinks such as tea (Figure 3.9). If you do not have one, you can use muslin or other cloth to separate the beads of jelly from the liquid.

Figure 3.9

- If you do not have pH probes, you can use strips of Universal Indicator paper to measure pH.

Safety considerations

- Learners should have read the safety guidance section within the workbook before carrying out this investigation.

- Standard laboratory safety procedures should be followed always.

- Although all enzymes can produce allergic reactions in a small minority of learners, the concentrations of urease used in this investigation are unlikely to pose any significant risk.

Carrying out the investigation

- It is important to ensure that the enzyme–alginate mixture is as uniform as possible, so that all beads contain the same concentration of urease. As previously described, make sure that it is sufficiently liquid to use in a dropper pipette.

- Learners may have difficulty in producing beads of similar sizes, although most are able to do this with a little practice.

- The jelly beads are quite fragile, and may be broken up if learners handle them too vigorously.

- The pH probes need to be calibrated shortly before the practical begins. Make sure that each probe is carefully cleaned between measuring the pH in one solution and the next. Even a tiny quantity of urease that has contaminated the probe will be able to break down urea that the probe later comes into contact with.

- If the urea solution runs through the column of beads too quickly, or if the spaces between the beads are too large, then not enough urea solution will come into contact with the urease in the beads, and only a little ammonia will be produced. This can be remedied by packing the beads more tightly (smaller beads pack better than large ones) and/or by reducing the rate of flow through the column by partly closing the clamp over the rubber tubing.

🕐 Learners who complete the investigation quickly and successfully could plan and carry out an investigation to try to answer one of the following questions:

- Does the activity of the urease in the beads remain relatively constant, or does it decrease as successive batches of urea solution are poured through the beads?

- When beads containing urease are added to urea solution, the gases produced form bubbles on the beads. These bubbles can cause the beads to rise to the surface. The faster the production of bubbles, the faster the beads rise. Use this information to devise a way in which the beads could be used to find the concentration of a urea solution.

Note that, for the second question above, it would be important to test the technique before doing the experiment. Carbon dioxide is a soluble gas and relatively dense, and if the beads themselves are also dense (as may happen if the sodium alginate solution is very thick) there may not be sufficient carbon dioxide adhering to them to cause a reduction in density below that of the urea solution – so the beads may not rise at all.

Sample results

Initial pH of urea solution	pH of urea solution after passing through the column of beads
7.7	9.0

Table 3.7

Answers to the workbook questions (using the sample results)

a The pH of the urea solution rose from 7.7 to 9.0 after passing through the beads. This happened because the urease broke down the urea, releasing ammonia which formed an alkaline solution and caused the pH to increase.

b It is likely that learners will find that some bubbles are formed, indicating that there is still urea present. Not all of the urea in the solution has been broken down by the urease in the beads, perhaps because not all of the urea molecules came into contact with the active site of a urease molecule.

Practical investigation 3.6:
Investigating the effect of an inhibitor on the action of bromelain

Learning objective: 3.2(a)

Skills focus

The following skill areas are developed and practised (see the skills grids at the front of this guide):

MMO — Making decisions about measurements: (g), (j)
Successfully collecting data and observations: (a)

PDO — Recording data and observations: (a), (b), (c)
Layout of data or observations:

ACE — Interpreting data or observations and identifying sources of error: (f), (g)
Drawing conclusions: (b)
Suggesting improvements or modifications to extend an investigation: (a), (b), (c), (e)

Duration

Making the copper sulfate solutions and setting up the Petri dishes will take about 45 min. You could reduce this time by providing learners with ready-made copper sulfate solutions.

Learners will need to return later on the same day, or the next day, to measure the diameters of the wells and record their results.

Preparing for the investigation

• Learners should have knowledge of enzyme inhibitors. Copper sulfate is a non-competitive inhibitor.

• The jelly (gel) for the Petri dishes should be made up the day before, and kept in a refrigerator until used. The jelly should be of a similar consistency to agar jelly – sufficiently solid to be able to cut wells that hold their shape. If it is very solid, however, this will slow down the digestion of the protein and it will take longer to obtain results. It is important to use jelly that is based on gelatin, not on agar (which is not a protein). In most countries, cubes or powder can be bought to make edible jellies – the packet should indicate if this contains gelatin. Use a strongly-coloured jelly if possible, as this makes it easier to measure the diameters of the wells.

(Note: in some countries, the word 'jelly' refers to a fruit preserve that can be spread on bread. This is *not* what is intended here.)

• The pineapple extracts should also be made up beforehand. Cut some fresh pineapple into chunks, liquidise, and filter through two layers of muslin. Take a small quantity of this fresh extract and boil, then cool.

• You should trial the investigation, to determine a suitable time for which to leave the dishes after learners have set up their experiment. Depending on the activity of the enzyme in the pineapple extract, and the ambient temperature, you might get results in as little as 1 h. It could, however, take considerably longer than this.

Equipment

Each learner or group will need:

• about 50 cm^3 of an extract made from fresh pineapple (see above)

• a small quantity of boiled pineapple extract

• five small Petri dishes containing coloured jelly, made using gelatin (see above)

• about 10 cm^3 of 1 mol dm^{-3} copper sulfate solution

- a cork borer
- a ruler to measure in mm.

Additional notes and advice

- If you do not have small Petri dishes, learners could use large ones and make several wells in each one. However, this does mean it is possible for wells to merge if the bromelain is very active and digests a lot of protein quickly.

Safety considerations

- Learners should have read the safety guidance section within the workbook before carrying out this investigation.
- Standard laboratory safety procedures should be followed always.
- Copper sulfate solution should be washed off with cold water if it gets onto hands or clothes.

Carrying out the investigation

- This is a relatively reliable investigation, as long as you are successful in making a suitable jelly.
- Learners may find it difficult to cut the wells neatly. You could provide a few spare dishes of jelly for them to practice. Twisting the cork borer slightly as you lift the core of jelly out can often work well.
- They may also have difficulty in deciding where the edge of the well is, when measuring its diameter. There is no easy fix for this, so it will need to be noted as a source of error.

Some learners may still not be confident in using serial dilution to make up solutions, although by now they will probably have done so on several occasions. You could provide a help sheet for them if needed.

Alternatively, ask learners to refer to the Practical Workbook, Figure 2.2. You may also like to refer to Figure 3.4 on page 23 in this Teacher Guide.

Learners who would benefit from a challenge could plan an investigation to compare the activity of bromelain from pineapple with proteases found in other fruits (e.g. pawpaw, kiwi fruit or figs). If time allows, they could carry out their planned investigation.

Sample results

Wells were cut with an 8 mm diameter cork borer.

0.8 cm^3 of pineapple extract and three drops of water or copper sulfate solution were added to each well.

Pineapple extract	Copper sulfate solution concentration / $mol \, dm^{-3}$	Diameter of well after 2 h / mm
boiled	0	8
fresh	0	37
fresh	0.001	16
fresh	0.01	9
fresh	0.1	8
fresh	1.0	8

Table 3.8

Answers to the workbook questions (using sample results)

a The wells containing boiled pineapple extract, and the fresh extracts to which 0.1 and 0.01 mol dm^{-3} copper sulfate solution had been added, were unchanged after 2 h.

The well containing fresh pineapple extract had increased in diameter to 37 mm, an increase of 25 mm. The well containing fresh pineapple extract and 0.001 mol dm^{-3} copper sulfate solution had also increased in diameter, but only by 8 mm, while the well containing fresh pineapple extract and 0.01 mol dm^{-3} copper sulfate solution had increased very slightly to 9 mm diameter.

b The wells increased in diameter because protease enzymes in the pineapple extract digested the protein in the jelly.

The enzyme in the boiled extract was denatured by boiling – the hydrogen bonds in the enzyme molecules were broken, so the active site lost its shape and could no longer form complexes with protein molecules. The protein around the well containing boiled extract was therefore not digested.

Copper sulfate has acted as an inhibitor. Even the lowest concentration of 0.001 mol dm^{-3} has reduced the activity of bromelain. Concentrations of 0.1 mol dm^{-3} appear to have completely prevented its activity, although it would be interesting to see if any activity did occur if the dishes were left for longer.

Copper ions act as non-competitive inhibitors. They bind permanently with the enzyme at a position other than the active site, distorting the 3D shape of the enzyme, so that its active site is no longer a complementary shape to the protein molecules that normally act as a substrate.

c The most significant source of error is likely to be the measurement of the diameter of the wells. The edges are often not clear-cut, and the wells and the digested areas may not be absolutely circular. Learners are likely to have had to make estimates of the diameters rather than precise measurements.

Another source of error is the volume of extract and/or inhibitor added to each well. These are very small volumes, and it is not easy to measure these accurately. Even small variations could affect results.

d The most obvious way to improve the investigation would be to use repeats. Three or five sets of dishes could be set up, and a mean diameter calculated for each well. This would allow any anomalous results to be detected more easily.

Chapter outline

This chapter relates to Chapter 4: Cell membranes and transport in the coursebook.

In this chapter, learners will complete practical investigations on:

- 4.1 The effect of salt solutions on eggs
- 4.2 Measuring the rate of osmosis using an osmometer
- 4.3 The effect of surface area : volume ratio on the rate of diffusion
- 4.4 The effect of temperature or concentration gradient on the rate of diffusion
- 4.5 Estimating the water potential of potato tuber cells
- 4.6 Estimating the solution potential of onion epidermis cells
- 4.7 Determining water potential using density
- 4.8 The effect of temperature on membrane permeability

Practical investigation 4.1:
The effect of salt solutions on eggs

Learning objective: 4.2(b)

Skills focus

The following AS skills are developed and practised (see the skills grids at the front of this guide):

MMO	Collecting data and observations: (a), (c), (e)
PDO	Recording data and observations: (c), (d)
	Displaying calculations and reasoning: (a)
	Layout of data and observations: (c), (d), (e)
ACE	Interpreting data or observations: (a), (e), (f), (g)
	Drawing conclusions: (b)

Duration

The hens' eggs need to be left overnight in the acid. This could be done by yourself or a technician, but it is a better learning experience for the learners if they do this themselves.

The practical activity will take about 50 min. The analysis and evaluation questions will take about 30 min.

Preparing for the investigation

- Learners should know and understand how osmosis takes place, and be confident in using water potential terminology.

Equipment

Each learner or group will need:

Day 1

- six hen's eggs
- a very large beaker to hold all six eggs
- a large spoon or other implement for lowering the eggs into the acid
- enough 1.5 mol dm^{-3} hydrochloric acid to cover the eggs in the beaker

Day 2

- a large spoon or other implement for removing the eggs from the acid
- about 400 cm^3 20% sodium chloride solution
- syringes or pipettes to measure 1 and 10 cm^3
- a timer (e.g. on a phone)
- 6 × 400 cm^3 beakers
- paper towel.

Access to:

- electronic balance
- distilled water.

Safety considerations

- Learners should have read the safety guidance section within the workbook before carrying out this investigation.

- Standard laboratory safety procedures should be followed always.

- The suggested concentration of hydrochloric acid, $1.5\,mol\,dm^{-3}$, is dilute – about the same concentration as stomach acid. However, learners should wash off any acid that comes into contact with skin or clothes. They should wear eye protection.

Carrying out the investigation

Some learners may need help with deciding how to make up the range of solutions. You could consider providing a help sheet, with Table 4.1 already completed.

Final concentration of solution / %	Volume of solution added / cm³	Volume of distilled water added / cm³
0	0	200
5	50	150
10	100	100
15	150	50
20	200	0

Table 4.1

Sample results

Concentration of sodium chloride solution / %	Initial mass of egg / g	Final mass of egg / g	Percentage change in mass / %
0	73.2	76.4	+4.37
5	70.9	71.5	+0.85
10	76.3	76.2	−0.13
15	76.1	72.9	−4.20
20	66.4	62.4	−6.02

Table 4.2

All of the eggs are likely to become fairly hard in the centre, which is probably caused by the acid in which they were bathed to remove their shells. The eggs left in low concentrations of sodium chloride solution (or in pure water) appear swollen. If cut open, a lot of watery fluid flows out. The eggs left in high concentrations of sodium chloride appear shrunk, and feel less 'puffy' than those in low concentrations. If cut open, some fluid does leak out, but it is not as watery as that emerging from the other eggs.

Answers to the workbook questions (using the sample results)

a See Table 4.2 for results.

b

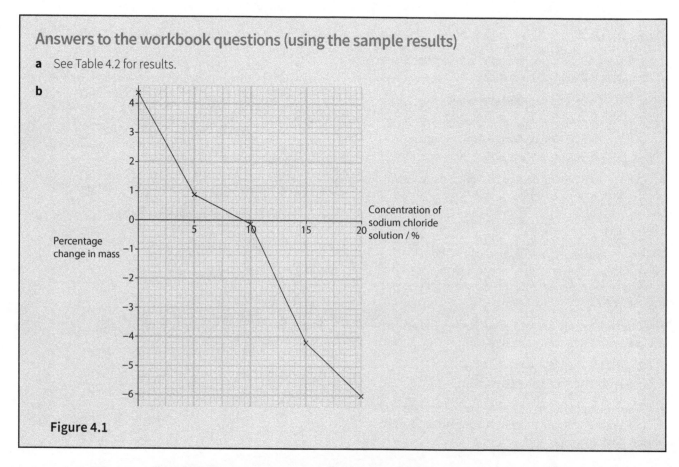

Figure 4.1

There are no anomalous results to identify in the sample results.

c When placed in concentrations of sodium chloride solution of 5% or less, the eggs gained mass. The lower the concentration of sodium chloride solution, the more mass they gained.

When placed in concentrations of sodium chloride solution of 10% or more, the eggs lost mass. The higher the concentration of sodium chloride solution, the more mass they lost. The egg in 10% solution changed only very slightly in mass.

d In water or a dilute sodium chloride solution, the water potential of the contents of the eggs is lower than that of the bathing solution. As these two solutions are separated by the partially permeable membrane surrounding the egg, water moves by osmosis down its water potential gradient, into the egg. This causes its mass to increase.

In a sodium chloride solution of 10% or more, the water potential of the contents of the eggs is higher than that of the bathing solution. As these two solutions are separated by the partially permeable membrane surrounding the egg, water moves by osmosis down its water potential gradient, out of the egg. This causes its mass to decrease.

e Important sources of error:

- The eggs may not have completely equilibrated with their solutions within 30 min. Eggs are large, and it takes a long time for water molecules to move all the way between the centre of the egg and the partially permeable membrane that separates it from the bathing solution.

- If learners have used an imprecise measuring instrument such as a syringe or a measuring cylinder when making up their sodium chloride solutions, the concentrations may not be exactly what they intended.

Practical investigation 4.2:
Measuring the rate of osmosis using an osmometer

Learning objective: 4.2(b)

Skills focus

The following AS skills are developed and practised (see the skills grids at the front of this guide):

MMO   Collecting data and observations: (b), (e), (f), (h)

PDO   Recording data and observations: (a), (b), (c)
             Layout of data and observations: (b), (c), (d), (e)

ACE   Interpreting data or observations: (f), (g), (h)
             Drawing conclusions: (a)

Duration

The practical work in Part 1 will take approximately 40 min, with perhaps another 15 min for the data analysis question. Part 2 will take another 60–90 min, plus another 20 min for the data analysis and evaluation questions. You could reduce the time for Part 2 by about 30 min by providing learners with a range of sucrose solutions, rather than asking them to make these up for themselves.

Preparing for the investigation

- Learners should already have used serial dilution to make a range of solutions of different concentrations from a stock solution.

Equipment

Each learner or group will need:

- Visking tubing

- about 100 cm^3 of a 2 mol dm^{-3} sucrose solution

- five 250 cm^3 beakers

- one 500 cm^3 beaker

- a piece of narrow glass tubing, approximately 30 cm long

- ruler marked in mm

- a retort stand, boss and clamp

- strong cotton thread

- a timer (e.g. on a phone)

- apparatus for measuring small volumes, e.g. two 5 cm^3 or 10 cm^3 syringes or two graduated pipettes

- a dropper pipette.

Access to:

- distilled water.

Additional notes and advice

- Visking tubing may be sold as dialysis tubing. If you cannot obtain Visking tubing or another type of dialysis tubing, you could try using cellophane as an alternative partially permeable membrane. This is often used in shops to wrap cakes or flowers. However, it is strongly recommended that you try out the cellophane beforehand, to ensure that it allows water molecules to pass through, but not sucrose. Some schools like to use animal intestines.

- The narrower the glass tubing that you use, the faster the meniscus will move up it, and the shorter time will be required for learners to collect a set of results. Capillary tubing is suitable, but any narrow glass tubing will work.

Safety considerations

- Learners should have read the safety guidance section within the workbook before carrying out this investigation.

- Standard laboratory safety procedures should be followed always.

- There are no additional significant safety issues with this investigation, although care needs to be taken with the glass tubing.

Method

Part 2

1 Learners will decide on a particular range of concentrations, and their table will reflect these choices. One possibility would be:

Concentration of solution / mol dm^{-3}	Volume of 1.0 mol dm^{-3} sucrose solution / cm^3	Volume of water / cm^3
0	0	100
0.5	25	75
1.0	50	50
1.5	75	25
2.0	100	0

Table 4.3

3 Two possible ways of measuring the dependent variable are:

- measure the time taken for the meniscus to move a pre-determined distance

- measure the distance moved in a pre-determined time.

The latter is the better option, as it means they can choose a time that will allow them to complete their collection of results within the lesson time.

4 Variables to be kept the same include:

- the volume of solution inside the tubing

- the volume and depth of water in the beaker

- the temperature

- the position at which the Visking tubing is tied to the glass tubing

- the diameter of the glass tubing.

Carrying out the investigation

- The most common difficulty is leakage between the Visking tubing and the glass tube to which it is tied. Use strong thread, and two people to tie it. Support the glass tube so that this join is above the level of the liquid in the beaker.

- In Part 2, learners will probably need to re-use the Visking tubing, so that the same piece is used for each concentration of sucrose. The tubing will need to be washed thoroughly, to remove all traces of sucrose from it. It will be difficult (perhaps impossible) to reattach it to the glass tubing in exactly the same position for each solution tested. This can be discussed as a source of error in the evaluation.

Learners may need guidance in selecting a suitable range of sucrose solutions in Part 2, and in preparing these by dilution.

They may need guidance in deciding how and when to measure the dependent variable. They should use their results from Part 1 to help them with this, by looking at the time taken for the meniscus to move a particular distance in the tubing.

Learners who require a further challenge could consider how they could use this apparatus to investigate the effect of temperature on the rate of osmosis. If time allows, they could do this experiment.

Sample results

Part 1

Time / min	Distance moved by meniscus / mm
0	0
2	4
4	8
6	13
8	16
10	18
12	19

Table 4.4

Part 2

Concentration of sucrose solution in tubing / mol dm⁻³	Distance moved by meniscus in 15 min / mm
0	0
0.5	4
1.0	10
1.5	16
2.0	25

Table 4.5

Answers to the workbook questions (using the sample results)

Part 1

a The graph should have:

- time on the *x*-axis, labelled Time / min, and with a suitable scale that goes up in intervals of 2 min and uses most of the graph grid

- distance on the *y*-axis, labelled Distance moved by meniscus / mm, and with a suitable scale that goes up in sensible intervals and uses most of the graph grid

- points plotted with a sharp pencil using neat, small crosses

- a line drawn with a sharp pencil, **either** carefully ruled between the exact centre of each cross using a ruler, **or** a smooth best fit line.

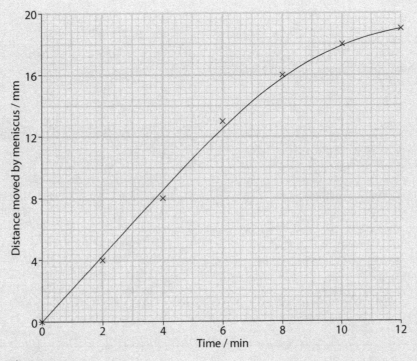

Figure 4.2

b $19 \div 12 = 1.6 \, \text{mm min}^{-1}$

c percentage error $= (1 \div 19) \times 100 = 5.23$

a

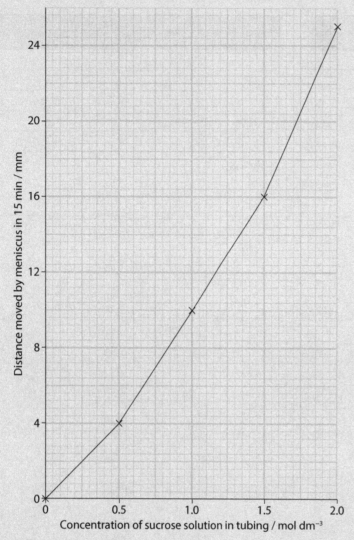

Distance moved by meniscus in 15 min / mm (y-axis)

Concentration of sucrose solution in tubing / mol dm⁻³ (x-axis)

Figure 4.3

b The greater the concentration of the sucrose solution, the faster the water moves up the tube. A concentrated sucrose solution has a lower water potential than a dilute sucrose solution. Therefore, the greater the concentration of the sucrose solution, the lower its water potential, and the steeper the gradient between the water in the beaker and the sucrose solution inside the Visking tubing. When the tubing contains water, the water potential of the liquids inside and outside the tubing is the same, so there is no water potential gradient and the rate of osmosis is 0.

c Significant sources of error include:

• Leakage of liquid from the join between the Visking tubing and the glass tubing. This is probably a systematic error within any one set up of the apparatus (if liquid leaks at an unchanging rate), but will be a random error when looking at the different set ups with the different concentrations of sucrose solutions. Leakage will affect the results by making the distance moved by the liquid up the glass tubing less than it should be, and so will make the rate of osmosis appear slower.

- Temperature changes in the room. This will be a random error. An increase in temperature will increase the kinetic energy of the water particles, which will increase the rate of osmosis. It will also cause expansion in the liquids, which will cause the liquid to move up the glass tube faster.

- Measurement of the distance moved by the liquid. This is difficult to do accurately, unless there is a scale marked on the glass tube. Inaccuracies in measurement are likely to be random errors.

- Inaccuracies in measurement of volumes when making up the sucrose solutions. These will be random errors, caused by the difficulty in measuring volumes precisely using syringes. The errors will be much less if graduated pipettes are used.

Practical investigation 4.3:
The effect of surface area : volume ratio on the rate of diffusion

Learning objective: 4.2(d)

Skills focus

The following AS skills are developed and practised (see the skills grids at the front of this guide):

MMO   Collecting data and observations: (a)

PDO   Recording data and observations: (b), (c)

ACE   Interpreting data or observations: (a), (f)

Duration

Allow about 1 h for the practical activity, and another 20 min for answering the questions.

Preparing for the investigation

No specific preparation is required for this investigation.

Equipment

Each learner or group will need:

- several transparent containers that can hold a cube with sides of 1 cm (e.g. boiling tubes or small beakers)

- a ruler to measure in mm

- a timer, for example, on a mobile phone

- a scalpel or sharp knife

- a white tile or other surface for cutting

- forceps

- approximately 250 cm^3 1.0 mol dm^{-3} hydrochloric acid solution (concentration is not critical)

- agar jelly containing ammonium hydroxide and cresol red.

Access to:

- distilled water.

Additional notes and advice

- Agar jelly should be made up from agar powder, which can be obtained from any biological supplier. It can also be bought as a cookery ingredient. Add 2 g of agar to 100 cm^3 of distilled water and heat gently until the agar dissolves. Add 5 cm^3 of cresol red solution (you can use phenolphthalein instead if you do not have cresol red) and 2 cm^3 2 mol dm^{-3} ammonium hydroxide. Mix thoroughly. While still warm, pour the mixture into a tray to a depth of 10 mm. It is helpful to smear the tray with a little oil first, to make it easier for learners to remove the jelly after it has set.

- To make up the cresol red solution, dissolve 0.5 g in 20 cm^3 of ethanol. Add distilled water to make up to 50 cm^3. To make up phenolphthalein, dissolve 1 g in 600 cm^3 of industrial denatured alcohol, then make up to 1 dm^3 with distilled water.

- Agar jelly is well known as a medium for growing microorganisms, so make up the jelly no more than a day or so before it will be used, and keep it in a cool place, such as a refrigerator, until required.

Safety considerations

- Learners should have read the safety guidance section within the workbook before carrying out this investigation.

- Standard laboratory safety procedures should be followed always.

- Learners should take care with the sharp blade.

- $1.0 \, mol \, dm^{-3}$ HCl is low hazard.

Method

2

Length of side / mm	Surface area / mm²	Volume / mm³	Surface area : volume
5	150	125	1.2 : 1
10	600	1000	0.6 : 1
15	1350	3375	0.4 : 1

Table 4.6

Carrying out the investigation

- It is difficult to determine the exact moment that all of the jelly has changed colour. There is not really anything that can be done about this; learners can discuss it as a significant source of error, and perhaps devise their own method of trying to minimise it.

  Learners who require a further challenge could additionally try using pieces of jelly that are not cubes – for example rectangular blocks with sides of 2 cm, 1 cm and 2 cm. They could also try using cylinders of jelly with different diameters (they will all have to be no more than 20 mm long, if you have provided jelly to a depth of 20 mm), cut out with different sizes of cork borers.

Sample results

Surface area : volume ratio	Time taken for whole cube to change colour / s			
	First trial	Second trial	Third trial	Mean
1.2 : 1	302	268	252	274
0.6 : 1	987	1000	976	988
0.4 : 1	1988	1909	2002	1966

Table 4.7

Answers to the workbook questions (using the sample results)

a The greater the surface area : volume ratio, the shorter the time taken for the acid to diffuse to the centre of the cube. Doubling the surface area : volume ratio from 0.6 : 1 to 1.2 : 2 causes the time taken to be almost 4 × less (988 ÷ 274 = 3.60).

b Points that learners could make include:

- Living organisms are not cubes. Small living organisms may have roughly spherical bodies. They may also have flattened bodies, which increases their surface area : volume ratios. However, this experiment does demonstrate how having a relatively large surface area : volume ratio does increase diffusion rate.

- The hydrochloric acid could diffuse into the cube across all of its surface. This relates well to simple organisms such as bacteria, protocista, cnidarians or annelids. However, for larger organisms such as fish or mammals, diffusion into and out of the body generally occurs only through specialised exchange surfaces such as alveoli or gills.

- Larger organisms have transport systems, so substances do not need to diffuse all the way into the centre of their bodies, only into the transport fluid (which is usually blood).

Practical investigation 4.4:
The effect of temperature or concentration gradient on the rate of diffusion

Learning objective: 4.2(b)

Skills focus

The following AS skills are developed and practised (see the skills grids at the front of this guide):

MMO   Making decisions about measurements: (a), (b), (e), (f), (h), (i)

PDO   Recording data and observations: (b), (c)
Layout of data and observations: (b), (c), (d), (e)

ACE   Interpreting data or observations: (e), (f), (g), (i)
Drawing conclusions: (a)

Duration

Learners need to plan their investigation before they do it. You may like to provide time for them to do this within the lesson, in which case they should need no more than 30 min. Alternatively, this could be given as a homework task.

The practical work itself can be completed within 1 h.

Preparing for the investigation

- See Practical investigation 4.3.

- If learners want to investigate the effect of temperature, they will need to find a way of keeping the dishes at a chosen temperature.

Equipment

Each learner or group will need:

- apparatus and materials as for Practical investigation 4.3

- syringes or calibrated pipettes for making a range of concentrations of hydrochloric acid solution.

Access to:

- distilled water

- thermostatically controlled water baths at five different temperatures, or the means to make water baths using beakers.

Safety considerations

- See Practical investigation 4.3.

Method

1–7 Learner answers will vary.

Carrying out the investigation

- See Practical investigation 3.3.

  Even though the instructions are quite structured, some learners will need help with the decision-making steps when planning their investigation. You may like to encourage them to work in groups, and discuss the plans together. They could then explain their plan to you (or write it down to be checked by you) before they begin their experiment.

- Remind learners that they need at least five values for their independent variable.

  Learners who require a further challenge could be asked to relate their findings to gas exchange in aquatic organisms. They could research and discuss this question: How might temperature changes affect the ability of an aquatic organism to obtain oxygen from its environment? They should discover that although high **temperature** increases the rate of diffusion of oxygen, the **concentration** of dissolved oxygen is less at higher temperatures.

Common learner misconception

- Some learners will want to change more than one variable – for example, they may want to change both temperature and concentration. Make sure that they understand they should have only one independent variable.

Sample results

Concentration of acid constant at 1.0 mol dm⁻³:

Temperature / °C	Mean time for cube with sides of 5 mm to change colour / s
0	too long to measure
10	847
20	394
30	195
40	102

Table 4.8

Temperature constant at 20°C.

Concentration of HCl / mol dm⁻³	Mean time for cube with sides of 5 mm to change colour / s
0.2	3473
0.4	2781
0.6	1385
0.8	764
1.0	403

Table 4.9

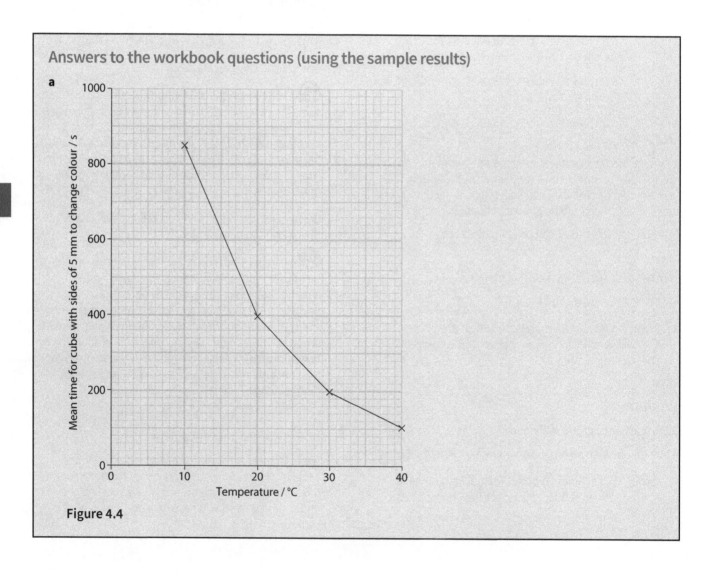

Answers to the workbook questions (using the sample results)

a

Figure 4.4

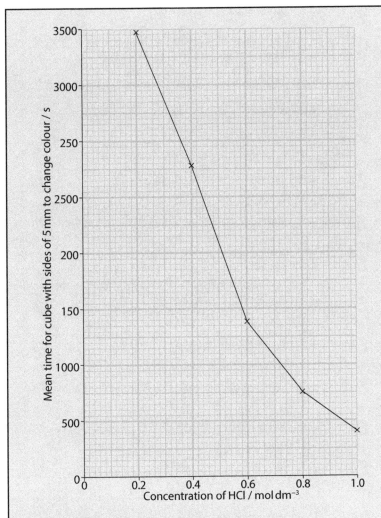

Figure 4.5

b For temperature: Increasing temperature increases the rate of diffusion. For the sample results, time roughly halves for a 10°C rise in temperature.

For concentration: Increasing the concentration gradient increases the rate of diffusion.

c The most significant errors are likely to be:

- measuring the time; it is very difficult to determine the precise moment at which the colour change is complete; random error; could result in random variation in the results.

- cutting the cubes; it is impossible to ensure that every cube has the same dimensions; random error; could result in random variations in the results.

- maintaining the different values of temperature absolutely constant; random error; could result in random variations in the results.

- making up different concentrations of hydrochloric acid; measurement of volume with syringes or measuring cylinders is not accurate; random error; could result in random variations in the results.

Practical investigation 4.5:
Estimating the water potential of potato tuber cells

Learning objective: 4.2(e)

Skills focus

The following AS skills are developed and practised (see the skills grids at the front of this guide):

MMO	Successfully collecting data and observations: (a)
PDO	Recording data and observations: (a), (c) Layout of data and observations: (b), (c), (d), (e)
ACE	Interpreting data or observations: (a), (b), (e), (f), (i)

Duration

If learners cut their own potato cylinders, allow between 75 and 90 min. If you prefer to provide them with cylinders that have already been cut, allow about 1 h. Although the instructions suggest leaving the cylinders in their solutions for 30 min, you could reduce this to 20 min if time is limited.

Preparing for the investigation

- Learners should have a good understanding of osmosis.

- They should appreciate that a potato tuber is made up of living plant cells.

Equipment

Each learner or group will need:

- a large potato

- a sharp knife or scalpel *or* a cork borer

- seven containers, for example, beakers, in which the potato cylinders can lie flat

- a white tile or other surface for cutting

- forceps

- paper towel

- about 50 cm³ of six different concentrations of sucrose solution, ranging from 0.1 to 1 mol dm⁻³

- a ruler to measure in mm and/or an electronic balance.

Access to:

- distilled water.

Additional notes and advice

- Cork borers are ideal for producing regularly shaped cylinders of potato tuber tissue with a constant diameter. If you do not have any, then learners can cut rectangular blocks of tissue using a scalpel or sharp knife. This makes it difficult to produce pieces of very similar dimensions, so it would be better to measure changes in mass rather than changes in length.

Safety considerations

- Learners should have read the safety guidance section within the workbook before carrying out this investigation.

- Standard laboratory safety procedures should be followed always.

- Care must be taken when using a sharp blade.

Carrying out the investigation

Some learners may need help in constructing the scale on the *y*-axis of their graph, because this needs to show positive and negative values.

Learners who require a further challenge could be asked to follow up their investigation by trying smaller intervals for more values of concentration of sucrose solution on either side of their estimated value for the water potential of the potato cells. This will allow them to add more points to their graph, to be more certain of the point at which the change in length or mass is zero.

Sample results

Concentration of sucrose solution / mol dm⁻³	Initial length of cylinder / mm	Final length of cylinder / mm	Percentage change in length / %
2.0	41	39	−4.88
0.8	47	46	−2.13
0.6	50	49	−2.00
0.4	51	51	0.00
0.2	50	51	+2.00
0.1	49	50	+2.00
0.0	45	48	+6.67

Table 4.10

Concentration of sucrose solution / mol dm⁻³	Initial mass of cylinder / g	Final mass of cylinder / g	Percentage change in mass / %
2.0	15.3	14.4	−5.88
0.8	16.7	16.0	−4.19
0.6	15.9	15.4	−3.14
0.4	15.4	15.3	−0.65
0.2	16.0	16.1	+0.63
0.1	15.5	16.4	+5.81
0.0	15.8	16.9	+6.96

Table 4.11

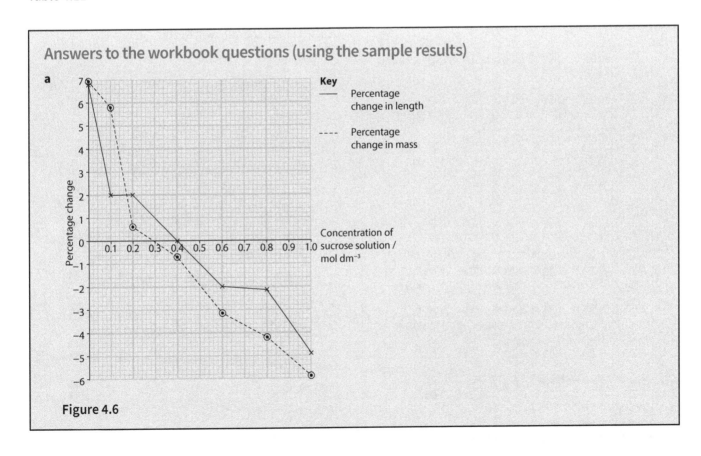

Figure 4.6

Practical investigation 4.6:
Estimating the solute potential of onion epidermis cells

Learning objective: 4.2(e)

Skills focus

The following AS skills are developed and practised (see the skills grids at the front of this guide):

MMO	Making decisions about measurements: (b), (l)
	Successfully collecting data and observations: (a), (d), (i)
PDO	Recording data and observations: (a), (c)
	Layout of data and observations: (b), (c), (d), (e)
ACE	Interpreting data or observations: (a), (b), (e), (f), (g), (i)
	Drawing conclusions: (a)

Duration

It will take learners approximately 30 min to make up their own range of solutions. This could be done a day or two before the main practical work. Alternatively, you could provide them with a range of solutions that have already been made up.

The remainder of the practical work can be done in 45–60 min, with another 15 or 20 min required to construct the graph and answer the questions.

Preparing for the investigation

- The concept of 'incipient plasmolysis' is quite a difficult one for learners to understand fully. Before they can begin to understand this concept (and therefore the

underlying principles of this investigation), learners need to be entirely comfortable with the concept of water potential, and appreciate that water moves from a high water potential to a low water potential. They then need to have a solid understanding of the effects of the loss or gain of water by osmosis on plant cells. You may therefore like to use a written or oral quiz to check understanding of these concepts before introducing this investigation.

Equipment

Each learner or group will need:

- an onion

- a sharp knife or scalpel

- several clean glass slides

- several cover slips

- a white tile or other surface for cutting

- forceps

- a seeker or mounted needle

- a dropper pipette

- filter paper or paper towel (for cleaning your slides)

- a microscope and light source

- about 50 cm^3 of 1 mol dm^{-3} sucrose solution

- syringes or pipettes to measure between 1 cm^3 and 10 cm^3.

Access to:

- distilled water.

Safety considerations

- Learners should have read the safety guidance section within the workbook before carrying out this investigation.

- Standard laboratory safety procedures should be followed always.

- Care must be taken when using a sharp blade.

Method

1

Concentration of solution / mol dm⁻³	Volume of 1 mol dm⁻³ sucrose solution / cm³	Volume of water / cm³
0.9	9	1
0.8	8	2
0.7	7	3
0.6	6	4
0.5	5	5
0.4	4	6
0.3	3	7

Table 4.12

Carrying out the investigation

- Some learners may find it difficult to prepare a slide where the epidermis is spread out, so that they can view a single layer of cells. However, this is something that they have practised earlier (see Practical investigation 1.1) so this is an opportunity to refine their technique.

⚙ Provide micrographs of plasmolysed and unplasmolysed onion epidermis cells, to help learners to identify these cells when they see them through the microscope.

⚙ If learners are having difficulty counting cells, show them how to tap with a pencil to record each cell that they 'count'. They can count up the number of dots they have made. Alternatively, you could provide a click counter.

⚙ Learners who would benefit from a further challenge could be asked to explain why this method allows us to estimate the **solute potential** of the contents of the onion epidermis cells, whereas the technique used in Practical investigation 4.5 estimates the **water potential** of the potato tuber cells.

Sample results

Concentration of sucrose solution / mol dm⁻³	Total number of cells counted	Number of cells that were plasmolysed	Percentage of cells that were plasmolysed / %
0.3	50	0	0
0.4	50	2	4
0.5	50	9	18
0.6	50	38	76
0.7	50	46	92
0.8	50	50	100
0.9	50	50	100
1.0	50	50	100

Table 4.13

Answers to the workbook questions (using the sample results)

a, b

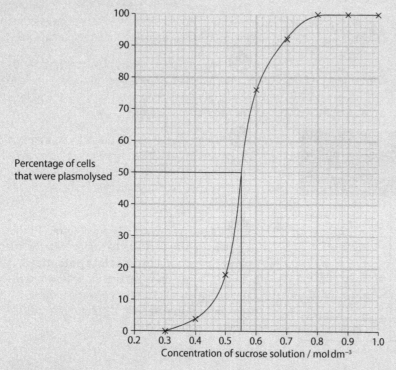

Figure 4.7

c The concentration read from Figure 4.7 is 0.55 mol dm⁻³, which is equivalent to a solute potential of approximately −1700 kPa.

d Learners may comment on some of the following issues, which reduce their confidence in their results and conclusion:

- the assumption that finding the concentration of solution that results in 50% of the cells being plasmolysed represents incipient plasmolysis – this assumes that the cells may differ slightly in their water potential; in practice, if the cells all have a similar water potential, then we might expect to find a sudden change from all being plasmolysed to all not being plasmolysed.

- any anomalous results that they have

- the fact that no repeats have been done

- the small number of data points on the graph, in particular only three values in the sample results that give values other than 0 or 100

- the possibility that the tissue samples may not have had time for osmosis to be completed before the counts were made

- the fact that only 50 cells were counted (in the sample results), which is quite a small sample of the total number of cells in the tissue pieces, and may not be fully representative

- difficulties in determining whether some of the cells were plasmolysed or not.

Practical investigation 4.7:
Determining water potential using density

Learning objective: 4.2(b)

Skills focus

The following AS skills are developed and practised (see the skills grids at the front of this guide):

MMO   Making decisions about measurements: (g), (i)
Successfully collecting data and observations: (a)

PDO   Recording data and observations: (a), (b)

ACE   Interpreting data or observations: (c), (f), (i)
Drawing conclusions: (a), (b)

Duration

This activity can be done in 60–70 min. Learners may need another 20 min to answer the questions.

Preparing for the investigation

- Each of the individual concepts that lie behind this investigation is relatively straightforward in itself, but learners may find it difficult to link everything together, and keep a clear picture in their mind of what they are doing, what is happening, and why. Make sure that learners understand each of the following concepts before beginning the practical activity:

  - A drop of liquid will sink in a liquid that is less dense than it is, and rise in a liquid that is more dense than it is.

  - A sucrose solution with a higher water potential (i.e. less sucrose) is less dense than a sucrose solution with a lower water potential (more sucrose).

  - When the banana pieces are placed in a solution that has a greater concentration (lower water potential), they will lose water, which means that the bathing solution gains water and therefore its water potential increases.

  - Similarly, the water potential of the bathing solution increases when the banana pieces have a higher water potential.

- It would be valuable to demonstrate the concept to learners using a range of sucrose solutions. Stain a medium concentration solution blue. Ask learners to predict what will happen to a drop of this solution if

you introduce it into a less concentrated solution. Do this – the drop should sink. Ask learners to explain why this happens. Also ask them how they could use the technique to find the concentration of an unknown sucrose solution.

- Trial the experiment beforehand, in order to determine the best range of sucrose solutions to use. Bananas can differ greatly in their water potentials, and you may need to use less or more concentrated solutions than those suggested below.

Equipment

Each learner or group will need:

- a banana

- a sharp knife or scalpel

- a white tile or other surface for cutting

- forceps

- a seeker or mounted needle

- 18 large tubes (e.g. boiling tubes)

- a dropper pipette

- syringes or pipettes to measure $5\,cm^3$

- a small quantity of methylene blue stain

- a range of sucrose solutions (e.g. 0.5, 1.0, 1.5, 2.0, 2.5 mol dm^{-3}).

Access to:

- distilled water.

Additional notes and advice

- Any plant tissue can be used instead of bananas – for example, apple, potato.

Safety considerations

- Learners should have read the safety guidance section within the workbook before carrying out this investigation.

- Standard laboratory safety procedures should be followed always.

- Care must be taken when using a sharp blade.

- Methylene blue is harmful and/or an irritant.

Carrying out the investigation

- The most difficult part of this investigation is introducing the blue drop carefully, so that it remains as a single drop and does not disperse. It is also very important not to disturb the liquids and introduce mass flow movements in them, or the drop may be carried upwards or downwards by mass flow, rather than because of its density. Practice and care will help learners to perfect this technique.

🛟 Some learners may need help in organising their tubes of solutions. You could suggest that they line up the test tubes containing the various sucrose solutions in sequence (for example, distilled water on the left, gradually increasing towards the most concentrated solution on the right). They could then organise a second row of test tubes, containing the same sequence of sucrose solutions, but this time stained blue.

⚙ Learners who require a further challenge could use this technique to compare the water potential of green (underripe), yellow and black (overripe) bananas. They could then research the changes that take place in a banana as it ripens, and use this information to explain their results.

Sample results

Concentration of sucrose solution / mol dm^{-3}	Behaviour of blue drop	
	First trial	Second trial
0.5	rose quickly	rose
1.0	rose very slowly	rose
1.5	sank very slowly	did not move
2.0	sank	sank
2.5	sank	sank

Table 4.14

Answers to the workbook questions (using the sample results)

a The drops of blue solution placed into the solution that had been bathing bananas in low concentrations of sucrose solution rose, while those placed into the solution that had been bathing bananas in high concentrations of sucrose solution sank.

b Points to be made include:

- banana pieces placed in low concentrations of solution gained water by osmosis, as the water moved down its water potential gradient. This reduced the water potential of the bathing solution, and increased its density. When a drop of the original (blue) solution was placed into this solution, it rose because it was less dense than the soaking solution.

- banana pieces placed in high concentrations of solution lost water by osmosis, as the water moved down its water potential gradient. This increased the water potential of the bathing solution, and reduced its density. When a drop of the original, (blue) solution was placed into this solution, it sank because it was more dense than the soaking solution.

c The solution in which the drop did not move – for the sample results this is about 1.5 mol dm^{-3} or just above.

d Points could include:

- discussion of the theory behind the method; in principle, this is all fine, and it is a valid way to measure water potential.

- significant sources of error, which could include: not enough time left for the water potentials of the banana pieces and sucrose solutions to equilibrate; possible differences between the concentrations of sugar in different parts of the solutions if they are not thoroughly mixed before sampling; difficulty in introducing the drop and determining whether it rises or falls.

- lack of repeats.

Practical investigation 4.8:
The effect of temperature on membrane permeability

Learning objective: 4.1(a)

Skills focus

The following AS skills are developed and practised (see the skills grids at the front of this guide):

MMO   Successfully collecting data and observations: (a), (e)

PDO   Recording data and observations: (a), (b), (d)

ACE   Interpreting data or observations: (f),
Drawing conclusions: (a), (b)
Suggesting improvements or modifications: (a), (b), (c), (d), (e)

Duration

The practical work and collection and recording of results can be done within 60 min. Allow another 30 min for answering the questions.

Preparing for the investigation

- An interesting approach to this investigation would be to avoid talking to learners beforehand about the effect of temperature on cell membranes. Instead, simply do the investigation, and then ask them to use their knowledge of the structure of cell surface membranes, and their results, to suggest reasons for the patterns that they find.

Equipment

Each learner or group will need:

- beetroot cylinders, outer peel removed, that have been soaking in water
- sharp knife or scalpel
- white tile or other surface for cutting
- forceps
- several test tubes and a rack to hold them
- a 250 cm³ beaker
- waterproof marker to label the test tubes
- syringe to measure 20 cm³.

Access to:

- distilled water
- water baths at a range of at least five different temperatures
- a colorimeter, if available.

Additional notes and advice

- The beetroot used for this investigation must, of course, be raw. Try to use red beetroot that is as fresh as possible. Remove the outer skin, and use cork borers to cut sets of cylinders of equal diameter. Place these in distilled water. This should be done just before the practical activity.

- Cutting the beetroot inevitably damages cells on the outer surface of the cylinders, and betalain leaks out from these into the water. Learners therefore need to wash off all of this 'loose' red pigment, ensuring that the only pigment remaining on the cylinders is inside undamaged cells, before they immerse the cylinders in the temperature-controlled water.

- If you have access to a colorimeter, this is a far better way of measuring the depth of colour, rather than making a visual comparison, as it provides quantitative results. Learners could then draw a graph of absorbance against temperature.

Safety considerations

- Learners should have read the safety guidance section within the workbook before carrying out this investigation.

- Standard laboratory safety procedures should be followed always.

- Care must be taken when using a sharp blade.

Carrying out the investigation

- Learners must take care not to damage cells on the external surface of the washed beetroot, or pigment will leak out.

- If no colorimeter is available, learners will need to find a way to describe the colours of the solutions. Encourage use of simple language: red, dark pink, light pink, colourless. Note that the word 'clear' does not have the same meaning as 'colourless'.

⚙ Some learners may need help in organising and structuring their answer to question **g**. This is effectively a planning exercise, and you could consider having a

55

template that you can provide to any learners who are struggling with constructing a logically organised answer.

🔧 As an extension activity, learners could research and report on (perhaps as a presentation or poster) the structure of cell surface membranes of thermophiles (organisms that are adapted to live in high temperature environments).

Sample results

If no colorimeter is available, learners should record the appearance of the liquid bathing the cylinders. Table 4.15 shows a typical set of these qualitative results, and also measurements from colorimetry.

Temperature / °C	Appearance	Absorbance of green light / a.u.
0	very pale red	17
15	very pale red	18
30	pale red	25
45	red	47
60	dark red	68
75	very dark red	97

Table 4.15

If a colorimeter has been used, learners could draw a line graph of their results.

Answers to the workbook questions (using the sample results)

a As temperature increases above 15°C, the depth of colour increases (and the absorbance of green light increases).

b This was caused by the loss of betalain from the beetroot cells.

c High temperatures cause the cell surface membrane to become permeable to betalain. As temperature increases, the kinetic energy of the phospholipid and protein molecules in the membrane increases. The phospholipid molecules may move so much that small gaps appear between them, large enough to allow betalain molecules to pass through. Protein molecules may lose their 3D shapes, as hydrogen bonds are broken; this also damages membrane structure and creates channels through which the betalain molecules can move.

d The pieces were washed to remove any betalain that might be on the surface, as a result of cutting through cells as the pieces were prepared. We need to know that any betalain in the water has come from previously undamaged cells.

Water from the water bath was used to fill the tubes so that the bathing solution of the beetroot pieces was at the measured temperature.

e Answers will depend on any differences found. Differences could be due to slight differences in technique, or in the beetroot samples used, or in colour perception (if a colorimeter has not been used).

f Repeats could be used, so that any anomalous results can be identified. Repeats also allow inspection of the range of variability between individual results, which provides information about how well other variables have been controlled.

If learners have not been able to use a colorimeter, they could explain how its use would enable an objective, quantitative measurement of the quantity of betalain in the water samples.

They could suggest using a better instrument for measuring the 20 cm³ of water, for example, a graduated pipette, which would give a more accurate measurement and therefore ensure that the volume of liquid is the same in each tube.

g Answers should include these points:

- The independent variable is concentration of ethanol. Learners should describe soaking the beetroot cylinders in a range of concentrations of ethanol, with at least five different values (one of these can be distilled water).

- The dependent variable is the same as before – that is, the depth of colour of the water after soaking the beetroot cylinders.

- Temperature is now a control variable. All the tubes should be placed in a water bath at a stated temperature *below* the temperatures known to increase the permeability of the membranes. Other control variables will be the same as before – including soaking all the cylinders in water beforehand, removing pigment from the outside of all the cylinders by washing in distilled water, immersing in the same volume of liquid and leaving for the same period of time.

56

Chapter outline

This chapter relates to Chapter 5: The mitotic cell cycle, and Chapter 6: Nucleic acids and protein synthesis in the coursebook.

In this chapter, learners will complete practical investigations on:

- 5.1 Making a root tip squash
- 5.2 Investigating mitosis using prepared slides

Practical investigation 5.1:
Making a root tip squash

Learning objective: 5.2(b)

Skills focus

The following skills are developed and practised (see the skills grids at the front of this guide):

MMO   Making decisions about measurements: (l), (n), (o)

PDO   Recording data and observations: (f)

Duration

If learners are successful first time, the investigation and drawings can be completed within 1 h. However, some learners may need to prepare a new slide if their first attempt is unsuccessful.

Preparing for the investigation

- Learners should be familiar with the different stages of the cell cycle. Ensure that they can recognise the stages of mitosis in plant cells from micrographs.

- They should be confident in preparing temporary slides and using a microscope.

Equipment

Each learner or group will need:

- a young seedling (e.g. fava bean, garlic)
- a clean microscope slide and a coverslip
- a scalpel, sharp knife or safety razor blade

- a means of gently heating the slide (Bunsen burner, spirit burner or hot plate)
- mounted needle
- filter paper
- a small bottle of $1 \, mol \, dm^{-3}$ hydrochloric acid, with a dropper
- a small bottle of orcein ethanoic stain (acetic orcein stain), with a dropper
- a watch glass or other small glass container
- a white tile.

Access to:

- distilled water.

Additional notes and advice

- Suitable root tips can be prepared by suspending a whole garlic bulb so that its base is in water. Keep the water topped up. Roots should appear within 1–10 days (depending on temperature and the variety and freshness of the garlic bulb.) It is a good idea to set some up about 10 days before you intend to do the practical, some eight days before, some six days before and so on. This should ensure a good supply of suitable root tips of various ages on the day.

- Alternatively, germinate fava beans (broad beans) in damp blotting paper or filter paper.

- Orcein ethanoic stain, also known as acetic orcein, can be obtained from any biological supplier.

- There is a variety of alternative techniques for making a temporary slide to show mitosis. If you would like to try a slightly different technique, visit the Nuffield Foundation website, and click on the Teachers tab, which will take you to the Practical Biology area of the site, where you will find detailed instructions for investigating mitosis in an allium root tip squash. This also contains instructions for making orcein ethanoic stain yourself, if you are able to obtain orcein and glacial ethanoic acid.

- Another excellent source of information is the Science and Plants for Schools website, where you can click on the Secondary tab and find detailed information about microscopy of mitosis in root tips. This includes a video of some of the stages in the preparation of the slide, as well as a Power Point, instructions for preparing for the practical, student notes and teacher notes.

Safety considerations

- Learners should have read the safety guidance section within the workbook before carrying out this investigation.

- Standard laboratory safety procedures should be followed always.

- The suggested concentration of hydrochloric acid, $1\,mol\,dm^{-3}$, is dilute. However, learners should wash off any acid that comes into contact with skin or clothes.

- Learners should wear eye protection.

- Orcein is low hazard. However, it will stain skin, so should be washed off immediately using cold water.

- The instructions recommend holding the watch glass in the fingers to pass it through the flame. This is to prevent learners letting it get too hot. However, they need to take care not to burn their fingers. Care also needs to be taken if a hot plate is used.

Carrying out the investigation

- Success can never be guaranteed with this investigation. Even if learners prepare their slide very well, it is not always possible to see chromosomes in dividing cells. Some plants may undergo mitosis at certain times of the day, so if you find you have no success when trying this practical in the morning, it is worth trying again in an afternoon session. For this reason, it would be very valuable to try this out yourself before setting the task for learners to do. See also the Troubleshooting guide, Table 5.1, in the workbook.

Many learners will not be successful in seeing chromosomes, and identifying stages in the cell cycle, on their first attempt. It is strongly recommended that you encourage them to use Table 5.1 to try to solve their problems themselves first, before asking you to intervene.

- Learners may need reminding of the guidelines for drawing good diagrams of cells. They may be tempted to

draw idealised diagrams of the different stages of mitosis, rather than what they can actually see.

Learners who are quickly successful in producing a slide on which they can see dividing cells could try comparing the number of cells in mitosis in garlic roots of different ages. (You have probably provided garlic bulbs that were set up on various days before the practical investigation.) They could use an eyepiece graticule to measure the mean size of a sample of cells in mitosis, and compare this with the mean size of cells in interphase.

Sample results

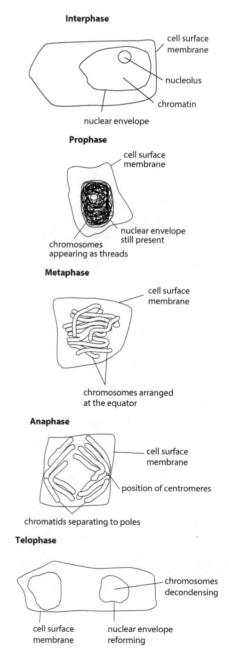

Figure 5.1

Practical investigation 5.2:
Investigating mitosis using prepared slides

Learning objective: 5.2(b)

Skills focus

The following skills are developed and practised (see the skills grids at the front of this guide):

MMO	Making decisions about measurements: (l), (o) Successfully collect data and observations: (a), (d), (i)
PDO	Recording data and observations: (a) Layout of data and observations: (f), (g)
ACE	Interpreting data or observations and identifying sources of error: (a) Suggesting improvements or modifications to extend an investigation: (c)

Duration

Counting the cells and completing the tally chart can be done in approximately 20–30 min. Another 30 min will be required for answering the questions.

Preparing for the investigation

- Learners should be familiar with the different stages of the cell cycle. Ensure that they can recognise the stages of mitosis in plant cells from micrographs.

Equipment

Each learner or group will need:

- a microscope

- a prepared slide of a root tip, stained to show cells undergoing mitosis.

Additional notes and advice

- Prepared slides of mitosis can be obtained from Cambridge. You can order these through the publications list, available through the cambridgeinternational.org website.

Safety considerations

- Learners should have read the safety guidance section within the workbook before carrying out this investigation.

- Standard laboratory safety procedures should be followed always.

- There are no additional significant safety issues associated with this investigation.

Carrying out the investigation

- If the prepared slide is of good quality, learners should have little difficulty in finding and identifying cells in various stages of mitosis.

- It must be remembered that the process of mitosis is a continuous one, so there is no sharp dividing line between each stage. Learners may therefore find it difficult to assign some cells to a particular stage. They should make a decision about this, and then try to make similar decisions for similar cells.

- Some stages are easier to pick out than others; for example, cells in anaphase tend to stand out more clearly than cells in prophase. This may mean that the number of cells in some stages is overestimated, in comparison with other stages.

- Learners who have difficulty in identifying cells on the prepared slide could be shown micrographs of groups of cells at a similar magnification to those in their field of view, and practise identifying and counting cells in the micrograph. (A web search will produce a number of examples of suitable micrographs.)

- If not done in Practical investigation 5.1, learners could use an eyepiece graticule to measure the mean size of a sample of cells in mitosis, and compare this with the mean size of cells in interphase.

- Learners who require a challenge could be asked to prepare a 'help sheet' for future biology learners, which provides annotated drawings or photographs of cells in each stage of mitosis, with a summary of what learners should look for when viewing a prepared slide, to identify which stage of mitosis a cell is in. This should be done using their own experience of viewing the slide.

Sample results

Stage	Interphase	Prophase	Metaphase	Anaphase	Telophase
Tally	̶I̶I̶I̶I̶ ̶I̶I̶I̶I̶ ̶I̶I̶I̶I̶ ̶I̶I̶I̶I̶ ̶I̶I̶I̶I̶ ̶I̶I̶I̶I̶ ̶I̶I̶I̶I̶ ̶I̶I̶I̶I̶ ̶I̶I̶I̶I̶ ̶I̶I̶I̶I̶ IIII	̶I̶I̶I̶I̶ ̶I̶I̶I̶I̶ I	̶I̶I̶I̶I̶ I	III	̶I̶I̶I̶I̶ IIII
Number	54	11	6	3	9

Answers to the workbook questions (using the sample results)

a Prophase, metaphase, anaphase and telophase.

b (11 + 6 + 3 + 9) ÷ 54 = 0.54

c Total number of cells counted = 83

percentage in interphase = 65.1

percentage in prophase = 13.3

percentage in metaphase = 7.2

percentage in anaphase = 3.6

percentage in telophase = 10.8

d Total time for one cell cycle = 9 h

= 540 min

Estimated time in interphase = 65.1% of 540

= 352 min

Estimated time in prophase = 13.3% of 540

= 72 min

Estimated time in metaphase = 7.2% of 540

= 39 min

Estimated time in anaphase = 3.6% of 540

= 19 min

Estimated time in telophase = 10.8% of 540

= 58 min

e

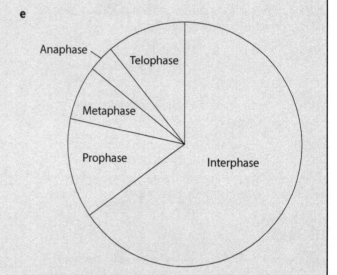

Figure 5.2

f There are likely to be considerable differences between the times calculated by different learners. The two main reasons are as follows:

- The prepared slides used are not the same – they may perhaps show different species of plant, different parts of the root tip, or have been made at a different time of day – note that in some plants the mitotic cell cycle can take place on a diurnal cycle, or be influenced by day length of temperature.

- Learners may have differed in their interpretations of the stages they can see. The stages are continuous, so there are justifiable reasons why one learner might consider a cell to be in metaphase while another thinks it is in anaphase.

g By far the most effective way of achieving more reliable results is to increase the sample size. Learners could count more cells on several different slides.

Chapter outline

This chapter relates to Chapter 6: Plant transport in the coursebook.

In this chapter, learners will complete practical investigations on:

- 6.1 Drawing low-power plan diagrams of prepared sections of stems and roots
- 6.2 Drawing high-power diagrams of cells and tissues
- 6.3 Estimating the rate of water loss through the stomata of a leaf
- 6.4 Using a potometer
- 6.5 Investigating the effect of one factor on rate of transpiration
- 6.6 Drawing sections and identifying the tissues of a typical leaf and a xerophytic leaf

Practical investigation 6.1:
Drawing low-power plan diagrams of prepared sections of stems and roots

Learning objective: 7.1(a)

Skills focus

The following skills are developed and practised (see the skills grids at the front of this guide):

MMO   Making decisions about measurements: (l), (m), (p)
        Successfully collecting data and
        observations: (e), (f)

PDO   Recording data and observations: (d), (f)
        Layout of data or observations: (h)

Duration

This investigation should take between 60 and 90 min to complete for both the practical and the analysis. Learners should be directed to do the drawings and measurements and can then carry out any calculations for a homework exercise. Learners should also be encouraged to not rush and to ensure that the quality of their diagrams is of importance.

Preparing for the investigation

- The practical work is quite simple provided learners have experience of using microscopes and eyepiece graticules. Prior to the lesson, the following topics and practical skills should have been covered:

  - setting up and using light microscopes and eyepiece graticules

  - a theoretical consideration of the structures of dicotyledonous stems, roots and leaves.

- Before the practical, the teacher should discuss with the pupils the instructions for drawing high-quality plan diagrams and general drawing skills. They should be shown some examples of stem and root structures so that they know where to look.

Equipment

Each learner or group will need:

- light microscope

- eyepiece graticule

- prepared sections of TS stem, and TS root of a dicotyledonous plant

- pencil, HB or 2H grade

- eraser

- pencil sharpener

- ruler.

Additional notes and advice

- Prepared sections may be obtained from a range of suppliers.

- Cambridge International also sells a range of sections. To view these visit the cambridgeinternational.org website.

- Suggested plants to use for the sections are *Ranunculus* and *Helianthus* (four weeks old).

- Other species with particular adaptations could be used for extension work including *Erica* stem, *Fagus* stem, *Menyanthes* stem, *Aesculus* stem, *Zea Mays* (maize) stem, *Zea Mays* root, plantain stem.

Safety considerations

- Learners should have read the safety guidance section within the workbook before carrying out this investigation.

- Standard laboratory safety should be followed when using microscopes.

- There are no additional significant safety issues associated with this investigation.

Carrying out the investigation

- This investigation should not be particularly demanding in terms of practical skills. If prepared sections of good quality are used, tissues should be very clear. Some sections may not, however, show all the tissue types.

  Many learners find using microscopes challenging and are unaware of how to draw biological diagrams. The teacher will need to circulate round the laboratory to ensure that learners are able to focus the microscope on appropriate tissues and are aware of how to follow the rules for drawing diagrams.

  It is worth making sure that all learners have set up the microscopes and are actually looking at sections during the initial period of the lesson – it is very easy for untrained learners to spend 10 min drawing dust and other anomalies because they have not set up their equipment properly. Some sections may not look like idealised textbook diagrams – learners will need reassuring that they should draw what they can see and not what they think they should see.

Some learners will need help in identifying each of the tissue types – it is worthwhile working through examples at the start of the lesson.

Some learners will need support carrying out the calculations. If these are set as a homework exercise, the teacher should talk through how to carry these out.

Learners who finish should be encouraged to look at a range of other plant sections (see Additional notes and advice). They should look at the sections and as an exercise in independent learning, research the plant to identify any adaptations that may be present.

Common learner misconception

- Learners may find identifying tissues difficult and mistake xylem tissue for sclerenchyma tissue. Showing diagrams of the tissues to the learners will help their understanding.

Sample results

The learners' results should be similar to the following data.

For the plan diagrams of stem and root, learners could draw the stem and root using a photograph available on the internet or Figures 6.1 and 6.3 in the workbook.

Part 1: TS stem

Vascular bundle	1	2	3	4	5	Mean
Length of vascular bundle / eyepiece units	7	8	6	7	6	6.8
Width of vascular bundle / eyepiece units	3	2	3	3	2	2.6

Table 6.1

Part 2: TS root

Diameter of stele: 12 eyepiece units

Diameter of root: 36 eyepiece units

Answers to the workbook questions (using the sample results)

Part 1

a   See Table 6.1.

b   i   Number of vascular bundles: 9

   ii   Maximum diameter of stem (eyepiece units): 45

c   i   Total area of vascular bundles:

      Mean length of vascular bundles = 6.8 e.u.

      Mean width of vascular bundles = 2.6 e.u.

      Mean estimated area of vascular bundles = 13.9 e.u.^{2}

      Total estimated area of vascular bundles = 125.1 e.u.^{2}

   ii   Cross-sectional area of stem:
      Maximum diameter of stem = 45 e.u.

      Total estimated area of stem = 1589.6 e.u.^{2}

   iii   Proportional area:

      Proportional area of stem composed of vascular bundles = 0.079

Part 2

a   Area of root: 1017.4 e.u.^{2}

   Area of stele: 113.0 e.u.^{2}

b   Proportional area of root = 0.11

c   The proportion may not be accurate because:

   • the shape of most vascular bundles is not an oval

   • the shape of the stem is not a circle

   • the vascular bundles measured are not representative and may be smaller or larger than most.

d   A proportion is the amount of something relative to something else and is a ratio. It is calculated by dividing one area by another area. If the units are the same, they effectively 'cancel' each other out, giving no units.

Practical investigation 6.2:
Drawing high-power diagrams of cells and tissues

Learning objectives: 7.1(b), 7.1(c), 7.1(d)

Skills focus

The following skills are developed and practised (see the skills grids at the front of this guide):

MMO	Making decisions about measurements: (l), (n), (q) Successfully collecting data and observations: (e), (g)
PDO	Recording data and observations: (d), (f) Layout of data or observations: (h)
ACE	Interpreting data or observations and identifying sources of error: (k)

Duration

The practical part of this investigation should take between 60 and 90 min to complete. The analysis sections should take approximately 30 min. Learners should be directed to do the drawings and measurements and can then carry out any calculations for a homework exercise. If learners are taking a great deal of time to identify all the structures, the practical could be split into two 1-h lessons. Learners should also be encouraged to not rush and to ensure that the quality of their diagrams is of importance.

Preparing for the investigation

• The practical work is quite simple providing learners have experience of using microscopes and eyepiece graticules. Prior to the lesson, the following topics and practical skills should have been covered:

   • setting up and using light microscopes and eyepiece graticules

   • a theoretical consideration of the structure and functions of the tissue and cells of dicotyledonous stems, roots and leaves

   • the difference between plan diagrams and high-power diagrams of tissues and cells.

• Before the practical, the teacher should discuss with the pupils the differences between high-power diagrams of tissues and cells and plan diagrams. The learners should have completed Practical investigation 6.1 prior to this practical. They should be also be shown some examples of the cells and tissues to help them appreciate what they are looking for.

Equipment

Each learner or group will need:

- light microscope

- eyepiece graticule

- prepared sections of TS stem, TS root, TS leaf, LS stem of a dicotyledonous plant

- pencil, HB or 2H grade

- eraser

- pencil sharpener

- ruler.

Additional notes and advice

- Prepared sections may be obtained from a range of suppliers.

- Cambridge International also sell a range of sections. To view these visit the cambridgeinternational.org website.

- Suggested plants to use for the sections are *Ranunculus* and *Helianthus* (four week old) TS and *Cucurbita* for LS.

- Other species with particular adaptations could be used for extension work including *Erica* stem, *Fagus* stem, *Menyanthes* stem, *Aesculus* stem, *Zea Mays* (maize) stem, *Zea Mays* root, plantain stem.

Safety considerations

- Learners should have read the safety guidance section within the workbook before carrying out this investigation.

- Standard laboratory safety should be followed when using microscopes.

- There are no additional significant safety issues associated with this investigation.

Carrying out the investigation

- This investigation should not be particularly demanding in terms of practical skills. If prepared sections of good quality are used, tissues should be very clear. Some

sections may not, however, show all the tissue types. The main problems that learners will encounter will be:

- identifying all the tissue types – some may not always be present or resemble an idealised textbook diagram (this is fine and learners should be encouraged to draw what they see)

- understanding how much of each tissue type to draw – five to ten cells of each type is fine.

- Many learners will consider that small diagrams are adequate.

- Many learners will think that they have to draw many cells.

Many learners find using microscopes challenging and are unaware of how to draw biological diagrams. The teacher will need to circulate round the laboratory to ensure that learners are able to focus microscope on appropriate tissues and are aware of how to follow the rules for drawing diagrams.

It is worth making sure that all learners have set up the microscopes and are actually looking at sections during the initial period of the lesson – it is very easy for untrained learners to spend 10 min drawing dust and other anomalies because they have not set up their equipment properly. Some sections may not look like idealised textbook diagrams – learners will need reassuring that they should draw what they can see and not what they think they should see.

Some learners will need help in identifying each of the tissue type. It is worthwhile working through examples at the start of the lesson.

Some learners will need support carrying out the calculations. If these are set as a homework exercise, the teacher should talk through how to carry these out.

Learners who finish should be encouraged to look at a range of other plant sections (see equipment). They should look at the sections and as an exercise in independent learning, should then research the plant to identify any adaptations that may be present.

Sample results

If slides are not available, there are many photographs available on the internet which could be drawn. The coursebook also has many figures that could be used (Figures 7.2, 7.7, 7.11, 7.13a, 7.14c, 7.23c, 7.23b, 7.31b, 7.31d).

Answers to the workbook questions (using the sample results)

The answers given for the comparisons of the structure are suggested possible differences and are not exhaustive. There may be other equally correct differences that learners identify from their sections.

a i xylem vessels and phloem (both TS and LS)

Xylem	Phloem
wider cross-section	narrower cross-section
thicker cell walls	thinner cell walls
lignin present in cell wall (if stain shows)	lignin absent in cell wall
regular shapes	less regular shapes
no cross walls	cross walls (sieve plates) present
no companion cells	companion cells and sieve tube elements present
more xylem vessels present	fewer sieve tubes present

Table 6.2

ii stem epidermis and root epidermis

Stem epidermis	Root epidermis
one or two cells thick	one or two cells thick
thin, rectangular cells	thin, rectangular cells
few hairs present	many root hair cells present

Table 6.3

iii lower and upper leaf epidermis

Lower epidermis	Upper epidermis
one cell thick	one or two cells thick
thin, rectangular cells	thin, rectangular cells
stomata present	no (few) stomata present
guard cells present	no guard cells present
no cuticle	waxy cuticle present

Table 6.4

iv palisade mesophyll and spongy mesophyll

Palisade mesophyll	Spongy mesophyll
long, rectangular cells	smaller cells, not rectangular
large numbers of chloroplasts	fewer chloroplasts
no air spaces	air spaces present
densely packed cells	less densely packed cells

Table 6.5

b Water cannot enter xylem or sclerenchyma cells so they die. Lignin is a strengthening tissue which:

- prevents xylem vessels collapsing
- provides the plant with strength to remain upright.

c i phloem

- sieve plates to withstand pressure due to translocation
- few organelles in sieve tube elements to allow more space for sucrose and less resistance to flow
- companion cells to provide metabolic processes for sieve tube elements
- no lignin present in cell walls to allow water flow through cell wall.

ii lower leaf epidermis

- stomata present to allow gas exchange (carbon dioxide diffusion into the leaf for photosynthesis, oxygen diffusion out)
- stomata allow water loss to provide transpiration stream
- guard cells regulate stomatal opening to reduce water loss.

iii root epidermis

- root hair cells providing larger surface area for osmosis of water and uptake of mineral ions.

iv collenchyma cells

- strengthening tissue with additional cellulose in cell walls
- thicker cell walls with more regular shapes.

d to allow sufficient light penetration so that image is not distorted by other layers of cells.

Practical investigation 6.3:
Estimating the rate of water loss through the stomata of a leaf

Learning objective: 7.2(e)

Skills focus

The following skills are developed and practised (see the skills grids at the front of this guide):

MMO   Making decisions about measurements: (k), (p)
       Successfully collecting data and observations: (a), (d), (i)

PDO   Recording data and observations: (a)
       Displaying calculations and reasoning: (a), (c)

ACE   Interpreting data or observations and identifying sources of error: (a), (f), (g)
       Drawing conclusions: (a), (b)
       Suggesting improvements or modifications to extend an investigation: (a), (e)

Duration

- This investigation needs to be set up over one week and done in two parts.

Part 1: Measuring the water loss (Days 1–7)

- In the first lesson, there is a very simple activity - placing the stem of a plant into a 100 cm³ measuring cylinder with water with a layer of mineral oil placed on top of the water. This should take about 20 minutes.

Parts 2 and 3: Estimating the leaf surface area and the total number of stomata (Day 7)

- After seven days (this may be adjusted to fit with lesson times), the second part of the practical is carried out – the leaf area is estimated and the stomatal density determined. If time is a problem, the practical should be carried out in groups with different learners carrying out different activities. It can also be carried out as a whole class practical with one branch placed into a measuring cylinder of water and each learner measuring the area and stomatal density of a leaf. The class results are then collated. The second part of the practical will take approximately to gather the data. Analysis of data can be carried out in a further lesson or for homework if necessary, and should take about 30 min.

Preparing for the investigation

Part 1: Measuring the water loss (Days 1–7)

- This practical will require the collection of several small branches of a suitable plant (such as laurel or privet). The branch should be long enough to fit the end into a measuring cylinder and have approximately ten leaves. This should be trialled to find a species that will work.

Part 2: Estimating the leaf surface area (Day 7)

- This can be carried out between four and nine days after Part 1. The volume of water in the measuring cylinder should be checked daily. If the leaves have a rapid transpiration rate, Part 2 will have to be carried out sooner; if the rate is low, Part 2 will have to be carried out later (or some water can be removed without learner knowledge!). Suitable plants that give a reasonable rate of transpiration should be trialled.

Part 3: Estimating total number of stomata (Day 7)

- This should be straightforward. It should be trialled to ensure that there is an expected pattern of stomatal distribution on the leaf surfaces (more on the lower surface than the upper surface).

Equipment

Part 1: Measuring the water loss (Days 1–7)

Each learner or group will need:

- a suitable branch of a plant with approximately 10 leaves

- a measuring cylinder, 100 cm³

- paraffin oil in a dropper bottle, 50 cm³

- a source of tap water.

Part 2: Estimating the leaf surface area (Day 7)

Each learner or group will need:

- a selection of gridded paper for tracing around the leaves, for example 10 mm, 5 mm, 2 mm and 1 mm. If gridded paper is not available, graph paper can be used.

Part 3: Estimating total number of stomata (Day 7)

Each learner or group will need:

- clear (transparent) nail varnish

- forceps

- mounted needle

- microscope slides
- coverslips
- light microscope
- stage micrometer.

Safety considerations

- Learners should have read the safety guidance section within the workbook before carrying out this investigation.
- Standard laboratory safety procedures should be followed always.
- There are no additional significant safety issues associated with this investigation.

Part 1: Measuring the water loss (Days 1–7)

- Standard laboratory safety procedures should be followed always. Check that learners are not allergic to plant species or that a poisonous species has not been selected.

Part 2: Estimating the leaf surface area (Day 7)

- As for Part 1.

Part 3: Estimating total number of stomata (Day 7)

- As for Part 1.
- Eye protection should be used when using nail varnish.

Carrying out the investigation

Part 1: Measuring the water loss (Days 1–7)

- It is important to select a species of plant that will have a reasonable rate of transpiration – several should be trialled.
- There should be no leaves along the lower stem of the branch so that it will fit into the measuring cylinder.
- The water level should be checked each day in case it is getting too low. It is possible to top up the water underneath the paraffin oil but the amount added should be recorded.

Parts 2 and 3: Estimating the leaf surface area and total number of stomata (Day 7)

- This part can be carried out at any point depending on the rate of transpiration from the leaves. If a period other than seven days is used, the later calculations will need adjusting.

- If there is insufficient time, this practical can be carried out in larger groups or as a whole class practical with each learner determining leaf surface area and stomatal density.

- Nail varnish should be allowed adequate time to dry before attempting to remove it. Only small sections are needed, not a whole leaf cast.

- Any method of generating random numbers can be used, for example, the random number generator function on many calculators, putting numbers into a bag and picking them out, or using the random number feature on spreadsheet packages.

⚙ Learners should find the practical skills well within their grasp.

⚙ Many will need support when carrying out the calculations. The calculations can be carried out as a group step by step if necessary, rather than letting learners do them individually. The different values that different groups obtained can be discussed as a group with reasons suggested for the differences. A great deal of data quality evaluation can be discussed and learners should be encouraged to think about the accuracy and reliability of random sampling, and why the transpiration rate would have varied over the seven-day period.

⚙ For extension work, learners could make nail varnish casts of different plant species such as *Nymphaea, Erica* and *Oleander*.

Sample results

The learners' results should be similar to the following data. This data can be used to answer the Data analysis and Evaluation questions if the learners are not able to do the investigation.

Part 1: Measuring the water loss (Days 1–7)

Volume of water in measuring cylinder after seven days: 45 cm³

Part 2: Estimating the leaf surface area (Day 7)

	Leaf number				
	1	2	3	4	5
Number of whole squares	6	4	5	7	3
Number of part squares	8	10	9	8	5
Number of part squares ÷ 2	4	5.5	4.5	4	2.5
Total number of squares	10	9.5	9.5	11	5.5

Table 6.6

Total number of leaves on branch: 16

Part 3: Estimating total number of stomata (Day 7)

Field of view number	Number of stomata in field of view	
	lower epidermis	upper epidermis
1	14	0
2	12	0
3	16	0
4	8	0
5	21	0
mean	14.2	0

Table 6.7

Diameter of field of view = 450 μm or 0.45 mm

Answers to the workbook questions (using the sample results)

Part 1: Measuring the water loss (Days 1–7)

a i Mean loss of water per day = 7.9 cm³ day⁻¹

ii Mean loss of water per hour = 0.33 cm³ h⁻¹

iii Mean loss of water per hour = 327 mm³ h⁻¹

Part 2: Estimating the leaf surface area (Day 7)

a i Mean leaf surface area = 9.1 squares

ii Area of one square = 100 mm²

iii Mean leaf surface area = 1820 mm

iv Total leaf surface area = 29 120 mm²

v Surface area of upper epidermis = 14 560 mm²

Surface area of lower epidermis = 14 560 mm²

Part 3: Estimating total number of stomata (Day 7)

a i Area of one field of view = 0.159 mm²

ii Mean number of stomata in lower epidermis = 14.2 stomata per field of view

Mean number of stomata in upper epidermis = 0 stomata per field of view

iii Mean number of stomata per square millimetre in lower epidermis = 89.3 stomata mm⁻²

Mean number of stomata per square millimetre in lower epidermis = 0 stomata mm⁻²

iv Total number of stomata on lower epidermis = 1 300 208 stomata

The total number of stomata on upper epidermis = 0

v Mean rate of water loss per stomata = 2.51×10^{-4} mm³ h⁻¹ stomata⁻¹

b Five leaves were selected at random to:

- give a representative sample

- avoid bias when selecting leaves

- reduce the workload of measuring all the leaves.

c i Total leaf surface area would be lower than the true value.

ii Estimated rate of water loss per stomata would be higher than the true value.

d Paraffin oil ensures that no water is lost due to evaporation from the surface of the water in the measuring cylinder. All water loss must be from the leaves.

e Four factors that could have caused differences in the rate of water loss are:

- light intensity changes: stomata open in the light and close in the dark

- temperature changes: increases in temperature increase the kinetic energy of water molecules and increase evaporation rate

- wind speed changes: increasing wind speed maintains a diffusion gradient, increasing rate of water loss

- humidity: reduced humidity increases the diffusion gradient, increasing rate of water loss.

f Three sources of inaccuracy in the experiment and suggested improvements could include:

  i Inaccuracy: gridded paper has large gaps between lines making estimation of leaf area inaccurate.

  Improvement: use smaller intervals between grid lines.

  ii Inaccuracy: fluctuations in abiotic factors (e.g. light intensity, wind speed, humidity, temperature).

  Improvement: suggest practical methods of controlling these factors.

iii Inaccuracy: area of leaf that stomata were counted on was not representative.

Improvement: measure more areas of leaf.

iv Inaccuracy: Leaves that were sampled were not representative.

Improvement: Increase number of leaves in sample / use a running mean to identify when sample size is correct.

v Inaccuracy: measuring cylinder increments are not fine enough.

Improvement: use alternative method for measuring volume, for example, volume potometer.

Practical investigation 6.4:
Using a potometer

Learning objective: 7.2(e)

Skills focus

The following skills are developed and practised (see the skills grids at the front of this guide):

MMO   Making decisions about measurements: (g) Successfully collecting data and observations: (a), (c)

PDO   Displaying calculations and reasoning: (a)

ACE   Interpreting data or observations and identifying sources of error: (f), (g)

Duration

- This practical should take approximately 60–90 min. This will depend on the ability of the learners to set up the potometers without leaks. If leaks and air bubbles appear, equipment needs to be taken apart and reassembled – this will add time to the practical.

- If some groups of learners are having problems after several attempts, it is often best to relocate them to groups where the potometers are working.

- The analysis sections should take approximately 30 min.

Preparing for the investigation

- This practical requires the purchase or manufacture of simple volume potometers. These are very simple to make and consist of a section of capillary tube (with an internal diameter measuring 1–2 mm) with a piece of clear silicon tubing attached to the end. The tubing should be transparent so that it is easy to see whether there are air bubbles inside it.

- Branches should have sufficient diameter to fit into the silicon tubing tightly so that there are no leaks. A range of species of plant should be trialled and these will vary according to time of year and location. Laurel bushes often work well. It is important to trial the practical before it is given to learners.

Equipment

Each learner or group will need:

- a branch with several leaves attached

- a potometer

- beaker, 250 cm³

- ruler, graduated in millimetres

- secateurs (to cut the branch)

- filter paper

- stopclock

- retort stand, two clamps and two bosses

- piece of stiff card, A4 size

- marker pen for glass.

Access to:

- deep sink or water trough
- tap water.

Safety considerations

- Learners should have read the safety guidance section within the workbook before carrying out this investigation.

- Standard laboratory safety procedures should be followed always.

- Plant species should not be poisonous and learners should be checked to ensure that they have no allergies.

- Cutting the plant stems underwater with secateurs – learners should be warned to take care.

- Potometers are glass and often fragile. Learners should take care not to force plants into tubes, breaking glass and causing injury. Ideally reinforced glass should be used.

- Eye protection should be worn when using the capillary tubing when putting apparatus together.

Carrying out the investigation

- Volume potometers are notoriously temperamental pieces of apparatus. There must be no leaks and there must be a continuous column of water throughout with no air bubbles. If a leak or major air bubble breaking the column of water is present, the apparatus must be taken apart and reassembled.

- The end of the branch must be cut at an angle under water.

- The whole apparatus must be assembled under water; if parts are taken out of the water, air bubbles will enter the xylem vessels of the branch and / or the capillary tube.

- Care should be taken when clamping the potometer to the stand so as not to break the glass. Additional clamps can be placed on the stand to support the branch – electrical cable ties can also be used to secure the branch.

- The leaves need to be carefully dried with tissue.

- It may be necessary to demonstrate to learners how to create a bubble at the base of the capillary tube.

- It is best to demonstrate to the learners how to set up the apparatus before the practical, stressing all the precautions that need to be taken.

Most learners will need some support setting up potometers. The teacher should circulate round the laboratory assisting and checking that there are no leaks or major airlocks in equipment.

- Demonstrating how to set up the potometer at the start and placing a functional experiment at the front of the room as a reference point for learners is useful.

If any learners are having repeated difficulties with equipment, it is best to allocate them to groups where the equipment is working. It is also valuable to share data with the rest of the class so that all groups have data to write up.

Learners should start thinking about the limitations of the equipment and begin the planning exercise for Practical investigation 6.5.

Sample results

The learners' results may be similar to the following data (there may be great variance!).

Time / min	Distance moved by air bubble / mm
5	11
10	12
15	9.3
20	9
25	12

Table 6.8

Radius of capillary tube: 1 mm

Answers to the workbook questions (using the sample results)

a Mean distance moved per 5 min interval = 10 mm

Mean distance moved per minute = 2 mm min^{-1}

b Volume of water lost per minute = 6.32 mm^3 min^{-1}

c The calculated value of volume of water lost per minute may not necessarily be the actual volume of water lost from the leaves because:

- some water is used in photosynthesis

- some water is stored within the plant cells.

d Functions of transpiration:

- cooling

- transport of minerals / water to leaves

- support.

e If air enters the xylem, the hydrogen bonds between water molecules will be broken, reducing the cohesive forces. The transpiration stream is broken and water will not move up the xylem.

f The leaves were dried as the surface water would inhibit water loss from the stomata and reduce the rate of transpiration.

g Changes in water loss rate could be due to fluctuations in light intensity, wind speed, humidity and temperature.

h Differences in rate of water loss could be due to:

- different abiotic factors (humidity, wind speed, temperature, light intensity)

- different leaf surface area

- genetically different plants

- different age of leaves

- different stomata density on leaves

- different hydration state of leaves.

Practical investigation 6.5: Planning

Investigating the effect of one factor on rate of transpiration

Learning objective: 7.2(c)

Skills focus

The following skills are developed and practised (see the skills grids at the front of this guide):

MMO	Making decisions about measurements: (a), (b), (d), (e), (f), (h), (i)
	Successfully collecting data and observations: (b), (c)
PDO	Displaying calculations and reasoning: (c)
	Layout of data or observations: (a), (b), (c), (d), (e)
ACE	Interpreting data or observations and identifying sources of error: (e), (f), (g)
	Drawing conclusions: (a), (b)
	Suggesting improvements or modifications to extend an investigation: (c)

Duration

This practical has two parts:

- Part 1: a planning exercise that can be carried out within a lesson or as a homework exercise. Allow approximately 60–90 min for this part.

- Part 2: a practical session to carry out the learner's investigation or the standard investigation included. This includes the data analysis. This should take between 60 and 90 min.

Preparing for the investigation

- This investigation should be introduced after carrying out Practical investigation 6.4. Learners should be familiar with how to use a volume potometer. They should then carry out the theoretical planning exercise. This should be marked and checked before the learners carry out the actual investigation. To help them with planning, talk them through:

  - the definitions of independent, dependent and control variables

  - the variables that will affect transpiration and the reasons why

- how to change different independent variables, for example:

  - wind speed: fans at different distances from plant or at different settings

  - temperature: heater at different distances from plant

  - light intensity: lamps at different distances from plant

  - humidity: placing plant in polythene bags with different masses of silica gel

- how changing these variables can alter other variables, for example, increasing wind speed can reduce the temperature

- how to measure the dependent variable accurately and reliably (i.e. repeats).

- how to analyse the data

- risk assessment: how to evaluate risks and suggest measures for minimising the risk

- results table design.

- If a learner produces an unsuitable plan, the method below investigating the effect of wind speed can be used.

- After the learners have carried out their investigations and collected data, the teacher should discuss the findings with the whole class and how to analyse the data. The quality of the data should be examined and whether it can lead to a valid conclusion. The design of the experiment should be evaluated and potential sources of inaccuracy identified along with possible improvements.

Planning

Factor affecting transpiration rate	Why it affects transpiration rate	How increasing it will affect transpiration rate	How you could change it in your practical
temperature	• affects kinetic energy of water molecules • affects speed of movement of water molecules • affects how saturated with water air is • affects evaporation of water	• increasing temperature increases rate of transpiration	• place plant at different distances from a heater, measuring the air temperature with a thermometer • use a heater that can have different settings • possible heat sources could be radiators / Bunsen burners
humidity	• alters the diffusion gradient from inside leaf to outside	• increasing humidity reduces rate of transpiration	• place plant in clear polythene bag • place different amounts of silica gel or mist with water inside bag
wind speed	• blows away water vapour affecting the gradient from inside leaf to outside	• increasing humidity increases rate of transpiration	• place fan at different distances from plant • fan plant with card at different rates
light intensity	• light causes stomatal opening	• increasing light intensity increases rate of transpiration	• place a lamp at different distances from plant

Table 6.9

Variables

1 **a** Learner answers will vary.

2 Possible control variables (will depend on the variable chosen to the be independent variable):

Variable	How I will keep it constant
light intensity	place lamp at constant distance from plant
temperature	maintain temperature with heater, monitoring using thermometer
humidity	carry out experiment at same location to ensure humidity does not change
wind speed	place barriers around plant to prevent wind affecting it
leaf surface area	use same plant each time

Table 6.10

Equipment

Each learner or group will need:

- potometer
- branch of plant with leaves
- beaker, 250 cm³
- blotting paper
- electric fan (ideally battery powered, rather than mains powered)
- bench lamp
- one metre ruler
- clear polythene bags and food ties
- solid silica gel
- 30 cm ruler
- A4-sized piece of stiff card
- stopclock
- small heaters or Bunsen burners
- secateurs.

Access to:

- sink or large water trough
- water supply.

Safety considerations

- Learners should have read the safety guidance section within the workbook before carrying out this investigation.
- Standard laboratory safety procedures should be followed always.
- Risks and what can be done to minimise them could include the following:

Risk	Minimising the risk
cutting with secateurs	• keep fingers away from secateurs blades
being burnt / risk of fire from Bunsen burners	• tie back long hair and wear lab coat • keep fingers away from flame / hot objects • use a yellow flame when not directly using Bunsen • wear eye protection
care with glass potometer as if broken it can cause cuts	• take care using potometer • clear away any breakages carefully
electrical appliances placed near large volumes of water	• extra care should be taken to ensure they are placed at a safe distance

Table 6.11

Method

A suggested method is as follows:

1 Fill a sink or water trough with tap water.

2 Place the branch under the water and using the secateurs, cut the end of at an angle of approximately 45.

3 Place the potometer underwater and fill all parts with water.

4 Keeping the branch and potometer underwater, carefully insert the cut end of the branch into the silicon tubing.

5 Remove the potometer and branch and secure upright with the stand, boss and clamp.

6 Dry the leaves carefully with tissue paper and blot the end of the capillary tube to introduce a bubble.

7 Use a ruler to measure the distance the end of the bubble has moved in a 5-min period and record in Table 6.12. Repeat two more times.

8 Fill the beaker with water and use it to generate another bubble in the capillary tube.

9   Use the A4 card to fan the plant at a rate of one 'fan' every 10 s for 5 min. Record the distance moved by the bubble and repeat two more times. Record the results in Table 6.8. Repeat the experiment three more times, 'fanning' the card at rates of one 'fan' every 5 s, one 'fan' every 2 s and one 'fan' every second. Record all results in Table 6.12.

Carrying out the investigation

- The same issues in setting up volume potometers that are outlined in Practical investigation 6.5 may occur. As learners will be using their own plans, they may need to modify them during the practical.

    Some learners will require more support than others when writing the plan. The plans will need checking and

some may require rewriting if there are major errors. The teacher should read the plans carefully and suggest improvements if appropriate.

- When carrying out the practical it is important to get learners to realise that they can modify their protocol if needed; for example, they may need to change the length of time that they measure the movement of water over. It is also important that learners appreciate that there is no such thing as a 'right' or a 'wrong' result – they should record the results they obtain and evaluate the quality of the data after.

    When learners have recorded their data, some may require assistance with data analysis and selecting the correct graphs to plot.

    Some may also need additional help evaluating the results and design of the experiment.

    For an extension activity, learners could plan investigations into other independent variables.

Sample results

The learners' results may be similar to the data below. This data can be used to answer the Data analysis and Evaluation questions if the learners are not able to do the investigation.

Independent variable: distance of fan from potometer / cm	Distance moved by bubble / mm				Volume of water lost / mm³	Time taken / min	Rate of water loss / mm³ min⁻¹
	1	2	3	mean			
5	15	17	14	15.3	12.0	10	1.20
10	12	13	11	12.0	9.4	10	0.94
15	8	13	7	7.5	5.9	10	0.59
20	6	8	7	7.0	5.5	10	0.55
25	4	5	5	4.7	3.7	10	0.37
30	3	2	4	3.0	2.4	10	0.24

Table 6.12

Diameter of capillary tube = 1 mm

Time taken for bubble to move: 10 min

Answers to the workbook questions (using the sample results)

a–d (see Table 6.12)

e

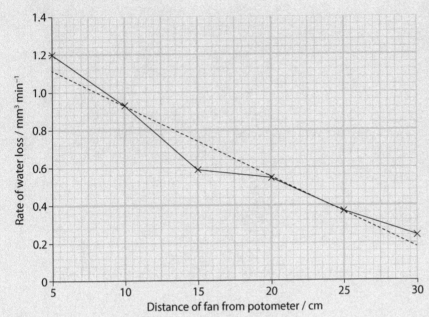

Figure 6.1

f This will depend on the results obtained by each learner.

g This will depend on the results obtained by each learner.

h • Changing temperature affects the humidity of the air and can create convection currents.

• Changing humidity by placing the branch in a bag will change wind speed and temperature.

• Changing light intensity can change temperature.

• Increasing wind speed can reduce the temperature.

Practical investigation 6.6:
Drawing sections and identifying the tissues of a typical leaf and a xerophytic leaf

Learning objective: 7.2(f)

Skills focus

The following skills are developed and practised (see the skills grids at the front of this guide):

MMO   Making decisions about measurements: (n)
Successfully collecting data and observations: (e), (f), (j)

PDO   Recording data and observations: (e)
Layout of data or observations: (h), (i)

ACE   Interpreting data or observations and identifying sources of error: (k)
Drawing conclusions: (c)

Duration

This practical should take about 1 h for the practical and about 20 min for the analysis work.

Preparing for the investigation

• Learners should be aware of all the leaf tissues and structures before this practical. They should also be aware of the term xerophyte and understand how different xerophytes have different adaptations. It is useful to provide as many different types of xerophyte in the laboratory to discuss each with the whole class. Pictures of the whole plant *Ammophila* should be shown to the learners.

- The practical itself is quite straightforward and reinforces drawing skills.

Equipment

Each learner or group will need:

- light microscope
- eyepiece graticule
- prepared sections of TS leaf of a dicotyledonous plant, TS leaf of *Ammophila*
- pencil, HB or 2H grade
- eraser
- pencil sharpener
- ruler.

Additional notes and advice

- *Fagus* and *Helleborus* are good leaves to use.

Safety considerations

- Learners should have read the safety guidance section within the workbook before carrying out this investigation.
- Standard laboratory safety procedures should be followed always.
- Ensure learners take care when using lamps and microscopes as the bulbs can become very hot.

Carrying out the investigation

- This is a relatively easy practical to carry out. Learners may find difficulty identifying tissue types.

  Some learners will need support identifying the different tissue types.

  Learners could also look at sections of other leaves and comment on their adaptions such as *Oleander*, *Rosemarinus* and *Pinus*.

Sample results

Photographs of cross-sections through leaves are available on the internet and could be used. Figures 7.7 and 7.22 from the coursebook could be also be used.

Answers to the workbook questions (using the sample results)

a Differences might include (any four):

- *Ammophila* is rolled up
- *Ammophila* has stomata in pits
- *Ammophila* has several layers of epidermis cells
- *Ammophila* has more lignin
- *Ammophila* has larger xylem vessels
- the vascular bundles are located in different area
- *Ammophila* has trichomes (hairs) on lower epidermis.

b
- Humidity is retained in the leaf by rolling the leaf up and having stomata in pits. This reduces the diffusion gradient, slowing rate of transpiration.
- Effect of wind speed is reduced by keeping stomata in pits and within the leaf. Trichomes also reduce wind effects.
- Exposed leaf surface is reduced, lowering rate of evaporation.
- The upper epidermis is thicker and has lignified tissue on the outside reducing evaporation of water through it.

Chapter outline

This chapter relates to Chapter 8: Transport in Mammals, and Chapter 9: Gas exchange and smoking in the coursebook.

In this chapter, learners will complete practical investigations on:

- 7.1 Identifying and drawing blood cells
- 7.2 Observing and drawing the structure of the heart
- 7.3 Observing and drawing the different structures of arteries, veins and capillaries
- 7.4 Observing and drawing the structure of the respiratory system and its tissues

Practical investigation 7.1:
Identifying and drawing blood cells

Learning objective: 8.2(a)

Skills focus

The following skills are developed and practised (the skills grids at the front of this guide):

MMO	Making decisions about measurements: (n) Successfully collecting data and observations: (e), (g)
PDO	Recording data and observations: (e)
ACE	Interpreting data or observations and identifying sources of error: (k)

Duration

This is quite a simple practical investigation that should not take more than 30–45 min for the practical work (provided learners are familiar with using microscopes), and 20–30 min for the analysis sections.

Preparing for the investigation

- There is little preparation for this investigation, although it is important that good quality slides are sourced.

- The teacher should begin the lesson by outlining the different cell types, their structures and their functions.

- If learners are not confident with microscopes and drawing diagrams, it is worth explaining how to use the microscope

and reading through the rules for drawing cells in the Quick skills section at the beginning of the workbook.

Equipment

Each learner or group will need:

- a light microscope
- prepared sections of blood
- pencil, HB or 2H grade
- eraser
- pencil sharpener
- ruler.

Safety considerations

- Learners should have read the safety guidance section within the workbook before carrying out this investigation.

- Standard laboratory safety procedures should be followed always.

- There are no additional significant safety issues associated with this investigation.

Carrying out the investigation

- This is a fairly straightforward practical investigation. One problem can be the quality of the microscope slides. If staining is not strong, it can be difficult to identify cells.

- Some learners may struggle to identify the types of white blood cell.

This should be a straightforward practical but some learners may need help setting up and focusing microscopes.

Some learners may need help to identify the white blood cells – this is often quite difficult. The teacher should clearly show the structure of the cells at the start of the lesson.

For extension work, learners could be asked to identify other cell types such as eosinophils and basophils.

Common learner misconception

- There could be some confusion over the term, 'phagocyte'. Many learners will use this term to describe white blood cells as a whole. They should be encouraged to use the terms monocyte and neutrophil and appreciate that phagocyte is a term used to describe those white blood cells that ingest pathogens.

Sample results

If no slides are available, learners can draw cells from the light micrograph in Figure 7.1 in the workbook.

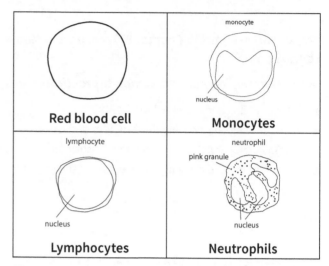

Figure 7.1

Answers to the workbook questions (using the sample results)

a

Cell type	Nucleus present (y / n)	Shape of nucleus	Colour	Other distinguishing features
red blood cell	n	n/a	red / pink	• biconcave disc • pale in centre • very abundant
monocyte	y	large, kidney-shaped	clear cytoplasm with stained (purple) nucleus	• large cells • low numbers
lymphocyte	y	circular	clear cytoplasm with stained (purple) nucleus	• smaller cells • low numbers • less cytoplasm
neutrophil	y	lobed	clear cytoplasm with stained (purple) nucleus	• large cells • large amount of cytoplasm

Table 7.1

b

Name of blood cell	Function
neutrophil	Transported around body in blood and ingests pathogens by phagocytosis.
lymphocyte	Exist in two major groups, T-cells and B-cells. Involved in the immune response including production of antibodies.
red blood cell	Contain hemoglobin and transport oxygen around the body.
monocyte	Transported around the blood eventually settling in organs to mature as macrophages, which ingest pathogens by phagocytosis.

Table 7.2

c i Leukaemia

Differences:

- large numbers of white blood cells
- fewer red blood cells.

Symptoms:

- tiredness due to less oxygen transport so tissues cannot respire as rapidly
- paleness due to lack of red blood cells.

ii Sickle cell anaemia

Differences:

- distorted (sickle) shaped red blood cells.

Symptoms:

- tiredness
- damage to tissues as blood vessels get blocked
- death of tissues due to lack of oxygen.

Practical investigation 7.2:
Observing and drawing the structure of the heart

Learning objective: 8.1(b), 8.1(c)

Skills focus

The following skills are developed and practised (the skills grids at the front of this guide):

MMO Successfully collecting data and observations: (a), (e), (f)

PDO Recording data and observations: (d)

ACE Interpreting data or observations and identifying sources of error: (k)
Drawing conclusions: (a)

Duration

This practical investigation should take about 1 h, with approximately 20 min needed for the analysis sections.

Preparing for the investigation

- Learners should be familiar with the structure and function of the heart. They should understand the circulation of the blood and the circulatory system map that shows the double circulation. The teacher should discuss the following at the start of the lesson:
  - structure and function of heart
  - roles of arteries and veins
  - circulatory map of the body, including the double circulatory system.
- The teacher should then introduce the practical and clearly explain the aims of dissection. Safe methods of cutting with scalpels should be demonstrated, encouraging learners not to 'saw' but to use sweeping strokes away from their fingers. It should also be stressed that dissection is about observation and the learners need to look and think about the structure of the heart.

- The importance of sterilising work surfaces and dissection equipment after the practical should also be discussed.

Equipment

Each learner or group will need:

- scalpel
- dissection scissors
- mounted needle
- forceps
- tray
- heart (sheep).

Access to:

- sink
- running water
- hand-washing facilities
- gloves if requested
- sterilising fluid and cloths.

Additional notes and advice

- It is recommended that sheep hearts are used. A reputable butcher will often supply hearts although it should be checked to ensure that it is 'disease-free'.

- The quality of hearts may vary. Sometimes the atria and blood vessels have been cut off or the ventricles sliced open. Purchasing from specialist suppliers will often guarantee 'dissection-grade' hearts.

Safety considerations

- Learners should have read the safety guidance section within the workbook before carrying out this investigation.

- Standard laboratory safety procedures should be followed always.

- Eye protection should be worn.

- Dissection equipment is sharp so caution should be taken. When using scalpels, keep fingers well away from the blade and only apply light pressure – demonstrate this technique to learners.

- Hands should be washed with soap and warm water afterwards. Gloves may be worn if required.

- After completing the dissection, all work surfaces should be washed down with disinfectant and dissection equipment placed into disinfectant.

Carrying out the investigation

- Problems you may encounter include hearts being of poor quality with no blood vessels and / or atria and learners cutting into tissue too quickly and so damaging the hearts without identifying the structures – they should be warned to take time.

- Some learners may wish to opt out of handling animal tissue due to religious or ethical reasons. They may wish to watch or to draw diagrams from textbooks.

  Some learners will need help in orienting the heart so that the ventral surface is uppermost. The position of the coronary blood vessels should help this.

  Many learners will find it difficult to identify the left and right ventricles and left and right atria. The teacher should circulate around the room pointing these structures out.

  Identifying the valves can be difficult for some learners – the teacher should help them locate and identify them.

- Try to ensure that dissection work is carried out carefully and methodically as many learners will try to start cutting immediately.

  To extend learners, they could take cross-sections of artery and vein tissue from the heart and compare the elasticity and strength.

Sample results

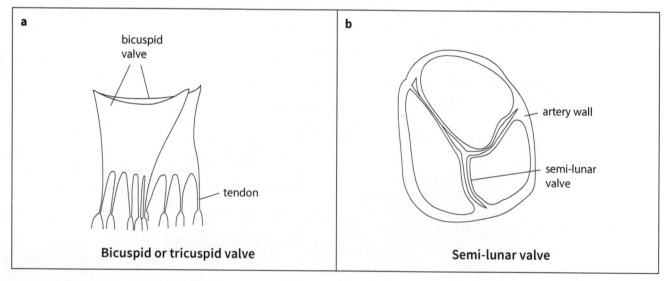

Figure 7.2

Maximum thickness of right atrium: 4 mm

Maximum thickness of left atrium: 4 mm

Maximum thickness of right ventricle: 15 mm

Maximum thickness of left ventricle: 35 mm

Answers to the workbook questions (using the sample results)

a i •	The left ventricle has a thicker layer of muscle.

• The left ventricle has to generate more pressure to force blood around the body / against gravity.

• The right ventricle only pumps blood to the lungs. If blood pressure is too high there is a risk of damage to capillaries in lungs.

ii • There is no significant thickness in the walls of the left and right atria. Both only pump blood into the ventricles so both generate the same pressure.

iii • The volumes of left and right ventricles are the same.

• The same volume of blood needs to leave each chamber.

• The larger left-side is due to the muscle thickness, not chamber volume.

b i Heart valves prevent backflow of blood / maintain blood flow in one direction.

ii The tendons prevent the valve leaking blood. They stop the valves being forced backwards and so maintain the valve in a closed position.

iii The semi-lunar valves are 'pockets' that fill with blood and so stretch across the artery, closing it.

Practical investigation 7.3:
Observing and drawing the different structures of arteries, veins and capillaries

Learning objective: 8.1(d)

Skills focus

The following skills are developed and practised (the skills grids at the front of this guide):

MMO	Making decisions about measurements: (m)
	Successfully collecting data and observations: (e), (f), (j)

PDO	Recording data and observations: (e)

ACE	Interpreting data or observations and identifying sources of error: (k)
	Drawing conclusions: (a), (c)

Duration

This practical should last approximately 45–60 min, with an additional 20–30 min for the analysis sections.

Preparing for the investigation

• Good quality prepared slides of TS artery and vein will need to be purchased. If possible, sections of capillary should also be included.

• Learners should be familiar with the structure and functions of arteries, veins and capillaries.

• Before beginning the practical, the teacher should discuss the different roles and structures of the blood vessels and relate this to the different blood pressures and blood velocities. The correct names and compositions of the inner layer, middle layer and outer layer should be introduced.

Equipment

Each learner or group will need:

• light microscope

• prepared sections of TS arteries, veins and capillaries

• pencil, HB or 2H grade

• eraser

• pencil sharpener

• ruler

• eyepiece graticule

• stage micrometer.

Safety considerations

• Learners should have read the safety guidance section within the workbook before carrying out this investigation.

• Standard laboratory safety procedures should be followed always.

• There are no additional significant safety issues associated with this investigation.

Carrying out the investigation

- The quality of sections can sometimes be an issue and good quality, well-stained, clear sections should be sourced.

- Obtaining good quality slides with capillary sections can be difficult. It may be necessary to use photomicrographs from the internet (Figure 8.7 in the coursebook has a photomicrograph of capillaries), there are also videos available on the internet showing blood movement through capillaries.

- It is often difficult to see the border between the middle layer and outer layer.

  Some learners will need assistance with identifying the different layers of the blood vessel walls. The teacher should circulate around the room ensuring that learners are clear about the layers.

Some learners will need assistance with the setting up and focusing of microscopes.

Learners can look at additional slides of arterioles and venules and compare the structures.

Learners can also look at other organs and tissues such as skin and try to identify the blood vessels found within them.

Common learner misconception

- Some learners will confuse the idea that the wall of the artery is thicker than the wall of the vein with the idea that arteries are wider blood vessels.

Sample results

Learners can use the photomicrographs from Figure 7.6 in the workbook chapter to draw their own plan diagrams.

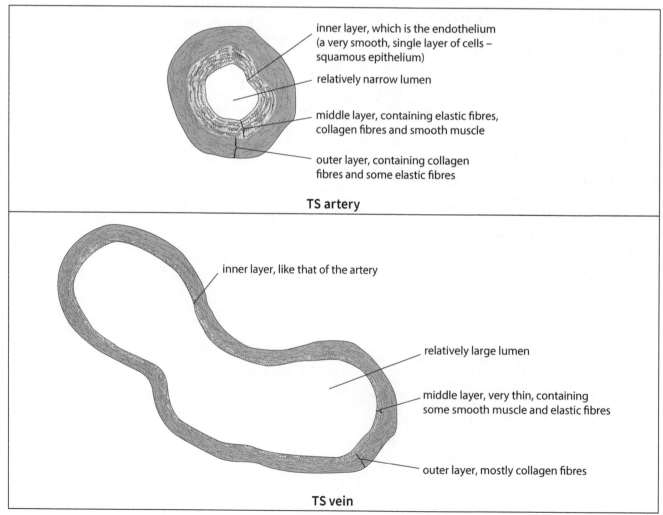

inner layer, which is the endothelium (a very smooth, single layer of cells – squamous epithelium)

relatively narrow lumen

middle layer, containing elastic fibres, collagen fibres and smooth muscle

outer layer, containing collagen fibres and some elastic fibres

TS artery

inner layer, like that of the artery

relatively large lumen

middle layer, very thin, containing some smooth muscle and elastic fibres

outer layer, mostly collagen fibres

TS vein

Figure 7.3

Blood vessel	Thickness of wall / μm	Maximum thickness of lumen / μm
artery	1000	1500
vein	500	5000
capillary	(one cell thick endothelium, approx. 1 μm)	approx. 10

Table 7.3

Answers to the workbook questions (using the sample results)

a Arteries:

- thick wall with elastic fibres, muscle and collagen

- blood is under high pressure and is pulsatile

- collagen adds strength and elastic fibres stretch to prevent bursting and recoil to smooth the blood flow

- the wall is impermeable so that blood does not leak

- muscle can contract and relax to control lumen diameter and blood flow.

Veins:

- thinner wall with some collagen but few elastic fibres and no muscle.

- blood is under lower pressure and is not pulsatile

- no need for elasticity as the pressure does not surge

- walls are impermeable to prevent blood leaking

- no muscle tissue.

Capillaries:

- single cell thick, endothelium wall

- permeable wall with no elastic fibres, collagen or elastic fibres

- wall allows transfer of tissue fluid / diffusion of substances from blood to tissues

- short diffusion path to tissues.

b • Arterioles have a higher proportion of muscle and lower proportion of elastic fibres and collagen. Arteries and arterioles have the same proportion of endothelium.

- less elastic fibres as blood pressure is lower

- muscle can contract / relax to enable vasoconstriction / vasodilation to occur. This will control the blood flow to tissues and organs.

c • Arteries have thicker layers of muscle, elastic fibres and collagen. The pressure in arteries is very high so the wall requires collagen and elastic fibres to prevent rupture. The elastic fibres recoil when pressure falls and this 'smooths' the flow of blood. The muscle can contract and relax to constrict and dilate the arteries - this regulates blood flow to different tissues.

- Veins have thinner layers of elastic fibres, collagen and muscle. This is because pressure is lower so that there is less risk of rupture. There is less need to control the exit of blood from tissues so there is less muscle in the wall. Blood is moved by skeletal muscle contraction so that there are valves present to prevent the backflow of blood.

- Capillaries consist of a thin endothelium that is permeable. Their function is to exchange molecules between tissues and blood so there is a short distance between blood and tissue. The pores enable small molecules such as glucose and oxygen to pass through the wall into tissues and molecules such as carbon dioxide to move back into the blood.

d i Velocity:

- is high and pulses in arteries. Falls along with increasing distance.

- falls in arterioles and loses pulse

- drops sharply in capillaries

- increases sharply in venules

- increases, but less sharply, in veins.

Pressure:

- is high and pulses in arteries. Falls along with increasing distance.

- falls in arterioles and loses pulse

- drops less steeply in capillaries

- shallow decrease in venules

- further decrease in veins.

Cross-sectional area:

- low in arteries

- increases in arterioles

- continues up to a peak at start of capillaries

- falls in venules

- falls further in veins.

ii • increase number of branches in arterioles and then capillaries results in a higher cross-sectional area.

iii • The force is constant but area increases in arterioles and capillaries. Force spread out over a larger area reduces pressure.

- Friction of blood vessel walls reduces pressure.

- Tissue fluid loss reduces blood volume which reduces pressure.

iv • As pressure falls in arterioles and capillaries, the blood velocity decreases.

- In veins, a negative suction pressure is created by skeletal muscle contraction and reduced thoracic pressure when inhaling.

Practical investigation 7.4:
Observing and drawing the structure of the respiratory system and its tissues

Learning objectives: 9.1(a), 9.2(b)

Skills focus

The following skills are developed and practised (the skills grids at the front of this guide):

MMO — Making decisions about measurements: (m), (n)
Successfully collecting data and observations: (a), (e), (f), (j)

PDO — Recording data and observations: (e), (f)

ACE — Interpreting data or observations and identifying sources of error: (k)
Drawing conclusions: (c)

Duration

This practical will take about 85 min. Approximately 20–30 min should be needed to answer the analysis questions. If learners draw slowly it may be necessary to separate the lesson into two sessions.

Preparing for the investigation

The practical is split into two sections:

- Part 1: Demonstration of dissection of the respiratory system of the sheep

- Part 2: Observation and plan drawing of the structure of trachea, bronchi, bronchioles and alveoli

Part 1: Demonstration of dissection of the respiratory system of the sheep

- The aim of this practical is to enable learners to appreciate the gross structure of the respiratory system to help them appreciate the sections through the structures on slides. The learners are to make notes on the following during the dissection:

  - overall appearance of lungs: colour, texture, elasticity, pleural membranes

  - trachea: shape of and function of the cartilage, diameter

  - bronchi: shape of and function of the cartilage, diameter

  - terminal bronchioles: shape and function, absences of cartilage, diameter.

- The teacher should begin by demonstrating the appearance of the two lungs, bronchi and trachea. If the heart is still attached, the pulmonary artery and vein should be demonstrated. The colour and appearance of the lungs should be discussed with the learners. The shiny pleural membrane on the outside of the lungs should be shown and its function in attaching the lungs to the inside of the ribcage explained.

- If the lungs are in good condition and not sliced open, it may be possible to insert a tube attached to a foot or hand pump. The lungs can then be inflated and the elasticity demonstrated. If the lungs are inflated, this should be carried out in a large, clear plastic bag to prevent the possible release of aerosols of mucus that may contain pathogens.

- The trachea should now be demonstrated. The structure and function of the C-rings of cartilage should be shown – it is easy to dissect out an individual ring with a sharp scalpel.

- The position where the bronchi emerge from the trachea should be demonstrated next. It will now be necessary to start to cut into the lung tissue to reveal the extent of the bronchi. The route of the bronchus into the lung should be revealed by cutting into the lung along its length. The smaller diameter and reduced cartilage compared to the trachea should be discussed.

- For the final part of the demonstration, a section of lung should be cut through in order to expose terminal bronchioles. The narrow diameter of these and lack of cartilage should be discussed.

Part 2: Observation and plan drawing of the structure of trachea, bronchi, bronchioles and alveoli

- Good quality, prepared slides should be purchased. The slides required are:

  ○ TS trachea

  ○ TS bronchus

  ○ TS bronchiole

  ○ TS lung tissue with alveoli.

- The slides need to be of good quality to enable the learners to identify tissue types.

- The teacher should explain the tissue types that each structure contains and how to identify them. Key features to stress include:

  ○ trachea: ciliated epithelium, goblet cells within the ciliated epithelium, a layer of smooth muscle, 'loose' tissue that may contain mucus glands and a thick strip of cartilage

  ○ bronchi: a thinner layer of ciliated epithelium, fewer goblet cells, a layer of smooth muscle, a thinner layer of cartilage that may be in the form of a block rather than a C-ring

  ○ bronchiole: fewer ciliated epithelial cells and goblet cells, a more folded epithelium, a layer of smooth muscle and no cartilage

  ○ a large surface area of squamous epithelia, no cartilage or smooth muscle. Some bronchioles may be present.

Equipment

Part 1: Demonstration of dissection of the respiratory system of the sheep

You will need:

- one set of sheep's lungs and trachea; this may have the heart still attached

- scalpel

- forceps

- pump with tube

- large, clear polythene bag

- pencil sharpener

- ruler

- eyepiece graticule

- stage micrometer.

Part 2: Observation and plan drawing of the structure of trachea, bronchi, bronchioles and alveoli

Each learner or group will need:

- light microscope

- prepared sections of TS trachea, bronchi, bronchiole, alveoli

- pencil, HB or 2H grade

- eraser

- pencil sharpener

- ruler

- eyepiece graticule

- stage micrometer.

Additional notes and advice

- Lungs and tracheas can usually be obtained from a butcher. The quality may be variable and ideally, they should have few cuts.

- It should be ensured that the lungs are not diseased and are fresh.

- Lungs must be stored in a refrigerator, as they will decompose rapidly.

Safety considerations

- Learners should have read the safety guidance section within the workbook before carrying out this investigation.

- Standard laboratory safety procedures should be followed always.

- Care should be taken when handling dissection equipment.

- All equipment and surfaces should be sterilised with a sterilising solution such as Virkon.

- If the lungs are inflated, they should be kept within a large, clear plastic bag.

- Hands should be washed with soap and water and disposable gloves may be worn.

- For the observation of the sections, standard laboratory safety rules should be followed.

Carrying out the investigation

Part 1: Demonstration of dissection of the respiratory system of the sheep

- Some learners may object to observing the dissection of the lungs and others may feel faint. Learners should be asked about their likely response to seeing the tissue

before the investigation and the teacher should monitor any learners who appear to look ill.

- The lungs may be of poor condition and may not inflate.

Part 2: Observation and plan drawing of the structure of trachea, bronchi, bronchioles and alveoli

- The quality of the microscope slide may vary, in particular it may be very difficult to identify cilia on the surface of the epithelium, or see goblet cells (depending on the stain used).

- Learners may find it difficult to identify the tissue types – the teacher should constantly circulate from group to group to help.

⚙ Some learners will need help identifying the different cells and tissues in the airway structures. The teacher should spend time at the start explaining which tissues and cells each structure contains.

⚙ Some learners will need help setting up and focusing microscopes.

- Learners should be reminded of the rules for drawing plan diagrams.

⚙ Some slides or photos of conditions such as emphysema, COPD can be purchased for learners to compare with the normal sections.

Sample results

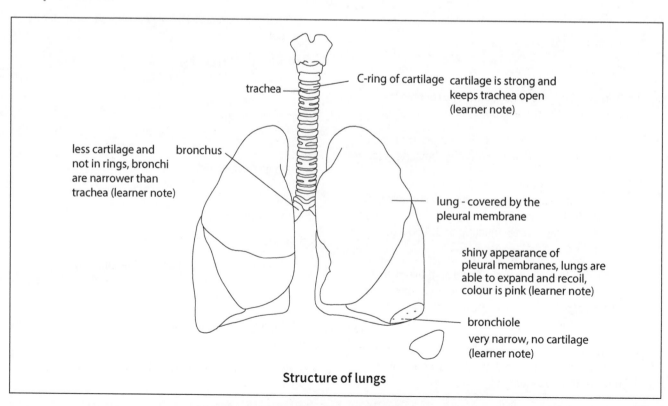

Structure of lungs

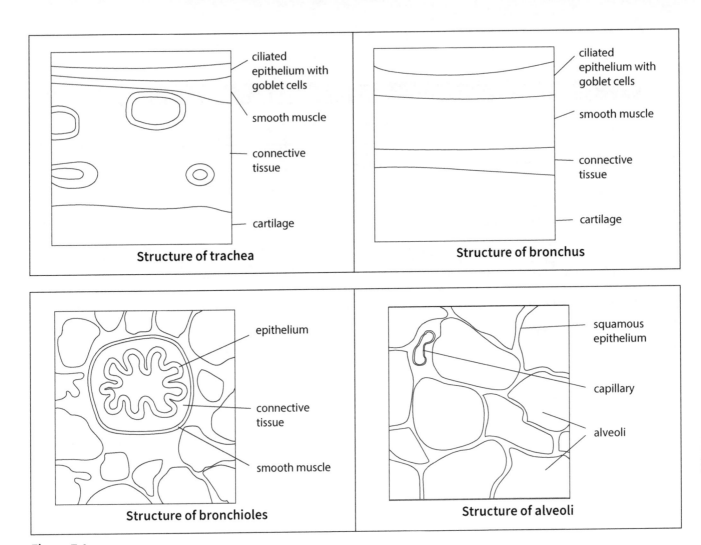

Figure 7.4

Answers to the workbook questions (using the sample results)

a

Airway	Cartilage	Ciliated epithelium	Goblet cells	Smooth muscle
trachea	yes	yes	yes	yes
bronchus	yes	yes	yes	yes
bronchiole	no	no (a few)	no (a few)	yes
alveolus	no	no	no	no

Table 7.4

b i
- 7.13b has larger air spaces
- 7.13b has less surface area of epithelia
- 7.13b has thicker alveolar walls

- less oxygen is absorbed into blood
- less respiration in tissues
- less energy
- less elasticity so less ability to ventilate and expel air.

ii Disease: emphysema

Effects: tiredness / inability to exercise / breathlessness due to:

- less surface area of alveoli
- longer diffusion path for oxygen into blood

Chapter outline

This chapter relates to Chapter 12: Energy and respiration in the coursebook.

In this chapter, learners will complete practical investigations on:

- 8.1 Using a simple respirometer to calculate the respiratory quotient of germinating seeds
- 8.2 The effect of temperature on the rate of respiration of an invertebrate
- 8.3 The effect of glucose concentration on the respiration rate of yeast using a redox indicator
- 8.4 The ability of yeast to use different sugars during fermentation

Practical investigation 8.1:
Using a simple respirometer to calculate the respiratory quotient of germinating seeds

Learning objective: 12.1(h)

Skills focus

The following skills are developed and practised (see the skills grids at the front of this guide):

P   Defining the problem: (e)
             Methods: (b), (f), (h)

ACE   Dealing with data: (b), (e)
             Evaluation: (a), (b), (g)
             Conclusions: (a), (b), (e)

Duration

This practical will require learners to return to collect data after 24 h and again after 48 h. Setting up the practical itself will require between 45 and 60 min. Obtaining the data and carrying out the analysis will take approximately 45 min. If 24 h and 48 h are not practicable, alternative times such as 20 h can be used.

Preparing for the investigation

- Seeds will need to be soaked for 24 h in water three or four days before the practical. If germination is too fast, they can be stored in a refrigerator.

- Learners will need to understand the idea of respiratory quotient (RQ) before the practical and the teacher should explain this at the start.

- It is advised that the teacher demonstrates how to set up the equipment at the start of the practical explaining how to test for leaks and how to use the three-way tap.

- Depending on the availability of equipment, different styles of respirometer can be used. Some very simple ones can be constructed (see Figure 8.1) although learners will need to be aware that there is no control experiment linked to it and will need separate controls to be set up. Ready-made respirometers may be purchased from some suppliers or constructed from scratch. Any set-up that allows the measurement of oxygen consumption is acceptable. They should be trialled before the practical and demonstrated to the learners.

Equipment

Each learner or group will need:

- four boiling tubes

- two U-tube manometers (1 mm bore, 5–6 mm diameter) filled with fluid

- four bungs containing connecting tubes

- glass beads, 20 g

- soda lime granules, 20 g

- two three-way taps

- two screw clips

- germinating seeds, 20 g

- four wire gauzes or cradles

- two sets of clamps, bosses and stands

- boiling tube racks

- eye protection

- marker pen for glass

- 30 mm ruler or scale.

- two syringes, 1 cm³

Access to:

- balance.

Additional notes and advice

How to make a U-tube manometer respirometer

Cut a 250 mm length of 6 mm diameter capillary tubing (bore 1 mm) and flame polish the ends (there must be no sharp glass). Place two marks with a pen 110 mm from both ends of the capillary tubing. Hold the tubing in a roaring blue Bunsen flame at the position of one mark and soften the glass. Remove from the flame and create a 90° bend in the tube by allowing the tube to bend under its own weight. Allow the glass to cool on a heatproof mat and then repeat at the second mark to create a U-shaped tube. Cut a piece of plastic or rigid cardboard, big enough to mount the U-tube on and cover with a piece of graph paper (to make a scale). You can attach the U-tube to the plastic or card by making small holes and passing cable ties through them, or simply attach using an elastic band (as shown in Figure 8.1).

100 mm lengths of silicon tubing (5 mm diameter) should be fitted over the ends of the manometer.

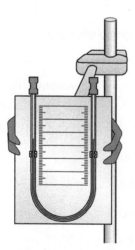

Figure 8.1

There are alternative methods of connecting the manometer to the boiling tubes. To make one pair of bungs, cut four 50 mm pieces of glass delivery tubing and flame polish the ends so there are no sharp edges. Carefully insert each through both holes of two two-hole rubber bungs. Attach a 100 mm piece of clear silicon tubing to one of the glass delivery tubes on each

bung. Attach a 40 mm long piece of clear silicon tubing to the other glass delivery tube on each bung and secure a three-way tap and 1 cm³ syringe as shown in Figure 8.2. If no three-way taps are available, it is possible to use clips.

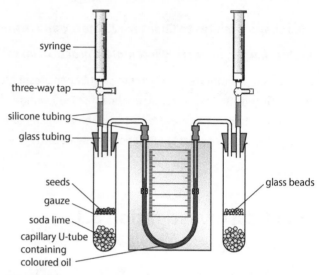

Figure 8.2

If manometers are not available, a simple respirometer such as that shown in Figure 8.3 can be used. This can be made in the laboratory. Cut a 300 mm long piece of glass capillary tubing (1 mm bore). Flame polish the ends to ensure that there are no sharp surfaces and make a right-angled bend approximately 70 mm along it. This should be inserted into a two-hole rubber bung for a boiling tube (as shown in Figure 8.3). A 50 mm length of glass delivery tube (5–6 mm diameter) should also be cut and the ends flame polished (again, ensure there are no sharp surfaces). This should be inserted into the other hole in the bung. A 50 mm length of clear silicon tubing (5 mm diameter) should be fitted over on the end. Three-way taps may be replaced by clips.

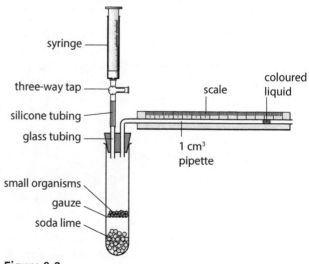

Figure 8.3

Other points to note:

- The fluid for the manometer should be water with some added cooking dye (such as cochineal substitute). A very few drops of detergent should be added. It should be injected into the manometer using a needle and syringe. It is essential that there are no large bubbles of air. Eosin in an ethanol solution is also a suitable liquid.

- The bungs must be made of rubber as cork will leak.

- It is worthwhile making pre-weighed, tied bags of muslin cloth that contain 5 g of soda lime. These can then be simply dropped into the boiling tubes and retrieved and reused at the end.

- There are many different types of seeds that can be used, such as, mung beans, peas, wheat, broad beans.

Safety considerations

- Learners should have read the safety guidance section within the workbook before carrying out this investigation.

- Standard laboratory safety procedures should be followed always.

- There is a risk of breakage of glass capillary and delivery tubes. Bungs and tubes should not be 'forced' and care should be taken to manipulate silicon tubing onto the ends of the glass delivery tubing.

- Soda lime is caustic and can cause severe burns. It is particularly dangerous to the eyes. It should be weighed out carefully and any spills cleared up. Eye protection must be worn and splashes on skin washed off with water. If it is splashed in eyes, irrigate with gently running tap water for 20 min and seek medical attention. It is worthwhile making pre-weighed, tied bags of muslin cloth that contain 5 g of soda lime. These can then be simply dropped into the boiling tubes and retrieved and reused at the end.

- Seeds that are non-toxic and non-allergenic should be used.

Carrying out the investigation

- Improperly sealed equipment will not function. Learners (and teachers) should check that the three-way tap is closed and that the level of fluid can be moved by depressing the syringe and does not immediately rise back up. If it immediately rises, there is most likely a leak and the equipment will need reassembling.

- Some learners will place bungs and the manometer on with the three-way tap in the wrong position. This will cause the fluid to squirt out of the manometer and it will need replacing.

- If soda lime is used too many times, it will become saturated and lose its ability to absorb carbon dioxide.

🔧 Many learners will find it difficult to calculate the carbon dioxide released when there is no soda lime present. They will often think that the distance moved by the fluid is the amount of carbon dioxide produced and not appreciate that they must compare it to the volume of oxygen consumed.

🔧 Some learners will find it difficult to understand why the RQ can exceed 1 if some anaerobic respiration occurs. They may think that organisms switch from aerobic to anaerobic instantly and do not appreciate that it is a gradual process.

🔧 This is quite a demanding practical and respirometers are often difficult to set up. The teacher should circulate around all groups and help check for leaks. Learners with dyspraxia will find connecting the equipment and using the taps difficult and may need help.

⏱ The experiment can be extended and different types of seeds used by different groups. A comparison of the respiratory substrates used by different seeds can then be carried out.

Common learner misconception

- Some learners will not understand that the soda lime removes carbon dioxide and think it removes oxygen.

Sample results

Time period / h	Distance moved by fluid during 24 h period / mm		
	with soda lime	without soda lime	with soda lime – without soda lime
24	35	2	33
48	42	7	35

Table 8.1

Internal diameter of U-tube manometer: 1 mm

Exact mass of seeds used = 5.2 g

Answers to the workbook questions (using the sample results)

a, b, c, d, e Sample results are shown in Tables 8.1 and 8.2.

Time period / h	Oxygen			Carbon dioxide		
	volume consumed / mm³	rate of consumption / mm³ h⁻¹	rate of consumption per mass of seed / mm³ h⁻¹ per gram	volume evolved / mm³	rate of evolution / mm³ h⁻¹	rate of evolution per mass of seed / mm³ h⁻¹ per gram
0–24	27.47	1.14	0.22	25.90	1.08	0.21
24–48	32.97	1.37	0.26	27.47	1.14	0.22

Table 8.2

f RQ between 0 and 24 h: 0.95

RQ between 24 and 48 h: 0.85

g Learners will need to compare their calculated RQ values with the values in the tables.

- If the RQ is equal to 1, it suggests that aerobic respiration of carbohydrate is occurring.

- Between 0.7 and 0.9 suggests lipids are used.

- Between 0.9 and 1.0 suggests proteins are used.

- If RQ > 1.0, some anaerobic respiration has occurred.

- In reality, the situation is not clear as there may be a mixture of substrates.

- Depending on the results, it may be that the seeds increase use of lipids or proteins as time goes on.

- The sample results suggest over the first 24 h that there is aerobic respiration of carbohydrate with a small amount of protein / lipid. Over the second 24 h there is increasing use of lipids / proteins.

h If oxygen levels fall, more anaerobic respiration will occur and the RQ will rise.

i To allow fair comparisons when analysing the data from the two experiments. Different masses of seeds would consume and produce different volumes of oxygen and carbon dioxide.

j As RQ is a comparison of carbon dioxide production and oxygen consumption, increasing the temperature would theoretically increase the rate of both so RQ would not change. It may change if temperature affected the rate of protein, lipid and carbohydrate use differently.

k Leaves would photosynthesise and would thus be using up carbon dioxide and releasing oxygen.

92

Practical investigation 8.2: Planning

The effect of temperature on the rate of respiration of an invertebrate

Learning objective: 12.2(m)

Skills focus

The following skills are developed and practised (see the skills grids at the front of this guide):

P   Defining the problem: (a), (b), (c), (d), (e)
       Methods: (a), (b), (c), (f), (g), (h), (j), (k), (l)

ACE   Dealing with data: (a), (b), (c), (d), (e), (n)
       Evaluation: (a), (b), (d), (e), (f), (h)

Duration

This investigation is carried out in two stages:

Planning: learners are to plan a valid investigation into the effect of temperature on respiration rate of invertebrates using respirometers (as in Practical investigation 8.1). This will take 60–90 min and can be carried out in a lesson and then completed independently.

Practical: learners complete a standard practical and analyse the results. The practical will take about 1 h. The analysis will take about 45 min and can be carried out in the next lesson or independently by learners.

Preparing for the investigation

- For the planning exercise, learners will need to be familiar with the terms: independent, dependent and control variables. The teacher should discuss with the class the idea of how to plan an investigation that will enable a valid conclusion to be reached. Learners should be clear that they need to explain all the practical steps that they need to take and state the values of the independent variable that they will test.

- The experiment uses live invertebrates and learners should be clear about the ethical issues of handling live organisms.

- When carrying out the standard practical (which is included in the Teacher's guide), learners should be issued with a photocopy of the equipment list and method. They will need to place this in their workbook.

- The teacher should demonstrate how to set up the equipment, use the three-way taps and check for leaks.

- If time allows, each learner or group can do all the temperatures. If time is limited, the teacher should allocate different temperatures to different groups and collate class data.

- If thermostatically controlled water baths are available, these should be used. The temperatures do not have to be tested in a particular order and so learners can move around the room where there are free water baths. Large water baths will need setting up around the laboratory and learners will use these rather than making their own. If thermostatically controlled water baths are not available, the learners will need sources of hot water, cold water and ice to maintain temperatures.

- The analysis requires some statistical testing (Spearman's rank correlation coefficient). Ideally, learners will have already covered this test. If they have not, the teacher should explain the role of the test and discuss how to carry it out.

Planning

Learner answers on hypothesis and justification will vary.

Variables

Learner answers to independent, dependant and control variables will vary.

Equipment

Each learner or group will need:

- four boiling tubes
- two U-tube manometers filled with fluid
- four bungs containing connecting tubes
- glass beads
- soda lime granules, 20 g
- two three-way taps
- two screw clips
- invertebrates
- four wire gauzes or cradles
- two sets of clamps, bosses and stands
- boiling tube racks
- thermometer.

Access to:

- balance

- thermostatically controlled water baths set at 10°C, 15°C, 20°C, 25°C, 30°C, 35°C

- hot and cold water, ice.

Additional notes and advice

- As in Practical investigation 8.1, different styles of respirometer may be used. Instructions for making suitable respirometers are given in Practical Investigation 8.1.

- It is worthwhile making pre-weighed, tied bags of muslin cloth that contain 5 g of soda lime. These can then be simply dropped into the boiling tubes and retrieved and reused at the end.

- Typical invertebrates could be blowfly larvae, woodlice or crickets.

- Empty tea bags can also be used if gauze is not available.

- If thermostatically controlled water baths are not available, water baths can be made using 250 cm³ beakers and the temperature maintained by using thermometers, warm water and ice.

Safety considerations

- Learners should have read the safety guidance section within the workbook before carrying out this investigation.

- Standard laboratory safety procedures should be followed always.

- Eye protection should be worn always.

- Hands should be washed after handling invertebrates.

Risks and methods to minimise these risks could include:

Risk	Methods to reduce risk
there is a risk of breakage of glass capillary and delivery tubes	<ul><li>bungs and tubes should not be 'forced'</li><li>care should be taken to manipulate silicon tubing onto the ends of the glass delivery tubing</li></ul>
soda lime is caustic and can cause severe burns; it is particularly dangerous to the eyes	<ul><li>it should be weighed out carefully and any spills cleared up</li><li>eye protection must be worn and splashes on skin washed off with water</li><li>if it is splashed in eyes, irrigate with gently running tap water for 20 min and seek medical attention</li></ul>

Table 8.3

Method

A suggested method is as follows:

1. Place 5 g of soda lime into two boiling tubes.

2. Place a cradle or gauze into both boiling tubes above the soda lime.

3. Weigh out approximately 5 g of invertebrates and place them into the cradle in one of the boiling tubes. Record the exact mass.

4. Weigh out an equal mass of glass beads and place them into the other boiling tube (this is the control tube).

5. Place the bungs with the connecting tubes into the boiling tubes securely so that there are no leaks. Do not attach the three-way tap yet. Place the boiling tubes into the 10°C water bath so that the water is covering the position of the invertebrates (do not put the water into the tube). For the invertebrates leave for 5 min to reach the correct temperature.

6. Clamp the U-tube manometer securely and then attach the connecting tubes from the boiling tubes.

7. Insert the 1 cm³ syringes into the three-way taps and check that the taps have the syringes 'closed'.

8. Turn the taps to seal the apparatus (close off the external air). Use the syringes to make the fluid in the manometer level. Record the position of the fluid on the scale of the U-tube manometer.

9. Record the distance that the manometer fluid travels after 5, 10 and 15 min.

10. Turn the three-way taps so that fresh air enters the boiling tubes and allow the invertebrates to 'rest' for 5 min.

11. Repeat the experiment at 15°C, 20°C, 25°C, and 30°C.

12. Record the internal diameter of the U-tube manometer.

Carrying out the investigation

- Improperly sealed equipment will not function. Learners (and teachers) should check that the three-way tap is closed so that the level of fluid can be moved by depressing the syringe and does not immediately rise back up. If it immediately rises, there is most likely a leak and the equipment will need reassembling.

- Some learners will place bungs and the manometer on with the three-way tap in the wrong position. This will cause the fluid to squirt out of the manometer and it will need replacing.

- If soda lime is used too many times, it will become saturated and lose its ability to absorb carbon dioxide.

- Some learners may object to using live animals. Germinating seeds can be used but this will take longer.

- Weighing out the animals into pots can be difficult. A disposable plastic spoon is useful for transferring blowfly larvae. Lids should be secured onto stocks of blowfly larvae as they can escape.

- Maintaining water bath temperature may not be easy. Ideally, thermostatically controlled water baths should be used but if they are not available, learners will need to maintain the temperature and will need access to hot and cold water and ice.

- Time may limit the number of temperatures that can be tested. If this is the case, class results should be collated to ensure that each learner has a full set of results. If time is very limiting, each learner or group could only test one temperature and then collate results.

⚙ Some learners will require help with the plan. Dyslexic learners may need support when writing the extended method and may find it easier to write in bullet points.

✋ This is quite a demanding practical and respirometers are often difficult to set up. The teacher should circulate around all groups and help check for leaks. Learners with dyspraxia will find connecting the equipment and using the taps difficult and may need help.

🔢 Learners who lack confidence with mathematics may need support with the statistical testing. They should be encouraged to follow the steps methodically and write down all their workings.

⏱ Extension work could focus on increasing the number of temperatures tested (within ethical boundaries) or comparing different invertebrate species.

📊 Learners could also evaluate their graph and decide whether a Pearson's correlation coefficient test could be used.

Sample results

Temperature / °C	Distance moved by fluid in manometer / mm			
	0–5 min	5–10 min	10–15 min	mean
10	8	7	8	7.7
15	7	6	9	7.3
20	11	13	12	12.0
25	16	19	18	17.7
30	23	24	21	22.7
35	34	37	32	34.3

Table 8.4

Mass of invertebrates: 4.75 g

Internal diameter of U-tube manometer: 1.0 mm

Answers to the workbook questions (using the sample results)

a Learners should have correctly calculated the means using their data and written them in Table 8.4 (see sample results for example).

b Learners should have correctly calculated the volumes using the formula for volume of a cylinder (see sample results for example).

c Learners should divide their answers from part **b** by 5 min to calculate the rate of oxygen consumption per minute (see sample results, Table 8.5, for example).

d Learners should divide their answers from part **c** by the mass of the invertebrates (see Table 8.5 for example).

Temperature / °C	Mean volume of oxygen consumed in 5 min / mm³	Mean rate of oxygen consumption / mm³ min⁻¹	Mean rate of oxygen consumption per gram of invertebrate / mm³ min⁻¹ per gram of invertebrate
10	6.0	1.2	0.2
15	5.7	1.1	0.2
20	9.4	1.9	0.4
25	13.9	2.8	0.6
30	17.8	3.6	0.7
35	26.9	5.4	1.1

Table 8.5

e Graphs should have (see sample results Figure 8.4):

- temperature on *x*-axis and rate of oxygen consumption on *y*-axis

- full labels including units on both axes

- linear scales that enable the plots to cover half the grid

- accurate plotting within half a small square

- a best-fit line or curve

- a title for the graph.

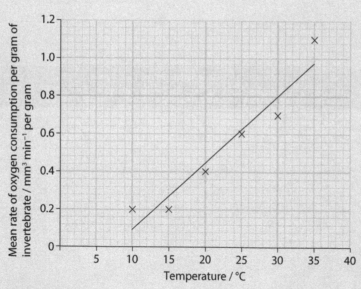

Figure 8.4

f i–vi A correct Spearman's rank calculation should have been carried out (see Table 8.6 for sample results). The results should be ranked correctly and the calculated value of r_s used correctly with the critical values table to reach a conclusion. This will depend on the data.

Temperature / °C	Rank for temperature, R_t	Rate of oxygen consumption / mm³ min⁻¹ per gram	Rank for oxygen consumption, R_o	Difference in ranks, D ($R_t - R_o$)	D^2
10	6	0.2	5.5	0.5	0.25
15	5	0.2	5.5	−0.5	0.25
20	4	0.4	4	0	0
25	3	0.6	3	0	0
30	2	0.7	2	0	0
35	1	1.1	1	0	0
					$\sum D^2 = 0.5$

Table 8.6

vii $r_s = 1 - ((6 \times 0.5)/(6^3 - 6)) = 0.986$

viii The calculated value of r_s is (**greater than**) the critical value (of 0.89).

This means that there is (**a significant correlation**) between temperature and mean rate of oxygen consumption.

g Learners should provide a detailed description of the pattern seen in terms of effect of temperature on rate of oxygen consumption. This should relate to the real data. The strength of the correlation should be discussed in light of the statistical test and how close points are to the line or curve of best fit. The sample results show an increase in rate.

Learners should provide an explanation of why temperature increases rate of respiration in terms of enzyme activity, faster movement of particles, higher kinetic energy, more frequent collisions between substrates and enzymes, more E/S complexes, faster use of oxygen.

h Learners should look at the raw data and correctly identify any anomalous values (there may not be any). Possible reasons could include: temperature fluctuations, invertebrates getting 'tired' and running low on energy substrates, altered gas concentrations, sudden changes in activity due to light intensity / sound / other factors.

i Learners should discuss the statistical test and how close the points are to the best-fit line or curve. They should discuss how similar their repeat measurements are (similar values suggest reliable data). Most variables are controlled but there are other factors that may have changed: light intensity, fatigue of invertebrates, gas concentrations, saturation of the soda lime.

j Most groups should show similar patterns but the values may be different. This may be due to the different invertebrates used (genetics), the basic trend of an increase should be the same as the values are calculated per gram of invertebrate.

k Systematic errors: balance consistently giving a reading that is too high or too low; ruler scale consistently showing an inaccuracy.

Random errors: sudden fluctuations due to changes in light intensity / sound, inconsistency in the diameter of the capillary tube bore.

Practical investigation 8.3:
The effect of glucose concentration on the respiration rate of yeast using a redox indicator

Learning objective: 12.2(h)

Skills focus

The following skills are developed and practised (see the skills grids at the front of this guide):

P   Methods: (d), (e)

ACE   Evaluation: (e), (g), (i)
            Conclusions: (a), (e)

Duration

This practical should take approximately 1 h with an additional 30–45 min for the analysis sections.

Preparing for the investigation

- Learners should be familiar with the importance of redox reactions in respiration. This should be discussed before the practical (either at the start or in preceding lessons).

- The role of methylene blue as an indicator should be explained.

- The reaction should be trialled before the lesson as different batches of yeast may yield different results. If the decolourisation is too rapid, lower concentrations of yeast / glucose should be used and if it is too slow, the concentrations should be increased.

Equipment

Each learner or group will need:

- 12 test tubes

- two large beakers, 500 cm³

- Bunsen burner, tripod and gauze or source of hot and cold water

- pipettes or syringes, 1 cm³, 5 cm³, 10 cm³

- thermometer

- 0.005% methylene blue solution, 20 cm³

- 10% glucose solution, 25 cm³

- distilled water, 100 cm³

- yeast suspension, 100 cm³

- boiled yeast suspension, 10 cm³

- stopclock

- bungs for test tubes

- marker pen for glass.

Additional notes and advice

- If thermostatically controlled water baths are available, they should be used, as otherwise many test tubes will be needed. Any method that can maintain 12 test tubes at a constant temperature may be used. It is possible for the reaction to occur at room temperature but it will take longer.

- As an alternative to methylene blue, 0.1% dichlorophenolindophenol (DCPIP) may be used.

Stock solutions

- 10% glucose: To produce 1000 cm³ of solution, 100 g of glucose should be dissolved in 1000 cm³ distilled water.

- 0.005% methylene blue solution: To produce 1000 cm³, 0.05 g should be dissolved in 1000 cm³ distilled water. If DCPIP is used, 1000 cm³ are produced by adding 1 g to 1000 cm³ distilled water.

- Yeast suspension: To produce 500 cm³ of yeast suspension, 100 g dried yeast should be added to 500 cm³ distilled water in a large beaker (it will need high sides as the yeast will froth). 1 g potassium dihydrogen phosphate (KH_2PO_4) should be added and the yeast aerated over one or two days. If an aeration pump is not available, it should be agitated manually. The suspension should be prepared one or two days before the practical.

- Boiled yeast suspension: Before the practical, some of the yeast suspension should be boiled for 2 min.

Safety considerations

- Learners should have read the safety guidance section within the workbook before carrying out this investigation.

- Standard laboratory safety procedures should be followed always.

- Care should be taken when using Bunsen burners.

- Methylene blue is classed as harmful and may be an irritant (particularly in a solid state), so any splashes on skin should be washed off. Eye protection should be worn and in the event of splashes in the eye, irrigate with gently running tap water for 20 min and seek medical attention.

- Glucose carries a low risk.

- Yeast is a living microbe and so hands should be washed after the experiment and laboratory coats worn.

Carrying out the investigation

- The methylene blue solution may not return to a blue colour easily when shaken.

- If learners agitate the mixture during the experiment, it will cause the methylene blue to return to a blue colour – this should be reinforced to learners.

⚙ Some learners will forget to replace the mixtures back into the water bath and will assume that the temperature will remain constant.

⚙ Some learners will find handling many test tubes simultaneously difficult and so it is often better to have them carry out the practical in a group.

⚙ Some learners may find judging the end-point difficult – this should be discussed as a limitation.

⚙ Some learners will not realise that the test tube with boiled yeast will not change colour.

⚙ An increased range of glucose concentrations could be investigated with learners calculating the dilutions and / or weighing out the glucose.

Sample results

Test-tube number	Glucose concentration / %	Time taken for blue colour to disappear / s			
		1	2	3	Mean
1	0.0	732	741	745	739
2	2.5	236	263	284	261
3	5.0	176	187	169	177
4	7.5	106	115	112	111
5	10.0	95	87	89	90
6	10.0*	n/a	n/a	n/a	n/a

Table 8.7

* Test tube 6 contained boiled yeast.

Answers to the workbook questions (using the sample results)

a Learners should calculate the means correctly leaving out any anomalous values (example shown in Table 8.7 for sample results).

b A line graph with either points joined or best-fit line or curve should be drawn (see Figure 8.5 for an example graph using sample results). Key points include:

- x-axis labelled as Concentration of glucose / %

- y-axis labelled as Time taken for blue colour to disappear / s

- points plotted ± half a square

- points joined with straight lines or a best-fit line or curve.

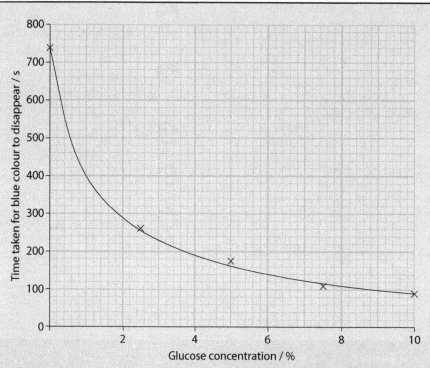

Figure 8.5

c A correct description of the graph should be given. It is expected that the time taken for the blue colour to disappear will decrease with increasing glucose concentrations. The graph may seem steep to start with (from the point with no added glucose).

d i Methylene blue acts as a hydrogen or electron acceptor and so becomes reduced (changing colourless). It could be receiving hydrogen or electrons directly from the electron transport chain, from respiratory substrates or from $NADH_2$ or $FADH_2$.

ii As glucose concentration increases, there is more substrate so glycolysis speeds up, also increasing the speed of Krebs cycle. This means that oxidation of substrates is faster and so hydrogen or electrons reduced methylene blue faster.

e Test tube 6 contains boiled yeast. There should be no respiration occurring and so it acts as a control experiment to demonstrate that the decolourisation of the methylene blue is due to respiration.

f There must be some respiratory substrates (e.g. glucose) already present in the yeast.

g i Shaking the tubes adds oxygen and so the methylene blue is re-oxidised.

ii To prevent methylene blue from returning to a blue colour due to oxidation.

h Learners should compare the repeats from the raw data – if the data is reliable the repeats and patterns should be similar. Learners should also consider how well-controlled the experiment is and discuss the problems with returning the colour to blue. Shaking the mixture to return the colour to blue is not accurate as it is impossible to obtain a definite concentration of re-oxidised methylene blue. If less oxidised methylene blue is present, the time taken to turn the mixture colourless will be less.

Practical investigation 8.4:
The ability of yeast to use different sugars during fermentation

Learning objective: 12.2(j)

Skills focus

The following skills are developed and practised (see the skills grids at the front of this guide):

P   Defining the problem: (e)
              Methods: (a), (g)

ACE   Dealing with data: (b)
              Evaluation: (b)
              Conclusions: (a), (e)

Duration

This is a long practical and will require at least 70 min and is best carried out over 90–120 min. Allow about 45 min for the analysis sections.

Preparing the investigation

- Learners should understand anaerobic respiration (fermentation) and be aware that it produces carbon dioxide gas. They should also be aware of different monosaccharides and disaccharides.

- The method used to measure carbon dioxide production will be unfamiliar to most learners. It should be trialled before the practical to ensure that the yeast is working fully and so that the teacher can demonstrate how to fill the fermentation tubes.

Equipment

Each learner or group will need:

- five test tubes

- five Durham fermentation tubes (50 mm × 6 mm)

- Bunsen burner, tripod and gauze or source of hot and cold water

- large beaker, 250 cm³

- 0.25 mol dm⁻³ glucose solution, 10 cm³

- 0.25 mol dm⁻³ fructose solution, 10 cm³

- 0.25 mol dm⁻³ sucrose solution, 10 cm³

- 0.25 mol dm⁻³ maltose solution, 10 cm³

- distilled water, 10 cm³

- pipettes or syringes , 1 cm³, 5 cm³, 10 cm³

- thermometer

- yeast suspension, 25 cm³

- stopclock.

Additional notes and advice

- If fermentation tubes are unavailable, 1 cm³ syringes may be used. 1 cm³ yeast suspension is drawn up into them and the plunger let in. The open-end of the syringe is then placed back into the mixture in the test tube.

- Thermostatically controlled water baths may be used. If time is an issue, these should be set up before the practical.

Stock solutions

- 0.25 mol dm⁻³ glucose: to make 1000 cm³, dissolve 45 g glucose in about 500 cm³ distilled water. The solution is then made up to 1000 cm³ with distilled water.

- 0.25 mol dm⁻³ fructose: to make 1000 cm³, dissolve 45 g fructose in about 500 cm³ distilled water. The solution is then made up to 1000 cm³ with distilled water.

- 0.25 mol dm⁻³ sucrose: to make 1000 cm³, dissolve 86 g sucrose in about 500 cm³ distilled water. The solution is then made up to 1000 cm³ with distilled water.

- 0.25 mol dm⁻³ maltose: to make 1000 cm³, dissolve 86 g maltose in about 500 cm³ distilled water. The solution is then made up to 1000 cm³ with distilled water.

Safety considerations

- Learners should have read the safety guidance section within the workbook before carrying out this investigation.

- Standard laboratory safety procedures should be followed always.

- Care should be taken when using Bunsen burners.

- Eye protection should be worn always.

- Glucose, fructose, sucrose and maltose carry a low risk.

- Yeast is a living microbe and so hands should be washed after the experiment and laboratory coats worn.

Carrying out the investigation

- Learners may find filling the Durham fermentation tubes difficult. The technique should be demonstrated before. If bubbles appear, the tube should be refilled. The diameter of the fermentation tubes should prevent the mixture from falling out.

- Yeast suspension will settle down if is not agitated so it should be stirred before taking samples.

- 🔘 Some learners, particularly any with dyspraxia will need help filling the Durham fermentation tubes. The teacher should demonstrate and help them to fill the tubes and place them into the mixture.

- ⚙ Additional carbohydrates such as lactose (yeast is unable to use lactose as it cannot synthesise lactase), trehalose or starch can be tested. The trisaccharide, raffinose, could also be tested.

Common learner misconceptions

- Some learners may not appreciate that carbon dioxide gas is released from fermentation.

- Some learners will not understand that glucose is a component of maltose and sucrose.

Sample results

Test tube number	Name of sugar	Length of bubble at time intervals / mm							
		10 min	20 min	30 min	40 min	50 min	60 min	70 min	80 min
1	glucose	2	12	19	28	37	49	54	59
2	fructose	0	2	8	16	27	36	43	53
3	sucrose	0	0	3	9	19	27	38	47
4	maltose	0	0	1	3	6	16	22	29
5	none	0	0	0	2	4	6	8	9

Table 8.8

Answers to the workbook questions (using the sample results)

a A graph that has:

- *x*-axis labelled as Time / s

- *y*-axis labelled as Length of bubble / mm

- appropriate linear scales so that the plots cover at least half of the grid

- plots correct ± half square

- plots joined with straight lines

- a key for each line.

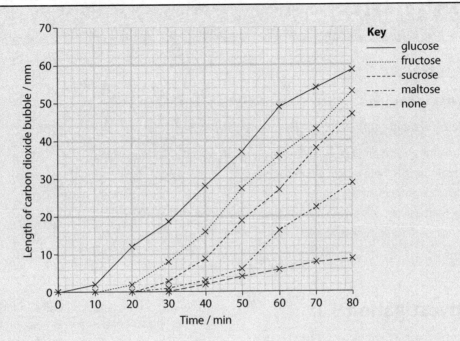

Figure 8.6

b Learners should give a full description of the patterns shown by each line and also compare the changes for each sugar, and the water. Some patterns may show a levelling-off effect at later times whilst others (sucrose and maltose) may take longer to start increasing the length but continue to increase. For example, carbon dioxide production increases at a steady rate when using glucose as a substrate between 10 and 60 min and then begins to slow down between 60 and 80 min.

c It is expected (although this may differ) that the length of the bubble when using glucose will increase at a faster rate and glucose will result in the most carbon dioxide production. This is because glucose is the primary substrate for respiration / fermentation.

Fructose may show a similar profile to glucose as fructose can also enter glycolysis.

Sucrose and maltose will have produced lower rates of increase and may have a time lag at the start before they start producing carbon dioxide. This is because yeast must start to produce sucrase / maltase to hydrolyse the sugars into glucose and fructose (glucose only when using maltose) before they can be absorbed and enter into respiration. It takes time for the yeast to produce the enzymes. Sucrose may work faster than maltose suggesting that yeast makes more sucrase at all times.

d To ensure that the temperature was even through the mixtures and that they had heated through thoroughly.

e Best-fit curves would be drawn and a tangent drawn at the point where the increase is steepest. The gradient of the tangent would be calculated (bubble length increase ÷ time).

Chapter outline

This chapter relates to Chapter 13: Photosynthesis in the coursebook.

In this chapter, learners will complete practial investigations on:

- 9.1 Identification and separation of photosynthetic pigments using paper chromatography
- 9.2 Effect of light intensity on the rate of photosynthesis
- 9.3 Gas exchange in a water plant
- 9.4 The effect of light wavelength on the light dependent reaction (Hill reaction)
- 9.5 The effect of carbon dioxide concentration on rate of photosynthesis

Practical investigation 9.1:
Identification and separation of photosynthetic pigments using paper chromatography

Learning objective: 13.1(e)

Skills focus

The following skills are developed and practised (see the skills grids at the front of this guide):

P	Defining the problem: (b), (c), (e)
	Methods: (b), (c), (g)
ACE	Dealing with data: (b)
	Evaluation: (g)
	Conclusions: (e), (f)

Duration

This practical will take approximately 75–120 min. It is possible to set up the chromatogram (which will take approximately 45 min) and learners can return between 30 and 60 min later to stop it running. The running speed can vary according to the temperature of the room – it will be slower if the conditions are cold. Allow approximately 30 min for the analysis sections.

Preparing for the investigation

- Learners should understand the technique of chromatography and how it separates substances on the basis of solubility.

- Learners should also know and understand the presence and functions of primary and accessory pigments.

- The teacher should demonstrate the application of the extract onto the chromatography paper.

- It is important that leaves are fresh and a range of leaf types should be trialled to see which give the best results. Fresh spinach and stinging nettles often give good results. Fresh, young grass leaves often contain high levels of pigments.

- The demonstration of fluorescence can be carried out as a class demonstration. When learners have set up their chromatograms, their extracts can be pooled into a test tube and the teacher can hold it into a light beam. The learners should stand at a 90° angle to the light – the extract should appear dark red / purple in colour.

Equipment

Each learner or group will need:

- pestle and mortar

- a small quantity of washed and dried sand

- muslin cloth

- test tube

- filter funnel

- scissors

- propanone, 50 cm³

- plant material

- pipette, 5 cm³ or teat pipette

- glass capillary tube

- chromatography paper, 80 mm long × 20 mm wide

- boiling tube with cork bung

- pin

- HB or 2H pencil

- solvent (one part propanone: nine parts petroleum ether (b.p. 80–100 °C), 20 cm³

- hairdryer or fan

- pipette, 10 cm³, and pipette filler.

Access to:

- centrifuge and two centrifuge tubes

- powerful light source such as an overhead projector (OHP).

Additional notes and advice

- If a pestle and mortar is not available, any other method of grinding the leaves so that a concentrated pigment is released may be used.

- Alternative methods of hanging the chromatography paper into jars so that only the base of the paper is in contact with the solvent may be used.

- It is possible to carry out the chromatography in propanone alone. However, separation will not be as effective.

- The leaves need to be ground sufficiently to produce a very dark extract – the darker the better. It is helpful if the teacher checks the extracts before they are filtered.

- If a centrifuge is not available to remove the sediment, sufficient time must be allowed to allow the sand and other solid matter to settle down. There should be no cloudiness.

Safety considerations

- Learners should have read the safety guidance section within the workbook before carrying out this investigation.

- Standard laboratory safety procedures should be followed always.

- Propanone and petroleum ether are highly flammable and should not be used near any naked flame.

- Propanone and petroleum ether are classed as harmful. Eye protection should be worn always, they should not be inhaled and any spills should be washed off with water.

- Glass capillary tubes are very fragile. The teacher should demonstrate the technique used for spotting the extract.

- Used solvents should not be poured down the sink but placed in a separate disposal bottle.

- Care should be taken when grinding the leaves as sand and extract can easily cause splashes.

Carrying out the investigation

- The importance of marking the origin with pencil rather than ink should be stressed.

- It is important not to use too much propanone to grind the leaves. It is tempting for learners to add more but this will result in a very dilute extract. If the volume added at the start is insufficient, extra may be added but in small volumes, bit-by-bit.

- When the learners remove extract with the glass capillary tube, care should be taken not to dislodge the sediment.

- It is important that each spot is dried before the next is added when placing the extract onto the chromatography paper. If insufficient drying time is allowed, the spot will become large and diffuse. Drying can be carried out with a hairdryer, fan or by wafting the paper in the air. Add 10–20 spots – this should be checked by the teacher to check that a sufficiently green spot has been created.

- It is important that there is not too much solvent in the base of the boiling tube. If the solvent comes over the pencil line, it will wash off the pigments.

- It is important that the learners cut the chromatography paper and test that it fits before placing the pigment on. The paper should not be buckled or touching the sides – this will cause the pigments to move in a skewed direction.

- The length of time that the chromatogram needs to run may vary according to the temperature. It may be necessary for learners to return after some time.

- Some pigments may not be visible. Chlorophyll a, chlorophyll b, and carotene are usually present; phaeophytin and xanthophyll may be less easy to detect. When analysing the results, if the extracts used were not concentrated enough, it will be difficult to see the pigments. If there was too much extract, the pigments tend to smear and it is difficult to measure where they have reached.

- Learners will need to be reminded to mark the solvent front as soon as they stop the chromatography as the solvent will rapidly evaporate and the solvent front will disappear!

  Some learners will need help to use the capillary tube to place spots on the paper.

  Some learners will need help deciding where to measure the spots to when the spots are large.

  Different species of plant and different ages of leaves could be compared.

  If possible, a chloroplast extract could be made (see Practical investigation 9.4 for protocol) and held up to the light to compare to the pure pigment extract. The intact chloroplasts should not fluoresce.

Sample results

Colour of extract in bright light: purple/red

Distance moved by solvent (solvent front): 60 mm

Distances moved by each pigment:

  pigment 1: 58 mm

  pigment 2: 50 mm

pigment 3: 43 mm

pigment 4: 39 mm

pigment 5: 28 mm

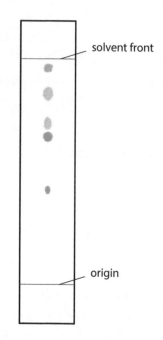

Figure 9.1

Answers to the workbook questions (using the sample results)

a, b Learners should have identified some of the pigments, calculated R_f values correctly and identified the pigments. The sample results are shown in Table 9.1.

Pigment number on chromatogram	R_f value	Identity of pigment
1	0.95	carotene
2	0.83	phaeophytin
3	0.71	xanthophyll
4	0.65	chlorophyll a
5	0.45	chlorophyll b

Table 9.1

c The chlorophyll absorbs light from the red and blue ends of the spectrum and electrons are energised and raised to a higher energy level. There are no electron acceptors in the extract so the electrons drop down to a lower energy level and give out the energy as light. If intact chloroplasts are used, the electrons are passed onto electron acceptors and so do not fluoresce.

d i The R_f value is a comparison of the distance the solvent moves compared to the pigment. If the solvent moves further, the pigments will also move proportionally further.

ii A longer chromatogram would give better resolution as it allows better separation of substances with similar R_f values.

e Learners should plan a fully controlled experiment that clearly states the independent, dependent and control variables. An accurate, consistent method should be indicated (i.e. consistently measuring to the centre of each pigment) that will generate reliable (i.e. repeated) data.

Independent variable = age of leaves

Dependent variable = pigments present (assessed by chromatography) and possibly quantity (using a colorimeter)

Control variables:

- Take equal masses of leaves of same species but different ages.

- Grind for same length of time with same volume of propanone (same solvent).

- Place same number of spots of extract onto chromatography paper.

- Same temperature when carrying out the chromatography.

Measuring the dependent variables:

- Either calculate R_f values to identify and compare pigments or run the two leaves side-by-side and compare.

- Use a colorimeter (set to red or blue light) to make a calibration curve with known concentrations of chlorophyll. Measure the absorbance of each leaf sample and use the calibration curve to determine chlorophyll concentration.

Practical investigation 9.2:
Effect of light intensity on the rate of photosynthesis

Learning objective: 13.2(e)

Skills focus

The following skills are developed and practised (see the skills grids at the front of this guide):

P   Defining the problem: (e)
           Methods: (b), (c), (g), (h), (j)

ACE   Dealing with data: (b), (c), (d), (e), (n)
           Evaluation: (a), (b), (c), (e), (h), (i), (j), (k)
           Conclusions: (a), (b), (e)

Duration

This practical should take between 60 and 90 min. If time is limiting, learners can do each light intensity once and class data can be collated. The data analysis will take a second lesson (about 45 min) or may be done by learners independently.

Preparing for the investigation

- Learners will need to understand the process of photosynthesis and understand that oxygen is a byproduct.

- Microburettes will need to be made. It is possible to modify the practical by just counting bubbles of oxygen produced by the pondweed.

- *Cabomba* tends to work best, along with *Elodea*. Other aquatic plants could be trialled if these are not available. There may be local restrictions on the use of *Cabomba*–

it is classed as an invasive species by some governments and so its cultivation is banned. Shoots with plenty of leaves should be selected and they should be illuminated under bright light for at least two minutes before the practical to check that bubbles are being produced.

- The pondweed should be kept under medium intensity illumination for 24 h prior to the practical.

- Learners should have carried out a Spearman's rank correlation coefficient test before the practical.

Equipment

Each learner or group will need:

- glass microburette

- 500 cm³, tall beaker

- sodium hydrogencarbonate solution (1 mol dm⁻³), 50 cm³

- distilled water, 50 cm³

- scalpel

- pondweed (*Elodea* or *Cabomba*)

- syringe, 5 cm³

- screw clip

- bench lamp

- clamp, bosses (two of each) and stand

- heatproof tile

- paper clip

- measuring cylinders, 10 cm³, 100 cm³

- one-metre ruler.

Additional notes and advice

- To make a microburette, cut a 300 mm long piece of capillary tubing (6 mm diameter, 1 mm bore). Flame polish one end of the tube and then heat the glass to soften it about 90 mm from the polished end. When the glass is soft, bend the section into a 'swan neck' shape and allow it to cool (see Figure 9.2). When cool, soften a section of glass 15 mm below the swan neck by heating it in a Bunsen flame. Pull the glass into a point and discard the end. Seal the end of the glass capillary and soften the end again in the Bunsen flame. Blow down the polished end of the capillary tube to form a bulb between 6 mm and 10 mm in diameter. Make a hole in the tube by heating the bulb and blowing very hard down the capillary tube – this may need two or three attempts to obtain a large enough hole (approximately 5 mm in diameter). Flame polish the end of the bulb and check there are no sharp edges.

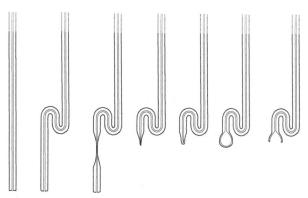

Figure 9.2

- If it is not possible to make or purchase a microburette, the practical can be carried out by counting bubbles of gas that are released by the cut end of the stem. Learners will need to be aware that it is not as accurate as measuring gas volumes as bubble sizes will vary.

- *Cabomba* and *Elodea* tend to be the best aquatic plants to use. Shoots should be cut for learners with one end intact. *Ceratophyllum* and *Potamogeton crispus* may also work but less well than *Elodea* and *Cabomba*.

Safety considerations

- Learners should have read the safety guidance section within the workbook before carrying out this investigation.

- Standard laboratory safety procedures should be followed always.

- The glass tubing is fragile so care should be taken with it.

- Sodium hydrogencarbonate is a low risk substance.

- Care should be taken not to splash cold water on hot bulbs as this can cause the glass to shatter.

- Eye protection should be worn always.

- Scalpels are very sharp and should be handled carefully.

Carrying out the investigation

- The main problem is pondweed that does not produce bubbles of oxygen. Several things can be tried:

  - re-cutting the end of the stem to help the bubbles escape

  - adding a tiny drop of detergent to the sodium hydrogencarbonate solution

  - tapping the beaker to help release the bubbles

  - if all else fails, changing the pondweed for a piece that is working.

  Learners may find positioning the cut end of the stem into the bulb difficult.

  A few learners may not appreciate that the bulb and the capillary tube need filling with the sodium hydrogencarbonate solution. The teacher should check that all learners have set up the equipment properly.

- Five minutes may not be long enough for the pondweed to adjust to the different light intensities.

- If there is insufficient time to carry out all the repeats, learners can do one set of results and class data can be collated.

- The time period for the collection of oxygen may need to be adjusted depending on the speed of photosynthesis (5 min is a suggested time). Learners will need to use the correct time when calculating the rate per minute.

  Some learners will need help positioning the cut end of the pondweed in the bulb.

  Some learners will need help with the Spearman's rank correlation coefficient test as there is no scaffolding in the exercise.

  A further experiment could be carried out with different concentrations of sodium hydrogencarbonate to see if carbon dioxide was a limiting factor.

  Learners could set up a similar experiment with oxygen probe, light meter and data logger if available. This could be left recording data for 24 h to observe changes in oxygen and light intensity. A correlation between oxygen concentration and light intensity could then be investigated.

Sample results

Distance of lamp from pondweed / mm	Light intensity / a.u.	Length of bubble produced in 5 min / mm			
		1	2	3	Mean
135	6	56	53	53	54.0
148	5	51	50	54	51.7
165	4	45	47	42	44.7
191	3	32	30	31	31.0
233	2	23	25	22	23.3
330	1	13	15	3	14

Table 9.2

Answers to the workbook questions (using the sample results)

a Means should be calculated correctly and given to the correct number of significant figures. The number of significant figures should be the same as the least accurate measurements or one further place when the mean has been calculated. Sample results can be seen in Table 9.2.

Distance of lamp from pondweed / mm	Light intensity / a.u.	Volume of oxygen produced in 5 min / mm³	Rate of oxygen production / mm³ min⁻¹
135	6	42.4	8.5
148	5	40.6	8.1
165	4	35.1	7.0
191	3	24.3	4.9
233	2	18.3	3.7
330	1	11.0	2.2

Table 9.3

b, c Learners should correctly calculate the volumes of oxygen and rates of oxygen production per minute. Sample calculations are shown in Table 9.3 for a capillary tube of 1 mm bore over a period of 5 min.

d A line graph should be plotted with light intensity on the x-axis and rate of oxygen production on the y-axis. A best-fit line/curve should be drawn or points joined with straight lines. The following should be present and correct:

- x-axis labelled as Light intensity / a.u.

- y-axis labelled as Rate of oxygen production / mm³ min⁻¹

- points plotted correctly (± half square)

- a correct best-fit line or curve or points joined with straight lines.

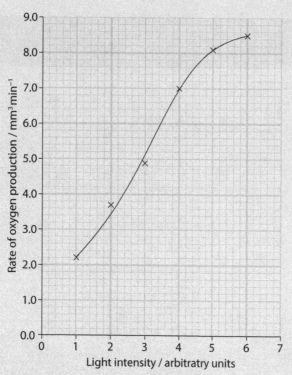

Figure 9.3

e Learners should give a correct description of the pattern shown by both graph and results.

It would be expected that as light intensity increases, rate of oxygen production also increases (a positive correlation). The graph may level off or begin levelling off with higher light intensities.

f Learners should explain:

- that as light intensity increases, more energy is available for the light dependent reaction

- more photooxidation of chlorophyll occurs

- more photolysis of water occurs as the chlorophyll receives electrons from water photolysis, resulting in more oxygen gas released

- eventually the graph levels off as another factor, such as temperature or carbon dioxide concentration, is limiting.

g Learners should carry out a correct Spearman's rank correlation test and correctly use the answer to state if there is a significant correlation. Sample results are shown in Table 9.4.

Light intensity / a.u.	r_{light}	Rate of oxygen production / mm³ min⁻¹	r_{rate}	D (difference in rank)	D²
6	1	8.5	1	0.0	0
5	2	8.1	2	0.0	0
4	3	7	3	0.0	0
3	4	4.9	4	0.0	0
2	5	3.7	5	0.0	0
1	6	2.2	6	0.0	0

Table 9.4

$r_S = 1 - 0$
$\quad = 1$

This value is greater than the critical value for six pairs of data and so there is a significant positive correlation between light intensity and rate of oxygen production at the $P < 0.05$ level.

h Sodium hydrogencarbonate provides a source of carbon dioxide so that it does not limit photosynthesis at lower light intensities.

i Anomalous values should be circled. Possible causes of anomalies include: temperature fluctuations, not allowing the pondweed long enough to adjust to light intensities, fluctuations in light intensities, reduction in carbon dioxide, bubbles 'getting stuck'.

j If the correlation coefficient gives a significant result, there is a probability of <0.05 that the correlation is due to chance. If the coefficient is lower than the critical value, there is a probability >0.05 that the correlation is due to chance. If the replicates of the results are similar it suggests they are reliable; if they are not similar or there are many anomalies it suggests that they are not reliable. If the Spearman's rank is significant and the data are reliable, their conclusion is likely to be valid.

k Variables could include (there may be others):

- Temperature: use a heat shield / water bath / monitor with a thermometer
- leaf surface area: use same pondweed
- same age / genetics of pondweed: use sections of same plant
- carbon dioxide: add same concentration of sodium hydrogencarbonate
- pH: place a buffer in the sodium hydrogencarbonate solution.

Practical investigation 9.3:

Gas exchange in a water plant

Learning objective: 13.2(d)

Skills focus

The following skills are developed and practised (see the skills grids at the front of this guide):

P	Defining the problem: (d) Methods: (f)
ACE	Evaluation: (i), (j) Conclusions: (g)

Duration

This practical should take between 60 and 90 min. Sufficient time must be allowed for the sodium hydrogencarbonate indicator to change colour – a longer time will give a better result. Setting up the experiment should be done as quickly as possible. Allow approximately 45 min for the analysis sections.

Preparing for the investigation

- Learners should have a basic understanding of the processes of photosynthesis and respiration and appreciate the basic equations. The teacher should display the equations and discuss the factors that affect the rates of photosynthesis (light intensity / temperature).

- Sodium hydrogencarbonate indicator should be made up to the correct colour before the practical.

- Learners will need to understand the colour changes that occur at different pHs.

Equipment

Each learner or group will need:

- five boiling tubes with rubber bungs
- hydrogencarbonate indicator solution, 200 cm³
- four pieces of pondweed (*Elodea* or *Cabomba*)
- bench lamp

- aluminium foil

- muslin cloth, three pieces

- boiling-tube rack (or large glass beaker)

- measuring cylinder, 20 or 50 cm³

- four rubber bands.

Additional notes and advice

To make 10 dm³ sodium hydrogencarbonate indicator:

- Dissolve 0.1 g cresol red powder and 0.2 g thymol blue in 20 cm³ ethanol. Dissolve 0.84 g sodium hydrogencarbonate in 900 cm³ distilled water in a 1000 cm³ measuring cylinder or volumetric flask. Mix the ethanol and sodium hydrogencarbonate solution and make up the volume to 1000 cm³ with distilled water. This is a concentrated stock and can be stored.

- About 1 h before the practical, samples of the stock are diluted for use by a factor of 10. For example, to make 1000 cm³, 100 cm³ stock is mixed with 900 cm³ distilled water. Air should be bubbled through the solution for at least 10 min (using an aquarium or filter pump) to bring the solution into equilibrium with the carbon dioxide concentration in the air. The indicator should be a reddish / orange colour.

Safety considerations

- Learners should have read the safety guidance section within the workbook before carrying out this investigation.

- Standard laboratory safety procedures should be followed always.

- Hydrogencarbonate indicator (thymol blue and cresol red) is listed as an irritant. Splashes on skin should be removed with water. If splashed in the eye, the eye should be irrigated with running water. Particular care should be taken with powdered thymol blue and cresol red and the concentrated indicator solutions.

- Eye protection should be worn.

Carrying out the investigation

- Glassware should all be very clean – traces of acid or alkali will alter the colour of the indicator.

- There needs to be sufficient time for the indicator to change colour – it is often worth setting up a demonstration practical before the lesson so that the learners can see the final expected results.

- Securing the muslin cloth can be difficult – adhesive tape of elastic bands can be used. If the experiment is going to be repeated many times, muslin cloth 'bags' can be made which fit over the boiling tubes and can be reused each time. If the wrapped tubes do not fit in a rack, they can be placed in a beaker.

- Some learners will need help in determining the colour changes. Learners who are colour blind will need to be in a group with learners who can differentiate between the different colours.

- If a colorimeter is available, the practical can be made more quantitative by determining the depth of the absorbance of red and blue light. If no colorimeter is available, learners could plan how they would use it to make a calibration curve using known carbon dioxide concentrations to quantify carbon dioxide concentrations.

Common learner misconceptions

- Some learners will not appreciate that the changes in pH are due to changes in carbon dioxide concentration. They will often think that an increase in pH is due to oxygen release and not a reduction in carbon dioxide.

- Some learners will assume that plants photosynthesise in the light and respire in the dark. They do not realise that respiration occurs all the time.

Sample results

Boiling tube number	Conditions	Hydrogencarbonate indicator colour
1	foil	yellow
2	one layer of muslin cloth	red
3	two layers of muslin cloth	orange
4	no covering	magenta
5	no pondweed or covering	red

Table 9.5

Answers to the workbook questions (using the sample results)

a With no light, the indicator turned yellow. With one layer of cloth, the colour remained red. With two layers, the indicator went orange. With two layers of cloth, the indicator went magenta. The control tube with no pondweed remained red.

b Learners should give a detailed conclusion explaining each of the colour changes:

Indicator colour: yellow / orange:

- acidity has increased (pH fallen)
- there has been a net release of carbon dioxide into the indicator
- respiration rate is greater than photosynthesis rate
- this is due to low light intensity.

Indicator colour: magenta / purple:

- acidity has decreased (pH risen)
- there has been a net reduction of carbon dioxide into the indicator
- photosynthesis rate is greater than respiration rate
- this is due to higher light intensity.

Indicator colour: red:

- acidity (pH) has not changed
- there has been no net increase or decrease of carbon dioxide in the indicator
- photosynthesis and respiration rates are equal
- this is the 'compensation point'.

c To prevent entry or loss of carbon dioxide which would alter the colour of the indicator.

d Detection of colour change is very subjective and different people would give different descriptions of the colours making it less accurate. The transmission of red and blue light through the indicator solution could be measured with a colorimeter. A calibration curve could be set up by determining transmission of indicator with different concentrations of carbon dioxide.

e **i** At night, photosynthesis would stop but respiration would continue. The plants would have a net intake of oxygen lowering concentrations in the hospital ward.

ii Respiration rate of the plants will increase with the higher temperature but photosynthesis will not as it is limited by the lower light intensity. The rate of glucose usage will exceed the rate of production causing the plants to die.

Practical investigation 9.4:
The effect of light wavelength on the light dependent reaction (Hill reaction)

Learning objective: 13.2(e)

Skills focus

The following skills are developed and practised (see the skills grids at the front of this guide):

P   Defining the problem: (a), (b), (c), (d), (e)
        Methods: (b)

ACE   Dealing with data: (b), (c)
        Evaluation: (c), (d), (e), (f)
        Conclusions: (d), (e)

Duration

This practical will take between 60 and 90 min, with an additional 45 min for the analysis work. It is best carried out in groups of two or three learners. One learner can focus on setting up the test tubes with the different light filters while the other prepares the chloroplast extract.

Preparing for the investigation

- This practical is notoriously difficult to obtain reproducible results from. The key to success is the quality of the isolation medium and keeping all solutions, the chloroplast extract and the glassware cold.

- Prepare the solutions a day in advance and store them in the refrigerator at 4°C. They should only be removed immediately before the practical work starts.

- If possible, all glassware should be kept in the freezer or refrigerator until the practical starts.

- Learners should have an understanding of the light dependent stage and the role of redox reactions in photosynthesis. If they have not already carried out Practical investigation 8.2 using a redox indicator (methylene blue) it will be necessary to outline the use of DCPIP as an indicator.

Equipment

Each learner or group will need:

- spinach leaves (approximately 10)
- measuring cylinder, 50 or 100 cm^3
- muslin cloth
- filter funnel
- small beaker (labelled '1'), approximately 100 cm^3
- medium size beaker (labelled '2'), approximately 250 cm^3
- large beaker (labelled '3'), approximately 500 cm^3 to use as an ice bath
- ice
- isolation medium, 100 cm^3
- DCPIP solution, 100 cm^3
- distilled water, 50 cm^3
- eight test tubes
- eight test-tube bungs
- test-tube rack
- pipettes, 1 cm^3 and 10 cm^3 and fillers
- bench lamp
- marker pen for glass
- aluminium foil 20 mm × 160 mm (or a size that will fold around a test tube completely
- coloured cellophane (light filters), purple, blue, green, orange and red (all approximately 20 mm × 160 mm or a size that will cover a test tube).

Access to:

- a blender
- a sink.

Additional notes and advice

- If no blender is available any other method of crushing up the leaves such as with a pestle and mortar may be trialled. If a pestle and mortar is used, it should be kept in the freezer before the practical.

- It is essential to use very fresh spinach leaves. The practical works best if the leaves are young and recently harvested. Green cabbage leaves can also be used.

- To make 500 cm^3 isolation medium:

  Dissolve 68.46 g sucrose and 0.38 g potassium chloride (KCl) in 300 cm^3 phosphate buffer solution. Add more phosphate buffer solution up to a total volume of 500 cm^3.

- To make 1000 cm^3 phosphate buffer solution:

  Dissolve 8.96 g $Na_2HPO_4·12H_2O$ and 3.4 g KH_2PO_4 in 1000 cm^3 distilled water.

- To make 500 cm^3 DCPIP solution:

  Dissolve 0.02 g DCPIP and 1.86 g KCl in 300 cm^3 phosphate buffer solution. Add more phosphate buffer up to a total volume of 500 cm^3.

- Syringes can be used if pipettes are not available.

- Coloured cellulose acetate light filters may be purchased from photographic and theatre suppliers. Coloured cellophane is also often sold in craft shops. Plastic wallets of different colours can be used and it is possible to even use the coloured cellophane found in sweet wrappers. A sufficient amount is required to cover a test tube. If the experiment is to be repeated several times, 'sleeves' of cellulose can be made by loosely wrapping a piece of cellulose around a test tube and securing it with tape so that the test tube can be easily placed in and out of the sleeve.

Safety considerations

- Learners should have read the safety guidance section within the workbook before carrying out this investigation.

- Standard laboratory safety procedures should be followed always.

- Eye protection should be worn at all times.

- DCPIP is classed as a low-risk substance.

- Isolation medium is a low-risk substance.

Carrying out the investigation

- As already mentioned, the main problem encountered in this practical is obtaining a functional chloroplast extract. This is far more likely if:

  ○ young, freshly picked leaves are used

  ○ all solutions are kept cold

- ○ glassware is kept cold before the practical
- ○ all solutions and the extract are kept on ice as much as possible.

- Learners should ensure that the test tubes are covered with foil or the light filters. There should be no extraneous light entering the tubes. It is common to see learners only wrap foil or a filter around the tube in the area where the chloroplasts are, allowing light to enter from above.

- Judging the end point can be subjective – learners, in groups, could discuss when they think the reaction has ended.

  The instructions for the practical are quite complex and so learners who find working methodically challenging may need help with organisation.

Some learners will need help with setting up the light filters.

Learners could plan how the practical could be carried out in a more quantitative way (using a colorimeter).

Learners could determine whether or not temperature affects the rate of decolourisation of DCPIP with light (with no coloured filter).

Learners could select and carry out a statistical test on the results to see if there is a significant difference (this could be standard error or t-test).

Sample results

Test-tube number	Colour of filter	Approximate light wavelength / nm	Time taken for DCPIP to decolourise / s
1	no filter	n/a	176
2	purple	425	254
3	blue	450	231
4	green	525	n/a
5	orange	625	378
6	red	675	223

Table 9.6

Answers to the workbook questions (using the sample results)

a i Class results should be entered correctly in the table and mean times calculated correctly. (Sample results shown in Table 9.7).

Test-tube number	Colour of filter	Approximate light wavelength / nm	Times taken for DCPIP to decolourise / s	Mean time taken for DCPIP to decolourise / s	Mean rate of decolourisation of DCPIP / s^{-1}
1	no filter	n/a	176, 143, 186, 154, 182	168.2	0.00595
2	purple	425	254, 234, 287, 287, 270	266.4	0.00375
3	blue	450	231, 210, 246, 245, 734	233.0	0.00429
4	green	525	n/a, n/a, n/a, 865, n/a	n/a	0.00000
5	orange	625	378, 342, 401, 385, 376	376.4	0.00266
6	red	675	223, 201, 254, 213, 224	223.0	0.00448

Table 9.7

ii Mean rates should be calculated correctly from the class results (sample results shown in Table 9.7).

b If learners plot a graph of rate of decolourisation of DCPIP against light colour, they should draw a bar chart (see Figure 9.4a). If the graph is rate of decolourisation against wavelength, a line graph with points joined with straight lines should be plotted (see Figure 9.4b). Key points include:

- *x*-axis labelled as Light colour or Wavelength of light / nm

- *y*-axis labelled as Rate of decolourisation of DCPIP / s^{-1}

- All points or bars plotted correctly (± half a square).

- Spaces between bars or lines drawn straight and through points.

- Linear scale for *y*-axis and for *x*-axis if wavelength is used. If a bar chart is drawn, each colour should be labelled.

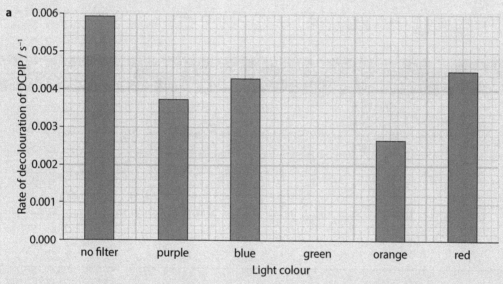

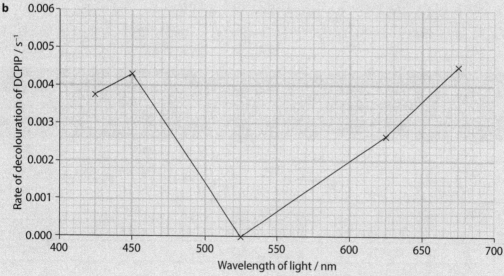

Figure 9.4

c Learners should describe their results and the graph obtained from the class results.

The expected results would show (although the results obtained by the learners may be different):

- rapid rates of decolourisation for red, purple, blue colours / wavelengths

- slower rate for orange light / wavelength

- no reaction or a very slow reaction with green light / wavelength

- full light should give the fastest rate of decolourisation

- the test tube that was covered in foil should not decolourise.

d
- Photosynthetic pigments absorb light most strongly in the blue / red areas of the spectrum and do not absorb green light.

- The results demonstrate that decolourisation of DCPIP does not occur in the green area of the spectrum / is fastest in the red and blue areas of the spectrum.

- This demonstrates that the light that is absorbed is used for the light dependent stage and the action and absorption spectra follow the same pattern.

- DCPIP decolourises when it becomes reduced (gains electrons).

- DCPIP could gain electrons either directly from photo-oxidation of chlorophyll or from $NADPH_2$ synthesised during the light dependent stage.

- DCPIP only decolourises when the chlorophyll absorbs light energy and is able to release energised electrons.

- DCPIP in the test tube with foil was not reduced as no photo-oxidation of chlorophyll occurred.

- DCPIP in full light decolourised most rapidly as it had access to all wavelengths of visible light.

e i Independent variable: wavelength of light / colour of light.

Dependent variable: time taken to (or rate of) decolourise DCPIP / reduce DCPIP.

ii Controlled variables include (there may be other correct responses): volume of DCPIP / species of plant used / same genetics of plant / same number and density of chloroplasts / same age of plant and chloroplast / same volume of solution / distance from the lamp.

Variables not controlled include (there may be other correct responses):

- temperature – use a water bath and monitor with thermometer

- light intensity – use a light meter to measure intensity and move lamp different distances (or alter power of bulb)

- pH – add a pH buffer to the solution.

f Learners should try to:

- identify anomalies

- compare the patterns obtained by different groups

- suggest whether the results and patterns give concordant results – if not, more repeats should be suggested.

g The major limitations include:

- Detecting the end-point. This could be improved by measuring absorbance with a colorimeter.

- No control test tube was added with DCPIP and no chloroplasts. This would show that light does not directly cause DCPIP to decolourise.

h **i** Ice-cold slows down enzymatic hydrolysis within the chloroplasts after and during the extraction.

ii Isotonic means that the water potential inside and outside the chloroplasts is the same. There is no net movement of water by osmosis so that the chloroplasts do not become damaged.

Practical investigation 9.5:
The effect of carbon dioxide concentration on rate of photosynthesis

Learning objective: 13.2(a), 13.2(b)

Skills focus

The following skills are developed and practised (see the skills grids at the front of this guide):

P   Defining the problem: (b), (c)
           Methods: (d), (e)

ACE   Evaluation: (g)
           Conclusions: (a), (b)

Duration

This practical should take approximately between 60 and 90 min to complete. If time is limiting, each concentration could be carried out once and the class data collated. Allow an additional 45 min for the analysis work.

Preparing for the investigation

- Learners will need to understand the role of carbon dioxide in photosynthesis and that carbon dioxide concentration can limit the rate of photosynthesis.

- The technique for filling up the syringes with sodium hydrogencarbonate solution, and for removing bubbles of oxygen from the leaf discs should be demonstrated.

- Good quality leaves such as spinach or green cabbage will need to be purchased in advance.

- The experiment should be trialled to ensure that the chosen leaves are able to photosynthesise.

Equipment

Each learner or group will need:

- 10 leaves (spinach or green cabbage leaves)

- syringe, 10 cm³

- cork borer or straw

- sodium hydrogencarbonate solution (1 mol dm⁻³), 100 cm³

- distilled water, 100 cm³

- six small beakers, 50 cm³

- modelling clay

- bench lamp

- stopclock.

Safety considerations

- Learners should have read the safety guidance section within the workbook before carrying out this investigation.

- Standard laboratory safety procedures should be followed always.

- Sodium hydrogencarbonate is classed as a low risk hazard.

- Eye protection should be worn.

Method

Concentration of sodium hydrogencarbonate / $mol\,dm^{-3}$	Volume of 1 $mol\,dm^{-3}$ sodium hydrogencarbonate / cm^3	Volume of distilled water / cm^3
1.0	10	0
0.8	8	2
0.6	6	4
0.4	4	6
0.2	2	8
0.0	0	10

Table 9.8

Carrying out the investigation

- Some leaf discs may not float or sink. If five are placed in the syringe, there should be a sufficient number that work to obtain a reliable mean time.

- Some learners may have difficulty cutting the leaf discs out – the technique should be demonstrated.

Some learners may need help calculating the dilutions. The teacher should check the calculations made by each learner before they begin to make the solutions.

The experiment can be repeated at different light intensities or temperatures.

Different species of plant could be investigated.

The method can be used as a planning exercise for learners to produce a detailed plan for determining the effects of light intensity and / or temperature on rate of photosynthesis.

A Spearman's rank correlation coefficient could be calculated to determine whether or not there is a significant correlation.

Sample results

Concentration of sodium hydrogencarbonate / $mol\,dm^{-3}$	Time taken for discs to float to surface / s					
	1	2	3	4	5	mean
1.0	191	193	194	194	203	195.0
0.8	198	200	210	211	215	206.8
0.6	222	222	231	233	233	228.2
0.4	275	276	293	295	304	288.6
0.2	301	310	319	321	321	314.4
0.0	321	332	333	365	387	347.6

Table 9.9

Answers to the workbook questions (using the sample results)

a i Learners should calculate the mean times correctly and include the table with a maximum of one decimal place. Anomalies should be circled and ignored when calculating the means. Sample means are shown in Table 9.9.

ii Learners should plot a line graph with either a best-fit line or points joined with straight lines. The following should be correct:

- *x*-axis labelled as Concentration of sodium hydrogencarbonate / $mol\,dm^{-3}$

- *y*-axis labelled as Mean time taken for disc to float / s

- all plots correct (± half square)

- linear scales used for both axes that allow plots to cover over half the grid.

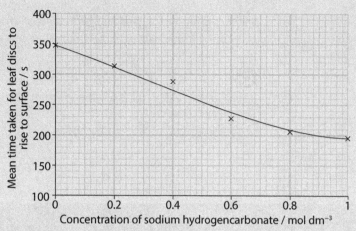

Figure 9.5

b Learners should correctly describe the graph and identify any turning points. For example:

- As concentration of sodium hydrogencarbonate increases, the mean time taken for the discs to float decreases. Around a concentration of 0.8 mol dm⁻³, the graph begins to level off.

c The leaves photosynthesise and oxygen gas is produced. This fills up inside the air spaces within the leaves, the density of the leaves fall and so they float.

d Sodium hydrogencarbonate increases the carbon dioxide concentration. Carbon dioxide is a raw material for photosynthesis so higher quantities increase the rate of photosynthesis. The graph begins to level off at higher concentrations of sodium hydrogencarbonate because another factor (such as light intensity or temperature) is limiting.

e i Variables include:

- length of syringe
- species of plant / same genetic individual
- light intensity / distance from lamp
- size of leaf disc
- number of leaf discs.

ii Uncontrolled variables include temperature or pH (there may be others suggested). A heat shield in front of the lamp could be used or the syringe placed in a water bath. A pH buffer could be included in the solution.

f Learners should identify if there are any concentrations where there are 'overlaps'. If there are overlaps, it will weaken the validity of the conclusion. It may be that the overlapping values are, however, anomalies.

Overlaps in the sample results are shown in bold in Table 9.10.

Concentration of sodium hydrogencarbonate / mol dm⁻³	Time taken for discs to float to surface / s					
	1	2	3	4	5	mean
1.0	191	193	194	194	**203**	195.0
0.8	**198**	200	210	211	215	206.8
0.6	222	222	231	233	233	228.2
0.4	275	276	293	295	**304**	288.6
0.2	**301**	310	319	321	**321**	314.4
0.0	**321**	332	333	365	387	347.6

Table 9.10

g • Set up the same apparatus but in water baths set at five or six different temperatures.

• Measure the time taken for five leaf discs to float.

Control variables:

• same concentration of sodium hydrogencarbonate solution at each temperature

• same volume of sodium hydrogencarbonate solution

• same distance from lamp

• same number of discs

• discs from same plant and leaf.

This Chapter relates to Chapter 14: Homeostasis, and Chapter 15: Coordination in the coursebook.

In this chapter, learners will complete practical investigations on:

- 10.1. The structure of the kidney
- 10.2. Analysis of urine
- 10.3. The role of gibberellic acid in the germination of barley seeds
- 10.4. The effect of light wavelength on phototropism in wheat seedlings
- 10.5. Investigating human reflexes

Practical investigation 10.1:
The structure of the kidney

Learning objective: 14.1(e)

Skills focus

The following skills are developed and practised (see the skills grids at the front of this guide):

P   Defining the problem: (a), (b), (c), (e)
          Methods: (a), (b), (c), (f), (g)

ACE   Conclusions: (e)

Duration

This practical is split into two halves which could be completed in two separate lessons. The dissection of the kidney should take approximately 30–45 min and the viewing and drawing of kidney sections another 30–45 min. Allow about 30 min for the analysis sections.

Preparing for the investigation

- Learners should understand the basic structure of the kidney and the nephron before beginning this practical.

- Identifying the structures of the nephron from slides is difficult and so it would be advisable if the teacher demonstrated them before the learners start.

- Learners should be warned to look at the kidneys carefully before rushing in with dissection equipment.

Equipment

Each learner or group will need:

- one fresh lamb's kidney

- scalpel

- forceps

- mounted needle

- tray (to keep the kidney in during the dissection)

- hydrogen peroxide, 20 volume, in a dropper bottle

- prepared microscope slides of kidney (TS cortex and medulla or TS kidney. These may be purchased from scientific suppliers or Cambridge Assessment).

Additional notes and advice

- Sheep kidneys should be used.

- The best quality kidneys (intact and with ureter and blood vessels) are encased in fat and it may be possible to request these from butchers in advance.

Safety considerations

- Learners should have read the safety guidance section within the workbook before carrying out this investigation.

- Standard laboratory safety procedures should be followed always.

- Hands should be washed with soap and water after handling the kidney. All surfaces should be wiped down with disinfectant after the practical.

- Hydrogen peroxide is classed as corrosive and an irritant, particularly to the eyes. Eye protection should be worn always, spills cleared up and any splashes on skin washed off with water. Learners should be warned of the risks. Technicians will need to wear protective equipment when diluting from concentrated stock.

- Scalpels, forceps and mounted needles should be handled with care as they can easily cause cuts.

Carrying out the investigation

- Kidney quality can be variable. As stated previously, it is best to order them in advance and request them to be encased in fat so that there is less chance they will be sliced and still have the ureter and blood vessels attached.

- If kidneys are not fresh, the tubules may not show up when hydrogen peroxide is added. It is not essential to add peroxide if it is not available and it is often possible to see some of the bigger tubules with a binocular dissecting microscope.

🔬 Some learners will need additional help focusing microscopes on the sections and identifying all the parts – the teacher should circulate around the room helping.

🔬 Many learners will need help identifying the features of the cortex and medulla on the sections. They will need to be patient and ensure that the microscope is well focused and set up.

🔬 If it is available, it is often possible to inject coloured latex into the ureter and renal vessels. The kidney should be first washed in warm 1% sodium chloride solution. Liquid latex or liquid rubber (which may be purchased from craft shops) can be dyed red, blue and yellow. The latex can be drawn up into 2 or 5 cm³ syringes and injected into the renal artery (red), renal vein (blue) and ureter (yellow). The latex should be left to harden for 24 h after which the kidney can be dissected. The latex should make the nephron structures easy to visualise. Sections of cortex and medulla can be removed and placed into sodium hydroxide solutions to dissolve away the tissues leaving the latex casts. You will need to check if there are any learners with latex allergies before doing this.

Common learner misconceptions

- Many learners are unaware that the different parts of the nephron have different functions. The functions should be discussed at the start of the lesson.

- Many learners do not appreciate how the nephrons are organised into the cortex and medulla – this practical is a useful way of explaining where the different parts are located.

123

Sample results

- If slides are not available, learners can draw the structures shown in Figures 10.2 and 10.3 in the workbook; sample diagrams are shown here in Figures 10.1, 10.2, and 10.3.

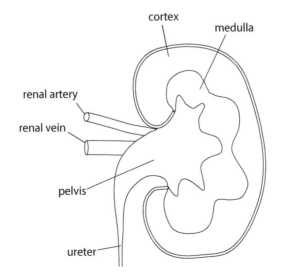

Note
medulla: pink / white;colour
cortex: brown / red colour;
pelvis: yellow colour

Figure 10.1

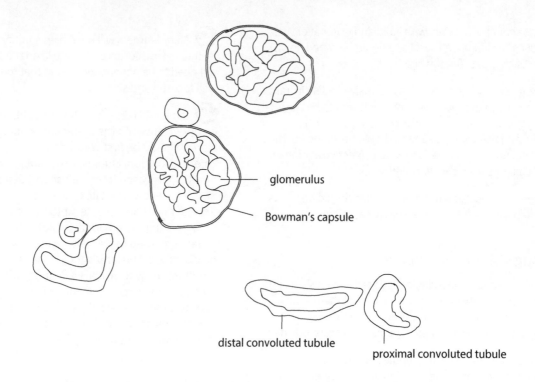

glomerulus

Bowman's capsule

distal convoluted tubule

proximal convoluted tubule

Figure 10.2

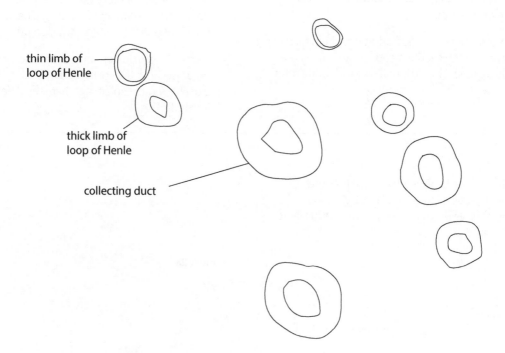

thin limb of
loop of Henle

thick limb of
loop of Henle

collecting duct

Figure 10.3

Answers to the workbook questions
(using the sample results)

a

Area of nephron	Structural features	Function
glomerulus and Bowman's capsule	• mass of capillaries • wider afferent arteriole than efferent to increase capillary blood pressure • thin layer of cells • basement membrane • podocyte cells wrap around capillaries	• ultrafiltration of blood by size • basement membrane acts as a filter
proximal convoluted tubule	• microvilli / brush border providing large surface area • many mitochondria in cells	• active transport of glucose and amino acids • osmosis of some water • diffusion of some salts • selective reabsorption
distal convoluted tubule	• no microvilli on cells • fewer mitochondria	• uptake of water by osmosis • some salt and pH regulation
loop of Henle	• counter-current loop • thin and thick sections • descending limb is water permeable • ascending limb is water impermeable but pumps out salt • thick limbs have cuboidal epithelial cells • thin limbs have flattened epithelial cells	• reabsorption of water • creates a salt gradient in the medulla • ascending limb actively pumps out salt • long to absorb large volumes of water
collecting duct	• thick, columnar epithelial cells • cells contain vesicles that have aquaporin proteins • ADH receptors on plasma membranes	• osmoregulation • ADH causes aquaporins to move to plasma membrane increasing water reabsorption

Table 10.1

b Tubules often appear in different shapes as they are cut in different planes – some will be transverse and some longitudinal whilst others will be oblique.

c Hypothesis:

- Increased dietary protein increases concentration of urea in urine.

Independent variable:

- Use five different protein levels in diet.

Dependent variable (method for measuring urea concentration):

- place equal volumes of urine in test tubes

- add equal volumes and concentrations of urease

- keep in 37°C water bath

- use a pH meter to measure fall in pH

- higher urea concentration will result in larger change in pH.

Control variables:

- same water volume in diet

- same exercise

- same sex and age subjects

- same temperature of room to prevent water loss

- same other dietary components

- urine taken at same times of day

- use water bath at 37°C when assaying with urease

- use pipettes / syringes to ensure volumes of solutions are same

- take urine samples at same time of day (and identical time after eating).

Reliability:

- repeat and calculate mean urea concentrations.

Practical investigation 10.2:
Analysis of urine

Learning objectives: 14.1 (e), 14.1 (l)

Skills focus

The following skills are developed and practised (see the skills grids at the front of this guide):

P	Methods: (d), (e)
ACE	Dealing with data: (d), (e)
	Conclusions: (a), (b), (e)

Duration

This practical should take 60–90 min, with an additional 30 min for the analysis work.

Preparing for the investigation

- The practical should be trialled before the lesson to ensure that the solutions give the desired results. Glucose protein and salt concentrations may be adjusted if necessary.

- Learners should understand the causes and symptoms of diabetes, why high blood pressure may lead to protein in the urine and the basic idea of a simple titration.

Equipment

Each learner or group will need:

- large beaker, 500 cm³

- 16 test tubes

- Bunsen burner, tripod and gauze (or hot water bath)

- biuret solution, 30 cm³

- Benedict's solution, 30 cm³

- four conical flasks, 250 cm³

- syringe, 5 or 2 cm³

- silver nitrate solution, 0.1 mol dm⁻³, 50 cm³

- potassium thiocyanate, 0.1 mol dm⁻³, 100 cm³

- saturated iron(III) nitrate solution in a dropper bottle, 10 cm³

- stopclock

- four samples of urine, labelled A, B, C, and D; 20 cm³ of each in labelled beakers

- pipette, 10 cm³.

Additional notes and advice

- Any method of making an 80°C water bath for the Benedict's test is acceptable. It is usually better if a communal water bath for the class is set up.

Stock solutions

- See Practical investigation 2.1 for recipes for biuret and Benedict's solutions.

- To make 250 cm³ 0.1 mol dm³ silver nitrate solution, dissolve 4.25 g silver nitrate powder in distilled water and make up to a total volume of 250 cm³.

- To make 1000 cm³ of 0.1 mol dm⁻³ potassium thiocyanate solution, dissolve 9.7 g of potassium thiocyanate in 500 cm³ of distilled water and make up to 1000 cm³ with distilled water.

- To make 100 cm³ saturated iron(III) nitrate solution, add approximately 100 g iron(III) nitrate powder to 100 cm³ water in a beaker. Keep adding iron(III) nitrate powder until no more dissolves. DO NOT HEAT THE SOLUTION.

- To make each 500 cm³ urine sample:

    A: Sodium chloride 3 g; albumin 10 g; water 500 cm³

    B: Glucose 10 g; Sodium chloride 3 g; water 500 cm³

    C: Sodium chloride 6 g; water 500 cm³

    D: Sodium chloride 3 g; water 500 cm³

- Each urine sample should be stained with some yellow / orange food dye or cold tea.

Safety considerations

- Learners should have read the safety guidance section within the workbook before carrying out this investigation.

- Standard laboratory safety procedures should be followed always.

- Biuret solution is classed as an irritant. When making the biuret solution, care should be taken with sodium hydroxide.

- Benedict's solution is classed as low risk.

- Urine samples are low risk.

- Potassium thiocyanate is classed as harmful by ingestion, in contact with skin and in contact with the eye. It is an environmental toxin and must not be heated as it can release harmful, very toxic gases.

- Silver nitrate solution is classed as harmful and an irritant at the concentrations used by the learners. At higher concentrations, it is classed as corrosive.

- Iron(III) nitrate is harmful in contact with skin, on ingestion and is an oxidising agent.

- Eye protection should be worn always and all splashes and spills cleared up with water.

Carrying out the investigation

- The biuret colour change can be difficult to judge at times. It should be trialled before the practical to ensure that it produces a purple colour. If there is no colour change, more albumin should be added and new biuret solution made.

- The Benedict's test should be tested on the urine to ensure that the glucose concentration is sufficient to give a clear result.

    For learners who do not study chemistry, the salt test may be difficult – it should be demonstrated at the start.

- The identification of each urine should be accessible to most learners.

    Learners who do not study chemistry may need support from the teacher with the back titration and salt concentration calculations. It can also be useful to assign learners to work in groups where at least one studies chemistry.

    A range of different glucose concentrations in different urine samples could be tested along with a semi-quantitative Benedict's test.

    If learners plan a method to test urea content, this could be trialled in the practical.

Sample results

Urine sample	Colour of Benedict's solution	Colour of biuret solution	Volume of potassium thiocyanate added / cm³
A	blue	lilac	6.6
B	red	blue	6.6
C	blue	blue	3.2
D	blue	blue	6.6

Table 10.2

Answers to the workbook questions (using the sample results)

a **i, ii** Learners should complete the calculations correctly and complete Table 10.3 (sample results are shown below).

Urine sample	Volume of potassium thiocyanate added (x) / cm³	Mass of chloride in 2 cm³ urine / g	Concentration of chloride ions in urine / g cm⁻³
A	6.6	0.012	0.006
B	6.6	0.012	0.006
C	3.2	0.024	0.012
D	6.6	0.012	0.006

Table 10.3

b

Urine sample	Presence / absence of glucose	Presence / absence of protein	Concentration of chloride ions in urine / g cm⁻³
A	absent	present	0.006
B	present	absent	0.006
C	absent	absent	0.012
D	absent	absent	0.006

Table 10.4

c **i** Excessive dietary salt

- urine sample C as the salt concentration is highest

- salt (sodium chloride) is absorbed into the blood plasma

- salt passes into the filtrate from the glomerulus into the Bowman's capsule

- less is reabsorbed by the proximal convoluted tubule and distal convoluted tubules

- more is released in urine.

ii Type 1 diabetes

- urine sample B which contains glucose

- lack of insulin causes high blood glucose concentration

- glucose passes from glomerulus into filtrate in Bowman's capsule

- active transport proteins in proximal convoluted tubule are overloaded and not all glucose is reabsorbed so it is released in urine.

iii High blood pressure

- urine sample A has protein

- high blood, hydrostatic pressure causes protein to be pushed out of glomerulus into Bowman's capsule

- no method of reabsorbing protein in nephron so it passes into urine.

iv No known conditions and a normal diet

- urine sample D which had no protein or glucose and low salt

- all the glucose has been reabsorbed and no protein has been released

- no additional salt has been released.

d **i** Glucose (Benedict's) test and protein (biuret) test are qualitative.

Salt assay is quantitative.

128

ii Glucose and protein tests:	Or
Make a series of known standard dilutions of glucose and carry out Benedict's and biuret tests. Match colours of urine sample Benedict's and biuret tests with known standards.	Measure absorbance with a colorimeter and make a calibration curve. Read concentration of glucose and protein in urine sample off calibration curve.

Practical investigation 10.3:
The role of gibberellic acid in the germination of barley seeds

Learning objective: 15.2(c)

Skills focus

The following skills are developed and practised (see the skills grids at the front of this guide):

P   Methods: (h), (i), (j)

ACE   Dealing with data: (a), (b), (d), (h)
         Evaluation: (a), (b), (i), (j), (k)

Duration

This practical will require some planning as it needs to be carried out in two separate lessons, approximately 36 h apart. The gap between the lessons can be between 24 and 48 h. The first lesson will take approximately 1 h and the second lesson approximately 45 min. Allow about 45 min for the analysis sections.

Preparing for the investigation

- Learners should understand plant growth regulators and the role of gibberellic acid in germination.

- It is important the sterile conditions are maintained.

- Learners will need to be shown how to cut the seeds and separate the sections with and without the embryos.

- The experiment should be trialled to optimise the concentrations of gibberellic acid and assess whether the starch agar plates can be pre-stained with iodine (see equipment).

Equipment

Each learner or group will need:

- six starch agar plates each containing a different concentration of gibberellic acid (0%, 1×10^{-6}%, 1×10^{-5}%, 1×10^{-4}%, 1×10^{-3}%, 1×10^{-2}%)

- scalpel or razor blade

- marker pen

- barley seeds (40) that have been soaked in water for between 6 and 8 h

- 3% sodium hypochlorite solution (bleach)

- forceps

- tea strainer or sieve

- iodine solution[4]

- pipettes, 1 cm³ and 10 cm³ and fillers

- three beakers, 50 cm³

- small, sterile bottles or containers with lids (such as McCartney bottles)

- tile for cutting on

- adhesive tape

- distilled water, 100 cm³ (this should be sterile).

Access to:

- incubator (or warm place) at a temperature of 20–30°C.

Additional notes and advice

- Gibberellic acid can be purchased from many scientific suppliers.

- To make the starch agar plates:

  First make up a stock of gibberellic acid (1×10^{-1}%) as follows:

  o Place 0.1 g gibberellic acid (GA_3) into a 100 cm³ volumetric flask (or other measuring apparatus).

  o Add 1 cm³ ethanol to dissolve the gibberellic acid and then add distilled water up to a total volume of 100 cm³.

  Carry out serial dilutions using distilled water to make stock solutions (between 20 and 100 cm³ of each

129

depending on how much will be needed) of the following concentrations of gibberellic acid:

- $1 \times 10^{-5}\%$
- $1 \times 10^{-4}\%$
- $1 \times 10^{-3}\%$
- $1 \times 10^{-2}\%$

Make the starch agar as follows (to make $100\,cm^3$):

- Dissolve 0.50 g soluble starch in a little water and make up to $100\,cm^3$ with distilled water.

- Heat the solution until boiling and add 2.0 g agar powder (or equivalent). Stir vigorously until all the powder is dissolved.

- Add the appropriate volume of gibberellic acid (see Table 10.5) and stir. Allow the mixture to cool to about 60°C and pour into Petri dishes to a depth of about 3 mm. Label the Petri dishes with the appropriate concentrations of gibberellic acid and store in fridge until needed.

Final concentration of gibberellic acid / %	Volume and dilution of gibberellic acid to add to starch agar
0	$10\,cm^3$ distilled water
1×10^{-6}	$10\,cm^3$ of $1 \times 10^{-5}\%$ solution
1×10^{-5}	$10\,cm^3$ of $1 \times 10^{-4}\%$ solution
1×10^{-4}	$10\,cm^3$ of $1 \times 10^{-3}\%$ solution
1×10^{-3}	$10\,cm^3$ of $1 \times 10^{-2}\%$ solution
1×10^{-2}	$10\,cm^3$ of $1 \times 10^{-1}\%$ solution

Table 10.5

- It is sometimes possible to pre-stain the starch agar plates by adding two or three drops of Iodine solution to the plates immediately after pouring. The mixture should be stirred vigorously in the plate to distribute the Iodine. This method is not, however, always reliable and enzyme activity may be affected by the presence of iodine. It should be tested before a class practical if the teacher wishes to use it.

- The barley seeds should be soaked in distilled water for 6–8 h before the practical.

- If sodium hypochlorite is not available, mild bleaches such as those used to sterilise baby bottles may be used.

- To make $1000\,cm^3$ iodine in potassium iodide solution, dissolve 6 g potassium iodide in $200\,cm^3$ distilled water. Add 3 g iodine crystals and add distilled water up to a final volume of $1000\,cm^3$.

Safety considerations

- Learners should have read the safety guidance section within the workbook before carrying out this investigation.

- Standard laboratory safety procedures should be followed always.

- Sodium hypochlorite solution is an irritant.

- Iodine solution is an irritant and a possible environmental hazard so should not be disposed of near natural water.

- Gibberellic acid is classed as low risk but may cause minor irritation.

- Razor blades and scalpels should be handled with care.

- Eye protection should be worn always. Splashes on the skin should be washed off with water and spills cleared up.

- After incubation, the starch agar plate should not be re-opened as it could represent a biohazard.

Carrying out the investigation

- This is quite a demanding practical and as always when using living organisms, may produce variable results.

  Learners may need help in deciding which end of the seeds contains the embryo – this should be demonstrated.

- Positioning the seeds on the agar is important. They need to have the cut-side touching the agar and they should be spread out evenly.

- It is possible to pre-stain the agar with iodine to avoid having to flood the plates at the end. This can be temperamental, however, and cause enzyme inhibition so must be trialled before the lesson.

- Visualising the clear areas may be difficult after staining. Learners should hold up the plates to the light and / or place on white paper. A light box (or OHP) is also useful.

- The clear areas may not be perfectly circular and if learners have placed seeds close together, they may overlap.

- If no source of gibberellic acid can be found, alternative experiments can be carried out by placing seeds with and without embryos on to starch agar plates to show the importance of the embryo and aleurone layers.

  Learners with dyspraxia may need help cutting the seeds and placing them on the agar.

Some learners could try placing the seeds halves with embryos and seeds cut vertically so that they have embryo, aleurone layer and endosperm onto the agar without gibberellic acid. This will show the interactions.

Another possible practical is to place embryo halves at different distances from endosperm halves to show that there is chemical diffusion of gibberellic acid from the embryo to the endosperm half.

Sample results

Concentration of gibberellic acid / %	Diameter of clear zone around each seed / mm					
	1	2	3	4	5	mean
0	1	0	0	1	2	0.8
1×10^{-6}	5	4	4	8	9	6.0
1×10^{-5}	26	27	21	24	25	24.6
1×10^{-4}	32	33	33	34	31	32.6
1×10^{-3}	39	38	38	39	37	38.2
1×10^{-2}	40	39	45	45	37	41.2

Table 10.6

Answers to the workbook questions (using the sample results)

a Correct calculations of means leaving out any anomalous data (sample results in Table 10.6 shows this).

b Correct bar chart with:

- y-axis labelled as Mean diameter of clear zone around seed / mm
- x-axis labelled as Concentration of gibberellic acid / %
- all bars labelled with concentrations
- mean values plotted correctly
- bars drawn with straight lines.

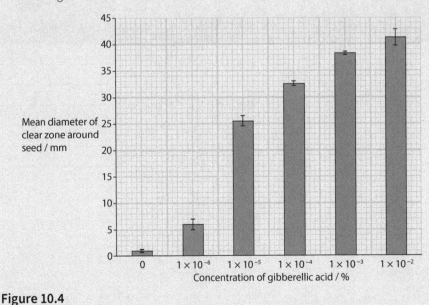

Figure 10.4

c Expected pattern would be mean diameter increases with increasing concentration of gibberellic acid. It may level off and there should be no clear zone with zero concentration.

d i, ii, iii, iv Learners should carry out the calculations and enter them in the table. Sample results are shown below.

Repeat number	(I) Diameter of clear zone around each seed (x) / mm	(II) ($x - \bar{x}$)	(III) ($x - \bar{x}$)^2
1	40	−1.2	1.44
2	39	−2.2	4.84
3	45	3.8	14.44
4	45	3.8	14.44
5	37	−4.2	17.64
			$\sum(x - \bar{x})^2 =$ 52.8

Table 10.7

v Learners should carry out correct calculation of standard deviation with their data.

Standard deviation for sample results = 3.63

vi Learners should carry out correct calculations of standard deviation for their data. They may choose to do this using the function on a calculator. Sample results are shown in Table 10.8.

e i, ii, iii, iv Learners should carry out calculations correctly using their data. Sample data calculations are shown in Table 10.8.

f Learners should add error bars to their graph correctly. Sample data error bars are shown on Figure 10.4.

g Learners should correctly compare the bars with the error bars. If there is no overlap, there is a 95% confidence that there is a significant difference in the means. If there is an overlap, they should state that the means are not statistically significantly different. The sample results show no overlap for any bars (i.e. significant differences) apart from concentrations as 1×10^{-3} and 1×10^{-4} (no significant difference).

Concentration of gibberellic acid / %	Mean diameter of clear zone / mm	Standard deviation	Standard error	2 × standard error	95% confidence limits (lowest ⟶ highest)
0	0.8	0.84	0.37	0.75	0.52 ⟶ 1.55
1×10^{-6}	6.0	2.35	1.05	2.10	3.90 ⟶ 8.10
1×10^{-5}	24.6	2.30	1.03	2.06	22.54 ⟶ 26.66
1×10^{-4}	32.6	1.14	0.51	1.02	31.58 ⟶ 33.62
1×10^{-3}	38.2	0.84	0.37	0.75	37.45 ⟶ 38.95
1×10^{-2}	41.2	3.63	1.62	3.25	37.95 ⟶ 44.45

Table 10.8

h In normal seeds, the embryo releases gibberellic acid which activates the aleurone layer. The aleurone layer releases amylase which then digests starch in the endosperm.

- The results should show that with no gibberellic acid there are no clear zones – this is because the seeds pieces have had the embryo removed and there is no gibberellic acid in the agar.

- As gibberellic acid concentration increases, the amount of amylase released from the aleurone layer increases.

- The amylase diffuses into the agar, digests the starch into maltose. The higher the concentration of amylase, the further it diffuses into the agar and digests the starch. The iodine will not stain blue where there is no starch.

- At higher concentrations it may level off as the aleurone layer has released amylase at its maximum rate (aleurone layer / amylase concentration is limiting).

i   Anomalous points should be circled. There are many possible causes including:

- dead seeds

- genetically different seeds

- the seed may have contained an embryo

- different sizes of seeds

- different ages of seeds

- wrong piece of seed placed on agar

- no / less / more endosperm present

- uneven concentration of starch / gibberellic acid.

Practical investigation 10.4:

The effect of light wavelength on phototropism in wheat seedlings

Learning objective: 15.2(b)

Skills focus

The following skills are developed and practised (see the skills grids at the front of this guide):

ACE   Dealing with data: (b), (c), (d), (e)
      Evaluation: (d)
      Conclusions: (a), (g)

Duration

This practical will require two lessons which are 24–48 h apart. The first lesson will take up to 1 h and the second one approximately 45 min. The analysis sections should take about 30 min.

Preparing for the investigation

- Learners should understand phototropism.

- There are many possibilities for alternative investigative practicals. Learners could plan and investigate other light colours and could also compare the responses of different species.

Equipment

Each learner or group will need:

- five shoe boxes with a 'window' cut out of the front (these may be shared between several groups)

- five Petri dishes containing wheat seedlings

- bench lamps

- ruler, 30 cm

- cellophane light filters; red, blue, green, clear

- small piece of black card to fit over the window of one box.

Additional notes and advice

- The practical suggests using shoe boxes with a window cut out. Any method that ensures that different coloured light can be used to illuminate seedlings from one direction can be used. Shared boxes can be used whereby several Petri dishes are placed into one box. It is also possible to place the seedlings into beakers covered in black paper with a window for light – a lid is then placed on the beaker.

- The practical suggests using wheat seedlings but there are many other alternatives such as oats, maize, cress, and mung beans.

  - To set up wheat seedlings:

- About one week before the practical, soak seeds in water for 24 h. Pour off the water and leave for 1–2 days.

- Look carefully at the seeds and select those which are beginning to germinate. Loosely place cotton wool in the base of Petri dishes, moisten it and place about 15 seeds on the cotton wool. Position the seeds so that they are evenly distributed.

- Place the Petri dishes into a cardboard box lined with foil and leave in the dark for between two and four days. Check the seedlings daily to ensure that they do not dry out. When the coleoptiles reach between 10 and 20 mm long, place them in the refrigerator.

- Any method of producing coloured light can be used. Cellophane light filters may be purchased from craft shops but coloured plastic stationary wallets or even coloured sweet wrappers can be used. It is even possible to fill beakers with water, add food dye and shine light through them. The black card should be sufficiently thick to prevent the entry of any light.

Safety considerations

- Learners should have read the safety guidance section within the workbook before carrying out this investigation.

- Standard laboratory safety procedures should be followed always.

- Learners should be checked for any allergies to plants and seeds.

Carrying out the investigation

- Sometimes the seedlings do not grow upright and tangle roots around each other, care should be taken when removing them not to dislodge others. Extra Petri dishes should be prepared.

- Measuring the coleoptiles can be difficult without damaging the plants. When measuring the final lengths, they can be removed from the Petri dish.

- It is important that the cotton wool does not dry out – it should be checked every day and water added if necessary.

- If seedlings are overwatered, it can cause fungal contamination. Extra dishes should be prepared in case some dishes are contaminated.

Learners with dyspraxia and problems with coordination will need help with removing seedlings.

Some learners will need help deciding how to modify the methods of analysis such as selecting appropriate statistical tests.

The basic method could be used as part of investigative planning on the responses of different species.

If the method is adapted to measure growth of individual seedlings, a t-test can be carried out. Error bars for the graph could also be calculated.

Other colours of light could be investigated.

Learners could research why different light colours cause different effects including the receptor pigment types that exist.

The light filters could be used to carry out investigations into light colour on the flowering or growth of plants.

Different species may exhibit different responses to the light colours. Learners could also design their own method for allowing unidirectional light through to the seedlings.

Common learner misconception

- Many learners will think that they will have to record the changes in length of individual coleoptiles. The practical looks for a change in mean length so they do not need to determine how much each individual one has grown.

Sample results

| | Starting length of coleoptile for each light colour / mm | | | | |
	no light (card)	clear	red	green	blue
	17, 16, 20, 18, 19, 19, 15, 18, 15	18, 16, 15, 17, 19, 14, 17, 19, 20, 18, 17	20, 15, 17, 17, 17, 18, 19, 20, 16, 15, 15, 16,	16, 16, 15, 18, 17, 18, 18, 19, 17, 19	17, 18, 19, 19, 20, 20, 15, 17, 18, 18, 17, 16, 15
mean	17.4	17.3	17.1	17.3	17.6

Table 10.9

	Final length of coleoptile for each light colour / mm				
	no light (card)	clear	red	green	blue
	25, 24, 27, 26, 25, 25, 27, 25, 27	23, 24, 23, 24, 21, 22, 23, 21, 22, 21, 20	24, 25, 26, 26, 25, 26, 25, 25, 26, 26, 26, 15	25, 26, 27, 26, 26, 25, 26, 25, 26, 27	23, 23, 24, 24, 21, 24, 21, 22, 22, 21, 22, 21, 20
mean	25.7	22.2	24.6	25.9	22.2

Table 10.10

Light colour	Number of coleoptiles that grow towards light source	Total number of coleoptiles	Percentage of coleoptiles that grow towards light source / %	Observations on curvature
no light (card)	0	9	0	• all coleoptiles grew straight up
clear	11	11	100	• all coleoptiles had bent towards light, many had become curved
red	5	12	42	• a few were leaning towards the light but the stems of the coleoptiles were not curved
green	1	10	10	• one was leaning towards the light – it may have 'fallen over' rather than grown that way
blue	12	13	92	• all except one were bent towards the light at a sharp angle • the stems were very curved

Table 10.11

Answers to the workbook questions (using the sample results)

a   Learners should calculate the mean lengths correctly and record them. This has been done for the sample data and is shown in Tables 10.9 and 10.10 – there may be some variance in the data obtained by the learners.

b   Learners should correctly calculate the percentages that are growing towards the light source. Percentages have been calculated for the sample results in Table 10.11 – this may be different from that obtained by the learners due to variation in seedlings and filters.

c   Learners should calculate the changes in mean length and record them. This is shown for the sample data in Table 10.12.

Light colour	Change in mean length of coleoptiles / mm
no light (card)	8.3
clear	4.9
red	7.5
green	8.6
blue	4.6

Table 10.12

d Learners should draw separate bar charts (or use two *y*-axes) to demonstrate the change in mean length and the percentage that grow in the direction of the light (the window). Graphs should have:

- both sets of axes labelled
- accurate plotting (±half square)
- neat bars with straight lines
- titles for the graphs
- labels for the bars.

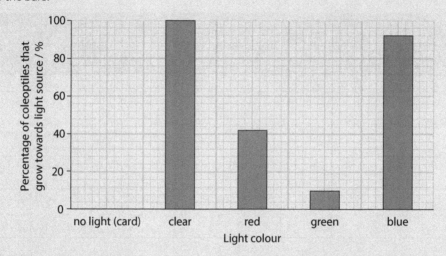

Figure 10.5

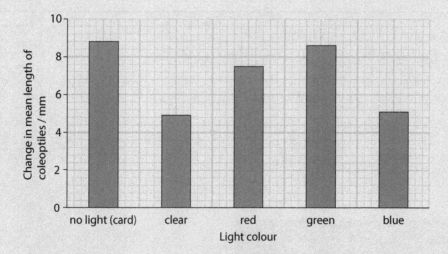

Figure 10.6

e The description will vary according to the results obtained by the learners. It would be expected that the seedlings / coleoptiles will sense the direction of light when a clear and blue filter is used but not (or not as effectively) when red and green are used. The sample results show that the seedlings / coleoptiles respond more to 'white (clear)' light and blue and red light than green light. The seedlings / coleoptiles grow more when kept in the dark or exposed to green light with no light terms.

f The comments will depend on the learners' results. The sample results suggest that the seedlings have a pigment that absorbs blue light but not green or red. The lengths may not vary greatly but may be longer in the dark and green light as they do not respond to green light; red light may result in slightly more elongation than blue light.

g Light intensity, temperature, genetics of seeds, age of seeds, humidity (any two).

h If there are large differences, there is more evidence for the conclusion. If the differences are small, they may not be significant differences but just due to natural variation. Only comparing mean lengths is a major limitation as some coleoptiles within a group may have grown more or less than others. Too few seeds were tested.

i The increase in length of individual coleoptiles should be examined. A standard deviation for increase in length could be determined allowing error bars to be added. If standard error is calculated, the significance of the differences in means could be measured. A t-test could also be carried out to determine whether the increases in length are significant. A chi-square test could be carried out to determine whether the number that bend towards the light (window) is significant.

Practical investigation 10.5

Investigating human reflexes

Learning objective: 15.1(d)

Skills focus

P   Methods: (g)

ACE   Dealing with data: (a), (b), (d), (e), (j), (k), (p)
          Evaluation: (a), (d), (i), (j)

Duration

This practical should take approximately 1 h. The analysis may take a further 30–45 min but could be carried out independently.

Preparing for the investigation

- Learners should understand the nature of reflexes, the reflex arc and synapses.

- Learners are expected to measure the distance the impulses take along the different pathways. They should do this as part of group and whole class discussion. The pathways are shown in a hint box in the workbook.

Equipment

Each learner or group will need:

- one-metre ruler

- a person to experiment on.

Safety considerations

- Learners should have read the safety guidance section within the workbook before carrying out this investigation.

- Standard laboratory safety procedures should be maintained always.

- There are no additional significant safety issues associated with this investigation.

Carrying out the investigations

- Learners need to make sure that the ruler is dropped vertically and that it is not thrown down.

- The ruler needs to touch the finger only when testing the touch reflex.

- The subject needs to be blindfolded for the touch and sound reflexes.

  ⚙ Many learners will find measuring the pathways difficult. The pathways are shown in a step b in the workbook.

  ⚙ Many learners will mix up the distance that the ruler fell and the distance of the impulse pathway – it is best to do all the ruler drops before measuring the pathways.

  ⚙ Some learners will forget to have the ruler touching the finger when carrying out the touch reflex. They should be reminded that it is not a test of extra sensory perception!

Some learners with mobility issues or conditions such as dyspraxia will find catching the ruler difficult and potentially embarrassing. It should be stressed that it is not a competition and that catching rulers quickly is not a major life skill! If some learners are unable to act as the subject, they should act as the experimenter or recorder.

- It may be better to work in groups of three (depending on the class) with one learner as the subject, one as the experimenter and one as a recorder. Learners can then swap round so they all obtain a set of data.

Learners can carry out a statistical comparison of the reaction times of the class.

Learners can investigate the effects of distracters on reaction times, for example, playing loud music when carrying out the sight or touch reflex, using scents when testing the reflexes. The effects of ingestion of caffeine from drinks could be investigated but this will need thorough risk assessment.

Learners could research theoretical maximum reaction times and explain why sprint athletes can be false-started even if they set off after the starting gun.

Sample results

Ruler drop number	Distances ruler fell and reaction times for different senses					
	Sight		Touch		Sound	
	distance / cm	reaction time / s	distance / cm	reaction time / s	distance / cm	reaction time / s
1	11	0.150	16	0.181	32	0.256
2	24	0.221	22	0.212	31	0.252
3	18	0.192	22	0.212	30	0.247
4	19	0.197	22	0.212	31	0.252
5	16	0.181	19	0.197	30	0.247
6	18	0.192	23	0.217	32	0.256
7	17	0.186	16	0.181	31	0.252
8	17	0.186	20	0.202	29	0.243
9	22	0.212	24	0.221	28	0.239
10	13	0.163	23	0.217	27	0.235
Mean	17.5	0.189	20.7	0.206	30.1	0.248
Standard deviation		0.021		0.015		0.007

Table 10.13

Answers to the workbook questions (using the sample results)

a   i, ii, iii Learners should correctly calculate the times taken and record the results in the table. Sample results are shown in Table 10.13.

b   i   Learners should correctly measure the distances that the impulses travel and record them. They should then correctly use the mean reaction times to calculate the impulse speed. Results with the sample data are shown in Table 10.14. Speeds will probably lie between 500 and 1600 cm⁻¹. Touch would be expected to have the fastest speed.

ii

Reflex type	Distance travelled by impulse / cm	Mean reaction time / cm	Impulse transmission speed / cm s⁻¹
sight	135	0.189	714
touch	295	0.206	1432
sound	135	0.248	544

Table 10.14

c   Learners should compare the speeds and reaction times.

- It would be expected that the touch reflex will have the fastest speed – this is due to the reduced number of synapses involved in the reflex. The impulse must cross synapses by chemical diffusion which is slower than the transmission of an electrical impulse.

- Sound and sight reflexes may have similar speeds. Sound may be slower than touch.

- The reaction times may be quite similar (touch may be the lowest). If the impulse speed were the same for all three types of reflex, it would be expected that touch would take longer as the pathway is longer.

d   i   There is no difference between *the reaction time for the sight and touch reflexes.*

  ii   Learners should correctly calculate the *t*-value for their data.

The *t*-value for the sample data is:

$t = 2.04$

  iii   Learners should calculate the degrees of freedom correctly:

The degrees of freedom for the sample data are 18.

iv   Learners should use the critical value table to correctly determine if the difference in reaction times is significant. For the sample data, the critical value for 18 degrees of freedom is 2.10 so the calculated value is less than this suggesting that there is no significant difference.

'The calculated *t*-value of 2.04 is {**less than**} the critical value of 2.10 for 18 degrees of freedom. This means there is a probability of {**>0.05**} that the difference in reaction time is due to chance. This means there is {**no significant**} difference and the null hypothesis {**is not rejected**}'

e   Learners should use their data to carry out *t*-tests correctly and reach the correct conclusions (they may or may not find significant differences – this is not a problem and reflects their results).

For the sample results:

  i   *t*-value = 8.22; significant difference so null hypothesis is rejected.

  ii   *t*-value = 8.45; significant difference so null hypothesis is rejected.

This chapter relates to Chapter 16: Inherited change, and Chapter 17: Selection and evolution in the coursebook.

In this chapter, learners will complete practical investigations on:

- 11.1 Studying stages of meiosis in an anther
- 11.2 Modelling the effects of selection pressure on allele frequency
- 11.3 Measuring and comparing continuous variation in two sets of leaves
- 11.4 Investigating tongue-rolling
- 11.5 Modelling the Hardy–Weinberg equations
- 11.6 The effects of selective breeding in *Brassica oleracea*
- 11.7 Comparing vitamin C content in two cultivars of *Brassica oleracea*

Practical investigation 11.1:
Studying stages of meiosis in an anther

Learning objective: 16.1(d)

Skills focus

This investigation does not involve planning or analysis.

Duration

Allow 45 min for this investigation.

Preparing for the investigation

- Learners should be familiar with the stages of meiosis.
- It will be helpful to have studied micrographs of cells in meiosis, and to have identified features of each stage that help in identification.

Equipment

Each learner or group will need:

- a microscope and light source
- a prepared slide showing cells in meiosis, for example, lily anther (locust testis is a possible alternative)

- reference micrographs (e.g. from the internet or textbooks) of cells in various stages of meiosis.

Safety considerations

- Learners should have read the safety guidance section within the workbook before carrying out this investigation.
- Standard laboratory safety procedures should be followed always.
- There are no additional significant safety issues associated with this investigation.

Carrying out the investigation

- The cells undergoing meiosis are small, and it can be difficult to see the chromosomes clearly. The better the microscopes that can be provided, and the better quality the slide, the more likely that learners will be successful. If possible, provide learners with ×100 oil immersion objective lenses.

  Learners who are having great difficulty in seeing or identifying cells may need help in focusing their microscopes, particularly if they are using oil immersion lenses. As a last resort, they could be given micrographs from which to make their drawings, rather than making these from a microscope slide.

  Learners who would benefit from a challenge could be asked to make low-power plans of the section through the lily anther, and annotate them to describe the structure and function of each tissue layer.

(⚙) They could also make a list of features that enable them to identify cells in each stage of meiosis.

Sample results

See Figure 11.3b in the workbook. Diagrams should be assessed using the normal criteria for high-power diagrams.

> **Answers to the workbook questions (using the sample results)**
>
> There are no questions for this investigation.

Practical investigation 11.2:
Modelling the effects of selection pressure on allele frequency

Learning objective: 17.2(a)

Skills focus

The following skills are developed and practised (see the skills grids at the front of this guide):

ACE   Dealing with data: (d), (e)
               Evaluation: (j)
               Conclusions: (a), (d)

Duration

Using beans to apply a selection pressure for six generations takes about 40 min. This is something that can be done outside the laboratory or classroom, if you prefer to use non-contact time for this activity.

Learners will need another 45–60 min to complete the calculations, draw the graphs, share data and answer the questions.

Preparing for the investigation

- Learners should be confident using the terms gene, allele, zygote, genotype, phenotype and population.

Equipment

Each learner or group will need:

- at least three different containers

- 100 beans of one colour and 100 very similar beans of a second colour.

Additional notes and advice

- The two types of beans should be as similar in size, shape and texture as possible, but should differ in colour.

- Mung beans (green) and adzuki beans (reddish brown) are suitable. However, some learners may find them small to work with; it is easy to drop them, or to pick up three at a time instead of two. You may prefer to use larger beans, such as kidney beans. Alternatively, any small objects of two different colours can be used, such as pieces of pasta coloured with dye, or beads or counters.

Safety considerations

- Learners should have read the safety guidance section within the workbook before carrying out this investigation.

- Standard laboratory safety procedures should be followed always.

- There are no additional significant safety issues associated with this investigation.

Carrying out the investigation

- The collection of data is straightforward. The main difficulty is that it is very repetitive, and it is easy to lose concentration and put pairs of beans into the wrong container, or to record them in the wrong place. Dealing with this issue is a good learning experience for learners; they will need to find a way of maintaining concentration and accuracy throughout the task. They can work either individually or in pairs.

- As this is a time-consuming exercise, it is recommended that you ask each learner, or pair of learners, to test only one selection pressure. If different groups test different selection pressures, they can then share results with each other.

The main difficulty that learners are likely to have is getting themselves organised so that they always know which beans are supposed to be in which container, and that they have a reliable method of scoring their results. It is best to leave them to work this out for themselves, only intervening if they are confused.

Tactics that can help are:

- Always put the population of beans from which you are selecting (i.e. the breeding population) into the same container.

- Always place the paired alleles (the offspring) into a different container, which is easily distinguished from the first one.

- Always place the discarded beans (those representing offspring that have died before they can reproduce) into a third container, again using one that looks different from the first two.

- If learners work in pairs, then the same person should always pick out the beans, and the second person can record the results.

- It is worth checking from time to time that you still have 100 beans of each colour altogether, and that you have not mislaid any.

Learners who need a challenge could use this technique to investigate one of the following:

- What happens to allele frequencies and phenotypic ratios if the selection pressure acts against the heterozygotes?

- Genetic drift: Set up a breeding population in which the frequency of one of the alleles is low. What happens to allele frequencies if a randomly selected small part of the population becomes isolated from the rest?

Sample results

Part 1: Investigating allele frequency with no selection pressure

Genotype	AA	Aa	aa
Tally	𝍐 𝍐 𝍐 𝍐 𝍐	𝍐 𝍐 𝍐 𝍐 𝍐 𝍐 𝍐 𝍐 𝍐	𝍐 𝍐 𝍐 𝍐 𝍐 𝍐
Number	22	46	27

Table 11.1

Part 2: Investigating allele frequency in subsequent generations while applying a selection pressure

Sample results for two selection pressures are given here. If you have enough learners in the group, you could include other selection pressures as well – for example, 20% and 50%.

10% selection pressure against **aa**

Generation	Number of AA genotype	Number of Aa genotype	Number of aa genotype	Number of a alleles discarded
1	27	46	27	4
2	27	46	25	4
3	29	42	25	4
4	29	42	23	4
5	25	53	13	2
6	29	40	21	4

Table 11.2

25% selection pressure against **aa**

Generation	Number of **AA** genotype	Number of **Aa** genotype	Number of **aa** genotype	Number of **a** alleles discarded
1	27	46	27	12
2	26	45	21	10
3	31	36	21	10
4	33	32	18	8
5	32	35	12	6
6	35	29	12	6

Table 11.3

Answers to the workbook questions (using the sample results)

Part 1: Investigating allele frequency with no selection pressure

a Approximately 1 AA: 2 Aa: 1 aa

b 3: 1 dominant feature : recessive feature

c 50%, or 0.5, for each allele.

d It would not change; it would remain as 1: 2: 1.

e It would not change; it would remain as 0.5.

Part 2: Investigating allele frequency in subsequent generations while applying a selection pressure

a For 10% selection pressure:

Generation	Number of **a** alleles remaining in the population	Total number of alleles remaining in the population	Percentage of **a** alleles in the population	Frequency of **a** alleles in the population
0	100	200	50	0.50
1	96	196	49	0.49
2	92	192	48	0.48
3	88	188	47	0.47
4	84	184	46	0.46
5	82	182	45	0.45
6	78	178	44	0.44

Table 11.4

For 25% selection pressure:

Generation	Number of **a** alleles remaining in the population	Total number of alleles remaining in the population	Percentage of **a** alleles in the population	Frequency of **a** alleles in the population
0	100	200	50	0.50
1	88	188	47	0.47
2	78	178	44	0.44
3	68	168	40	0.40
4	60	160	38	0.38
5	54	154	35	0.35
6	48	148	32	0.32

Table 11.5

b, c

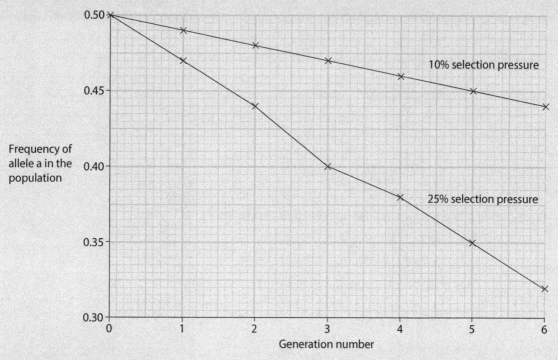

Figure 11.1

d Points that could be made include:

- In each generation, the frequency of the **a** allele decreases.

- The greater the selection pressure, the greater the rate of decrease.

- Some reference to the data – for example, that in six generations the frequency decreases from 0.50 to 0.44 (a difference of 0.06) with a 10% selection pressure, and from 0.50 to 0.32 (a difference of 0.18) with a 25% selection pressure.

- In Table 11.2, we can see that the number of organisms with genotype AA increases in each generation, and the number of heterozygous organisms decreases. (Learners could calculate these numbers as a percentage of the total number of 'offspring' in each generation.) The rate of change is greater with greater selection pressures.

- In the sample data above, the Generation 5 row for a 10% selection pressure could be identified as an anomalous result, as the proportion of heterozygotes to homozygotes is a lot higher than would be expected according to the general trend.

e No. Heterozygous organisms would still survive and breed, so some **a** alleles would still be passed on to the next generation. (If there is time, learners could model this scenario.)

f Points that could be made include:

- This technique results in the overall number of organisms in each generation decreasing, which is not what would happen in a real population. However, as we are interested in allele *frequencies*, and not in actual numbers of organisms, this model does provide a reasonable illustration of what might happen in a real population.

- In reality, individual alleles do not breed together. In reality, organisms (each with two alleles) breed together, producing more than one offspring each. In this model, we are effectively selecting 'gametes', each with one allele, from the population. Once again, as we are interested in the relative *frequencies* of the two alleles in the population, this technique does provide a valid model.

- The technique selects beans at random, so it represents random mating (i.e. each individual is equally likely to mate with any other individual).

- Learners may comment on any perceived sources of error in their investigation. For example, the learners who obtained the sample results above found that they were more likely to pick up adzuki beans (representing allele **a**) than mung beans (allele **A**), possibly because the adzuki beans were very slightly larger. This appeared to result in a relatively high number of **aa** offspring as they first began to pair alleles from the breeding population, which in turn may have resulted in a relatively low number of **Aa** offspring. If more **aa** offspring were produced, then more **a** alleles would be removed from the population, which would mean that the frequency of the **a** allele would decrease faster than if mating were truly random.

Practical investigation 11.3
Measuring and comparing continuous variation in two sets of leaves

Learning objective: 17.1(c)

Skills focus

The following skills are developed and practised (see the skills grids at the front of this guide):

ACE   Dealing with data: (b), (c), (e), (h), (k), (o), (p)
           Conclusions: (c)

Duration

Collecting the leaves is likely to take around 20 min. This could be done before the lesson, but it is best if learners collect their own leaves, rather than being presented with leaves that have been collected by someone else.

Measuring the leaves is time-consuming, and could take another 20 min. This can be done during non-contact time.

Analysing the results, including the calculations, can again be very time-consuming, and could take around 45 min. Again, this could be done in non-contact time.

Preparing for the investigation

- It would be helpful if learners are familiar with standard deviation, error bars, the concept of a null hypothesis and the *t*-test. However, step-by-step instructions are given for calculating and using each of these.

Equipment

Each learner or group will need:

- ruler to measure in mm.

Access to:

- a tree on which one side is exposed to more sunlight than another, and on which leaves can be easily reached.

Additional notes and advice

- Taking leaves from a single tree is best, as all the leaves will be genetically identical, meaning that differences are caused by the environment. However, if you do not have easy access to a suitable tree, you can use any biological material that shows continuous variation, and where two populations may have different ranges of variation. For example, you could use bean pods from two different varieties of the same species of bean; snail shells from the same species from two different habitats; flowers from the same species of plant growing in wet / dry, or sunny / shady habitats.

Safety considerations

- Learners should have read the safety guidance section within the workbook before carrying out this investigation.

- Standard laboratory safety procedures should be followed always.

- When collecting specimens, learners should always work in pairs.

- Ensure that they can easily reach the leaves without having to climb.

Method

1   Answers will depend on learners' choice of environments.

2   Answers will depend on learners' choice of environments. See the first bullet point in 'Carrying out the investigation' below.

145

Carrying out the investigation

- Step 2 asks learners what they will do to ensure that the only difference between their leaves is the factor they are investigating. This is difficult, because the leaves will also be different ages. One solution is to pick, for example, the third leaf from the tip of a shoot each time. These leaves are likely to be approximately the same age.

Learners are most likely to have difficulties with the calculations. The instructions give step-by-step guidelines, and they could ask you, or another learner, to check each step before they go on to the next one.

Learners could be asked to research differences between shade leaves and sun leaves, and relate their findings to the possible advantage to the tree of having leaves that differ in these different environments.

Sample results

All lengths in mm.

Leaves from sunny side of tree

155, 146, 162, 159, 173, 140, 142, 155, 129, 124, 123, 130, 139, 136, 137, 141, 145, 146, 146, 142, 141, 146, 149, 151, 158, 157, 165, 166, 166, 179

Leaves from shady side of tree

157, 132, 170, 153, 141, 146, 144, 156, 143, 148, 181, 151, 152, 159, 158, 157, 151, 154, 155, 139, 156, 161, 164, 169, 166, 145, 172, 178, 137, 159

	Length / mm						
	120–129	130–139	140–149	150–159	160–169	170–179	180–189
Sunny side	3	4	11	6	4	2	0
Shady side	0	3	6	13	4	3	1

Table 11.5

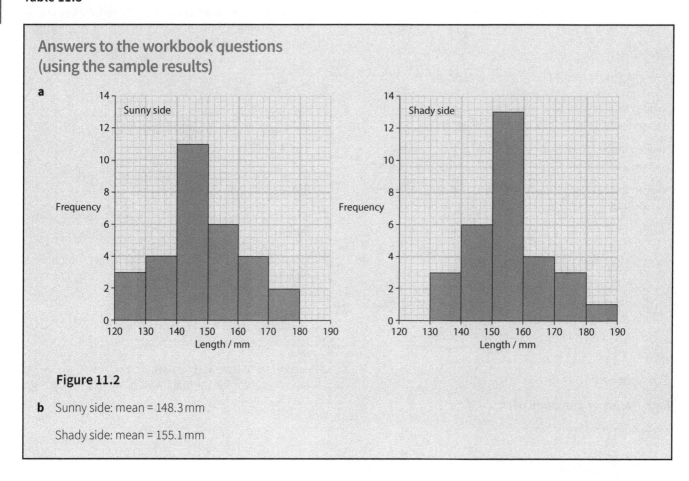

Answers to the workbook questions (using the sample results)

a

Figure 11.2

b Sunny side: mean = 148.3 mm

Shady side: mean = 155.1 mm

c

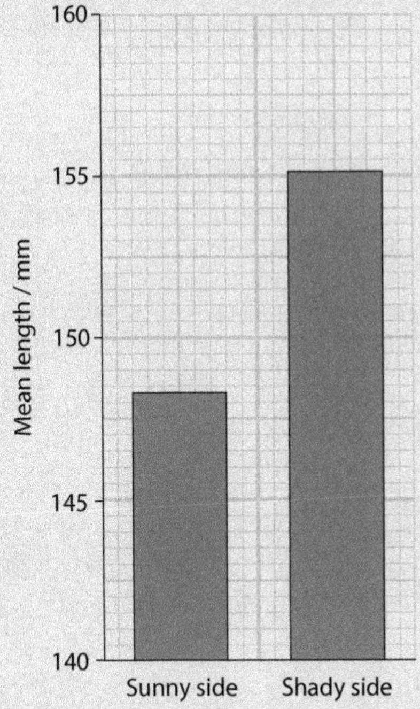

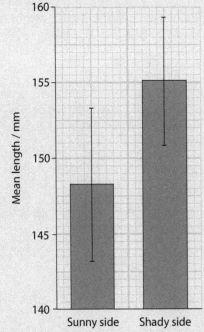

Figure 11.3

d Sunny side: standard deviation = 13.92

Shady side: standard deviation = 11.82

e Sunny side: standard error = 2.54

Shady side: standard error = 2.16

f

Mean length / mm

Figure 11.4

g The error bars do overlap. This means that the difference between the means of the two samples is not statistically significant.

h

$\bar{x}_1 - \bar{x}_1 = 148.3 - 155.1$

$= 6.8$ (the minus sign is ignored)

$$\frac{s_1^2}{n_1} = \frac{13.92^2}{30} = 6.46$$

$$\frac{s_2^2}{n_2} = \frac{11.82^2}{30} = 4.66$$

$$\frac{s_1^2}{n_1} + \frac{s_2^2}{n_2} = 11.12$$

square root of $11.12 = 3.33$

So $t = \dfrac{6.8}{3.33} = 2.04$

i Degrees of freedom: $30 + 30 - 2 = 58$

j 2.04 lies between probabilities 0.05 and 0.01 in the more than 30 row of the table.

This indicates that the probability of the null hypothesis being correct is between 0.01 and 0.05.

k We can say that the difference between the means of the lengths of the leaves from the sunny side and the shady side of the tree is significant.

147

Practical investigation 11.4: Planning
Investigating tongue-rolling

Learning objective: 17.1(a)

Skills focus

The following skills are developed and practised (see the skills grids at the front of this guide):

P   Defining the problem: (a), (b), (c), (e)
           Methods: (a), (b), (c), (g), (j), (k), (l)

ACE   Dealing with data: (a), (b), (c), (d), (e), (h), (i)
           Evaluation: (d), (g), (h), (i), (j), (k)
           Conclusions: (a), (c), (d), (g)

Duration

Initial planning of the investigation is likely to take around 20–30 min. This could possibly be done in non-contact time.

The collection of data for this investigation is best done in non-contact time. Learners can then collect observations from a wider range of subjects than just their own class.

Preparing for the investigation

- Learners should have a firm understanding of the differences between continuous and discontinuous variation.

- You could also ask them to research tongue-rolling on the internet. They are likely to find different information about this, with some sites suggesting that it is a discontinuous feature, controlled entirely by genes, and others providing evidence that it is affected by environment – in particular, by learning.

Equipment

No equipment is required for this investigation.

Safety considerations

- Learners should have read the safety guidance section within the workbook before carrying out this investigation.

- Standard laboratory safety procedures should be followed always.

- Learners should work in pairs when collecting their data.

- Ensure that all learners are aware that they must obtain consent from each subject.

- They should not touch someone else's tongue.

Carrying out the investigation

- This will largely depend on the plan constructed by the learner.

- They may have problems in finding enough subjects.

- It can also be difficult to decide whether or not a tongue is rolled – learners will need to decide on criteria for making this decision.

     Learners could be asked to hand in their plans for you to check, before they carry them out.

     They could be given a 'help sheet' with leading questions to help them to construct their plan.

     Learners who require a challenge could be asked to plan their investigation with a statistical test in mind, and use this to test the significance of any difference that they find between the two groups of subjects.

Sample results

No sample results are provided, as these will depend on the learners' plans.

When marking the work, look for these features:

- The plan is clearly and logically presented, and easy to follow. Someone else could use the plan to carry out the investigation.

- The learner has used a valid method of determining whether environment can affect the ability to roll the tongue. The most likely method is to ask one set of subjects to practise rolling the tongue, while another set is not asked to practise.

- The learner has identified their independent variable (e.g. whether the subjects have practised) and dependent variable (whether they can roll their tongue).

- Attempts are made to control other variables, such as the age of the subjects and the conditions in which they are tested.

- There is a suitable number of subjects – for example, at least 10 and preferably 20 in each group.

- There is a suitable method of determining whether or not the tongue is rolled.

- Results are clearly tabulated, and results tables meet all the appropriate criteria.

- If results have been collected in a suitable form, they are displayed in an appropriate graph.

- Valid conclusions have been drawn from the data.

- The reliability of the conclusions is evaluated appropriately.

Practical investigation 11.5:
Modelling the Hardy–Weinberg equations

Learning objective: 17.2(d)

Skills focus

The following skills are developed and practised (see the skills grids at the front of this guide):

P   Defining the problem: (a)
Methods: (g), (h)

ACE   Dealing with data: (a), (b), (c), (d)
Evaluation: (a), (d), (g), (i)
Conclusions: (a), (c), (d), (g)

Duration

Part 1 is likely to take around 30 min to collect the results, plus more time for analysing the data.

Part 2 will take a similar time, but you will also need to allow time for learners to plan their investigation (which could be done in non-contact time) and to share their results with other groups.

Preparing for the investigation

- It is advisable for learners to have carried out Practical investigation 11.2 before beginning Practical investigation 11.5. If this is not the case, they should refer to the description of the method for that investigation.

Part 1: Modelling the equations with all conditions satisfied

Equipment

Each learner or group will need:

- 150 beans of one type, and 50 of another; the two types of beans should be as similar in size, shape and texture as possible, but should differ in colour

- several containers, for example, beakers

Additional notes and advice

- Mung beans (green) and adzuki beans (reddish brown) are suitable. However, some learners may find them small to work with; it is easy to drop them, or to pick up three at a time instead of two. You may prefer to use larger beans, such as kidney beans.

- Alternatively, any small objects of two different colours can be used, such as pieces of pasta coloured with dye, or beads, or counters.

Safety considerations

- Learners should have read the safety guidance section within the workbook before carrying out this investigation.

- Standard laboratory safety procedures should be followed always

- There are no additional significant safety issues associated with this investigation.

Carrying out the investigation

- See Practical investigation 11.2.

  Learners could be asked to consider how measuring allele frequency in a wild population of organisms could provide evidence about whether the feature affected by that gene is subject to natural selection.

Sample results

Generation 1

Genotype	AA	Aa	aa
Tally	卌 卌 卌 卌 卌 卌 卌 卌 卌 卌 卌 || 卌 卌 卌 卌 卌 卌 卌 卌 卌 ||||
Number	52	44	4

Generation 2

Genotype	AA	Aa	aa
Tally	‖‖ ‖‖ ‖‖ ‖‖ ‖‖ ‖‖ ‖‖ ‖‖ ‖‖ ‖‖ ‖‖ ‖‖	‖‖ ‖‖ ‖‖ ‖‖ ‖‖ ‖‖ ‖‖	‖‖ ‖‖‖‖
Number	59	32	9

Generation 3

Genotype	AA	Aa	aa
Tally	‖‖ ‖‖ ‖‖ ‖‖ ‖‖ ‖‖ ‖‖ ‖‖ ‖‖ ‖‖ ‖‖	‖‖ ‖‖ ‖‖ ‖‖ ‖‖ ‖‖ ‖‖ ‖‖	‖‖
Number	55	40	5

Answers to the workbook questions (using the sample results)

a

Generation	Total number of offspring	Percentage of AA offspring	Frequency of AA offspring	Percentage of Aa offspring	Frequency of Aa offspring	Percentage of aa offspring	Frequency of aa offspring
1	100	52	0.52	44	0.44	4	0.04
2	100	59	0.59	32	0.32	9	0.09
3	100	55	0.55	40	0.40	5	0.05

Table 11.6

b $p = 0.75$ (because there are 150 beans representing the **A** allele, out of a total of 200)

c $q = 0.25$

d $p^2 = 0.5625$

e The mean value for the frequency of **AA** offspring in the three generations is 0.553. This is close to the calculated value of p^2.

f $q^2 = 0.0625$

g The mean value for the frequency of **aa** offspring in the three generations is 0.060. This is close to the calculated value of q^2.

h $2pq = 2 \times 0.75 \times 0.25 = 0.375$

i The mean value for the frequency of **Aa** offspring in the three generations is 0.387. This is close to the calculated value of $2pq$.

Part 2: Modelling the equations with one or more conditions *not* satisfied

The modelling could be carried out as follows:

There is non-random mating

Learners could use two different sizes of beans, so that it is much easier to pick up one type than another – for example, large beans are more likely to 'mate' with other large beans rather than with small beans.

Alternatively, learners could make a conscious decision about which beans 'mate' with which – for example, ensuring that four times out of five, a red bean 'mates' with another red bean rather than with a green bean.

A new mutation arises

Groups could model new mutations that produce more of an allele already present. This would involve replacing, say, two red beans with two green beans in the breeding population. Another approach would be to model a different mutation, by replacing, say, a red bean with a black bean.

There is immigration or emigration

Immigration can be modelled by introducing new beans, perhaps with different proportions of alleles than the original population. Emigration can be modelled by removing a number of beans from the population.

There is natural selection

This has already been modelled in Practical investigation 11.2. There is no need to do this again. Learners could, however, analyse their results from that investigation in terms of p and q.

Sample results

No sample results are provided, as there is a wide range of possibilities depending on the decisions made by the learners about how to carry out their investigation.

Practical investigation 11.6:
The effects of selective breeding in *Brassica oleracea*

Learning objective: 17.2(f)

Skills focus

This investigation does not involve planning or evaluation skills.

Duration

Allow approximately 1 h for studying the plants, collecting and recording information. Question **a** could be done later, and will require no more than 10 min.

Preparing for the investigation

- Learners should understand how selective breeding is carried out.

Equipment

Each learner or group will need:

- at least three different varieties of *Brassica*. These should be fresh, so the varieties will be determined by whatever you can obtain locally. If possible, try to provide complete plants.

- ruler to measure in mm.

Safety considerations

- Learners should have read the safety guidance section within the workbook before carrying out this investigation.

- Standard laboratory safety procedures should be followed always.

- There are no additional significant safety issues associated with this investigation.

Carrying out the investigation

- There are unlikely to be any significant problems with this investigation.

  Some learners may need guidance in selecting suitable features for comparison, and constructing a suitable table.

  Learners who require a challenge could use the internet to research the possible origins of the different cultivars of *B. oleracea*.

Sample results

No sample results are given, as these will depend on the varieties of *Brassica* that you are able to supply.

Look for these features in the comparison table:

- Results are presented in a table drawn with ruled lines.

- Columns are clearly headed. Where measurements are included, units are in the table headings and each value is given to the same number of decimal places.

- Comparable points are written in the same row.

- At least five different points of comparison are made.

- Descriptions are clear, brief and accurate. Biological terminology is used throughout.

Answers to the workbook questions (using the sample results)

a The description of selective breeding will depend on the variety that is chosen by the learner. Points to be made should include:

- selection of parents with the desirable feature

- how the two parents are bred together (e.g. pollen taken from one to fertilise the other; prevention of pollination by other pollen by removing anthers from the flower to be pollinated, and covering it)

- collection of seeds

- sowing seeds

- growing plants to maturity

- selecting mature plants showing the desirable feature to the greatest degree

- repetition for several generations.

Practical investigation 11.7: Planning

Comparing vitamin C content in two cultivars of *Brassica oleracea*

Learning objective: 17.2(f)

Skills focus

The following skills are developed and practised (see the skills grids at the front of this guide):

P   Defining the problem: (a), (b), (c), (d), (e)
           Methods: (b), (c), (d), (g), (h)

ACE   Dealing with data: (a), (b), (d), (e), (h), (i), (j), (k), (o), (p),
           Evaluation: (d), (i)
           Conclusions: (a), (b), (c), (d), (g)

Duration

Learners are likely to need around 30 min to initially plan their investigation.

If they test just one sample from each cultivar, this will take around 15 min. However, if their plans include testing multiple samples (as they should if they plan to carry out a statistical analysis of their results), this could take up to 1 h.

Analysis of results can be done in non-contact time and will require approximately 30 min.

Preparing for the investigation

- Learners may have met the DCPIP test for vitamin C (ascorbic acid) at IGCSE. However, it would be a good idea to demonstrate this test to them. Details can be found at:

  Details can be found on the Nuffield Foundation website; click on the Teachers tab, and then search in the Practical Biology section.

- Another good source of information relevant to this investigation is:

  Another good source of information relevant to this investigation is the Science and Plants for Schools website, where you can find detailed instructions for measuring changes in ascorbic acid concentration in ripening fruit and vegetables.

Planning

The null hypothesis could be:

There is no significant difference between the vitamin C content of the two *Brassica* cultivars.

Variables

- The independent variable is identified as the two different types of *B. oleracea*.

- The dependent variable is identified as the concentration of vitamin C, measured through the volume of DCPIP that is decolourised.

- Key variables to be controlled are identified as the mass of *Brassica* used, the volume of water it is mixed with and the concentration of DCPIP used. Other control variables might include the freshness of the *Brassica* samples, and the temperature.

Equipment

Each learner or group will need:

- two different cultivars of *Brassica*

- pestles and mortars and/or food processor

- pieces of muslin for filtering the samples

- freshly-made solution of DCPIP, 1% (2,6-dichlorophenol-indophenol; this can be bought as a powder)

- a selection of test tubes and/or boiling tubes and racks

- small conical flasks

- a selection of apparatus for measuring volume, to include syringes, measuring cylinders of different sizes, burettes and calibrated pipettes

- glass rods

- timers.

The diagram of the apparatus should include:

- apparatus for producing an extract from the *Brassica* plants, for example, pestle and mortar, or a liquidiser

- glassware or other containers that will allow measured volumes of the *Brassica* extract to be added to a measured volume of DCPIP **or** a measured volume of DCPIP to be added to a measured volume of *Brassica* extract; one of these liquids could be in a conical flask, beaker or test tube, with the liquid to be added in a burette or graduated pipette.

Additional notes and advice

- If only one type of *Brassica* cultivar can be obtained, learners could compare the vitamin C content of two parts of the plant, for example, cauliflower florets and leaves. A third possibility is to investigate the effect of storage time or method on vitamin C concentration.

Safety considerations

- Learners should have read the safety guidance section within the workbook before carrying out this investigation.

- Standard laboratory safety procedures should be followed always.

- There are no specific safety concerns with this investigation, other than those that are always present when handling glassware.

Carrying out the investigation

- The *Brassica* extracts, even when filtered, may not flow easily. It is therefore best to measure a set volume of extract into a test tube or conical flask, and then add DCPIP using a burette, rather than trying to add the extract to a measured volume of DCPIP. This also avoids having to clean the burette between samples.

- If the volumes of DCPIP that are added before the endpoint is reached are very small, learners could try using a 0.1% solution of DCPIP instead of 1%. If the volumes of DCPIP used are very large, try diluting the *Brassica* extracts.

- The endpoint is often not easy to determine precisely. It may be helpful to set up two reference tubes, showing the DCPIP colour with and without vitamin C present.

   Minimum guidance is given for this planning exercise, and some learners may need structured support to help them to construct a plan. You could provide this as a 'help sheet'. However, it may be better for learners to work in pairs or groups of three, so that they can discuss their ideas with each other.

   If you are able to obtain pure ascorbic acid (vitamin C) powder or tablets, learners who require a challenge could be asked to make up a range of solutions with different concentrations of vitamin C, using serial dilution. They can then measure how much DCPIP solution is decolourised by a standard volume of each concentration. They can then construct a calibration curve, with concentration (or mass) of vitamin C on the *x*-axis and volume of 1% DCPIP decolourised on the *y*-axis. They can then use this curve to find the concentration (or mass) of vitamin C in their *Brassica* samples, and convert this to mg of vitamin C in g of *Brassica*. (They should find that 1 cm³ of 1% DCPIP is decolourised by about 6.1 mg of vitamin C. Typical values for vitamin C concentration in *Brassica* leaves range between 100 and 450 mg per 100 g of leaf, but lower and higher values than these may be encountered.)

Sample results

25 g of leaf mashed with 250 cm³ of water.

1% DCPIP solution added until decolourised.

Brassica cultivar 1

Sample	Volume of 1% DCPIP decolourised / cm³
1	9.6
2	9.9
3	9.6
4	9.5
5	9.7
6	9.7
7	9.8
8	9.8
9	9.7
10	9.6

Table 11.7

mean = 9.7 cm³

standard deviation = 0.120

standard error = 0.038

Brassica cultivar 2

Sample	Volume of 1% DCPIP decolourised / cm³
1	9.5
2	9.2
3	9.3
4	9.5
5	9.5
6	9.4
7	9.3
8	9.4
9	9.6
10	9.6

Table 11.8

mean = 9.4 cm³

standard deviation = 0.134

standard error = 0.042

For the plan, look for the following points:

- The method for obtaining equivalent samples of *Brassica* is clearly described. This should involve measuring a standard mass and mashing it into a standard volume of water, followed by filtering. For example, 25 g of *Brassica* leaf could be crushed with 250 cm³ of distilled water and then filtered through muslin.

- Repeats are used, with at least five samples taken from each *Brassica* cultivar.

- Suitable choices are made of apparatus for measuring volume. Ideally, the DCPIP solution should be placed into a burette, so that measured volumes can be added to the *Brassica* extracts. The volume of *Brassica* extract can be measured using calibrated pipettes (if it does not contain pieces of plant tissue, which might get stuck in the narrow tube), small measuring cylinders or syringes.

- A suitable method is chosen for adding DCPIP solution to a measured volume of *Brassica* extract, and determining the endpoint. For example, the *Brassica* extract could be placed into a conical flask, and DCPIP added from a burette. The endpoint is reached when the DCPIP keeps its colour.

- Results are clearly tabulated (see sample results).

- The mean volume of DCPIP decolourised is calculated for each of the two *Brassica* cultivars.

Answers to the workbook questions (using the sample results)

a   A bar graph is drawn to show the mean values for the two cultivars. Standard error is calculated, and used to draw error bars on the graph. Some learners may also decide to carry out a *t*-test to determine if the means are significantly different.

b   The evaluation identifies major sources of error (uncertainty) that affect the reliability of the results. These should include the difficulty of achieving uniformity in the samples taken (there will be variability in how fully the tissue is mashed and how well it is filtered) and difficulty in determining the precise endpoint. Learners may also comment on uncertainty in reading volumes. If a *t*-test has been carried out, its results are correctly applied to determine whether any difference between the two samples is significant.

Chapter 12:
Ecology

Chapter outline

This chapter relates to Chapter 18: Biodiversity, classification and conservation in the coursebook.

In this chapter, learners will complete practical investigations on:

- 12.1 Using frame quadrats to assess abundance of organisms
- 12.2 Using frame quadrats to compare biodiversity in two habitats
- 12.3 Using a transect to investigate distribution and abundance of species
- 12.4 Investigating a possible correlation between species distribution and an abiotic factor
- 12.5 Estimating the population size of a small, mobile invertebrate

Introduction

The five investigations included in this chapter all relate to Section 18.1 in the syllabus, *Biodiversity*. They provide opportunities for learners to meet the requirements of learning objectives **18.1(c)**, **(d)**, **(e)** and **(f)** through first-hand experience.

The instructions for the investigations are, by necessity, quite general. The exact nature of the investigations that learners can carry out depends on the areas where they are able to work, and the type of organisms that they will find there. It is almost always possible to find an area where ecological investigations can be done. For example, you may be able to take learners out from school for a day to visit a rocky shore, a patch of grassland or a woodland. There may be a suitable area in the school grounds, such as a lawn, a playing field or a cultivated patch of ground that has weeds growing on it. If there are no large-scale areas available, then perhaps there may be a wall or a tree trunk with moss, lichens or algae growing on it where sampling can be done on a small scale.

Ecology investigations can be very time-consuming. You may need to allow time to travel to the area to be sampled, and learners can take a long time to collect data. You could therefore consider collecting data for two or more investigations on one visit. For example, on a one-day visit to a suitable site, learners could collect data for Practical investigations 12.1, 12.2 and 12.3.

No instructions are provided for investigations relating to Chapter 19, because it is difficult for most schools to obtain apparatus and materials for this topic. However, if you would like to do investigations relating to PCR (19.1c) or gel electrophoresis (19.1d), kits and detailed protocols are available in the UK through the website of the National Centre for Biotechnology Education, based in Reading, UK.

Practical investigation 12.1:
Using frame quadrats to assess abundance of organisms

Learning objective: 18.1(d)

Skills focus

The following skills are developed and practised (see the skills grids at the front of this guide)

ACE	Dealing with data: (g)
	Evaluation: (d), (i)
	Conclusions: (g)

Duration

Depending on the nature of the site that learners will be sampling, it could take as little as 1 h or as much as half a day to collect data. Alternatively, you could share out the work between different groups, so that each group collects data from just one or two quadrats, and then pool the data.

You could consider combining this investigation with Practical investigation 12.2, if it is possible to sample two different areas within the same time period.

Data analysis is likely to take around 45–60 min.

Preparing for the investigation

- You will need to familiarise learners with the organisms that they will find in their quadrats. If possible, provide keys and names for the organisms you expect them to find. If organisms cannot be named, learners can simply identify them as species A, species B and so on.

Equipment

Each learner or group will need:

- quadrat with sides of 0.50 m

- two long measuring tapes

- a set of random numbers, or a means of generating them (e.g. a phone app).

Safety considerations

- Learners should have read the safety guidance section within the workbook before carrying out this investigation.

- Standard laboratory safety procedures should be followed always.

- Check the area to be studied beforehand, to ensure that it is free of risks such as broken glass or poisonous plants.

- Learners should work in pairs, so that if one has an accident there is always someone close by to help out.

Carrying out the investigation

- The main difficulty is likely to be the identification of the different species within the quadrat. Good preparation beforehand can make this manageable.

- Decision-making about percentage cover can be tricky. Using a quadrat divided into smaller squares, as shown in Figure 12.2 in the workbook, is very helpful.

- If learners are assessing percentage cover in a well-vegetated area, explain to them it is acceptable to record values that add up to more than 100%. Also, if the vegetation does not cover all of the ground, they could record values of percentage cover of 'bare ground'.

  All learners are likely to need support when first attempting to identify organisms within a quadrat, and estimating their abundance.

- For this first ecology investigation, it is best if all learners simply collect data about the abundance of different species of organisms within their quadrats, rather than attempting to do anything more complex.

  Learners who need a challenge could try collecting data in two formats – for example, percentage cover and an abundance scale such as Braun–Blanquet – and then discuss the advantages and disadvantages of each.

Sample results

The results provided in Table 12.1 are for quadrats on a rocky shore, where organisms were counted as individuals.

Quadrat	Number of individuals				
	species A	species B	species C	species D	species E
1	6	5	0	0	2
2	0	7	14	0	0
3	12	3	0	0	0
4	2	6	1	1	3
5	0	2	18	0	0
6	0	2	12	0	1
7	15	5	0	4	0
8	0	8	23	0	0
9	0	4	13	0	0
10	1	3	2	0	2
mean	3.6	4.5	8.3	0.5	0.8

Table 12.1

Answers to the workbook questions (using the sample results)

a See Table 12.1. Note: means should be calculated to the same number of decimal places, or one more than, the individual results.

b Quadrats used had sides of 0.50 m.

   i total area of habitat = 480 m²

   ii total area sampled = $0.5 \times 0.5 \times 10 = 2.5\,m^2$

   iii Estimated number of organisms of species A in the whole habitat $= \dfrac{3.6 \times 480}{2.5} = 691$

c The most important sources of error are likely to be:

- Only a small number of samples were taken within a very large area, so we cannot be sure that the sample is genuinely representative of the whole area.

- If percentage cover or an abundance scale were used, it is not possible to estimate these precisely.

d The suggested improvements should relate to the major sources of error identified in the answer to **c**. These could include collecting more data from more samples, and improving the method for estimating percentage cover, for example, by taking high-definition photographs of the contents of each quadrat, and then analysing them systematically on a computer screen or printout.

Practical investigation 12.2:
Using frame quadrats to compare biodiversity in two habitats

Learning objectives: 18.1(d), 18.1(f)

Skills focus

The following skills are developed and practised (see the skills grids at the front of this guide)

ACE   Dealing with data: (f)
        Evaluation: (d), (j)
        Conclusions: (g)

Duration

If suitable, you could use the data collected in Practical investigation 12.1 as the first set of data, so that learners need only collect data from one more area rather than from two.

As for Practical investigation 12.1, you may need to allow up to half a day for the collection of data. Again, you could share out the work between different groups, so that each group collects data from just one or two quadrats, and then pool the data.

Data analysis is likely to take around 45–60 min.

Preparing for the investigation

- It is important to select two suitable areas for this investigation. Select a habitat where it is possible to count individual organisms (rather than using percentage cover), as this is required for the calculation for Simpson's diversity index. Learners are likely to gain most from their investigation if two areas that are basically similar, but with a clear difference between them, are chosen. Examples could include:

   ◦ a sheltered rocky shore and an exposed rocky shore (count sedentary animals)

   ◦ two different areas of woodland (use large quadrats marked out with measuring tapes, and count understory shrubs and/or trees)

- If no large areas are available, then consider sampling a much smaller habitat. For example, learners could compare the biodiversity of lichens on a north-facing and a south-facing surface, or on the trunks of two different species of tree. This has the advantage that data can be collected in a relatively short period of time.

- You will need to familiarise learners with the organisms that they will find in their quadrats. If possible, provide keys and names for the organisms you expect them to find. If organisms cannot be named, learners can simply identify them as species A, species B and so on.

Equipment

Each learner or group will need:

- quadrat with sides of 0.50 m (or as required for the selected area)

- two long measuring tapes.

157

Safety considerations

- Learners should have read the safety guidance section within the workbook before carrying out this investigation.

- Standard laboratory safety procedures should be followed always.

- Check the area to be studied beforehand, to ensure that it is free of risks such as broken glass or poisonous plants.

- Learners should work in pairs, so that if one has an accident there is always someone close by to help out.

Carrying out the investigation

- When collecting data to calculate Simpson's index, it is important that all relevant species encountered are counted.

- As the total range of species of all classification groups is likely to be unmanageably large, it is usually a good idea to restrict learners to a particular group of species – for example, just animals (ignoring seaweeds) on a rocky shore.

Sample results

The results provided below are for two rocky shores. They include the results from Practical investigation 12.1 and a new set.

Answers to the workbook questions (using the sample results)

a

Species	Number in Area 1	Number in Area 2
A	36	60
B	45	41
C	83	27
D	5	0
E	8	0
F	0	14
G	0	21
H	0	1

Table 12.2

b For Area 1:

total number of individuals of all species, N, in Area 1 = 177

c

Species	Number, n	$n \div N$	$(n \div N)^2$
A	36	0.203	0.041
B	45	0.254	0.065
C	83	0.469	0.220
D	5	0.028	0.001
E	8	0.045	0.002

Table 12.3

d $\sum(n \div N)^2 = 0.329$

e $1 - \sum(n \div N)^2 = 0.671$

f For Area 2, $N = 164$

Species	Number, n	$n \div N$	$(n \div N)^2$
A	60	0.366	0.134
B	41	0.250	0.63
C	27	0.165	0.027
F	14	0.085	0.007
G	21	0.128	0.016
H	1	0.006	0.000

Table 12.4

$\sum(n \div N)^2 = 0.247$

$1 - \sum(n \div N)^2 = 0.753$

g This analysis shows that Simpson's diversity index for Area 2 is greater than that for Area 1. We can say that the biodiversity of Area 2 is greater than that for Area 1.

h The most likely way of increasing confidence in these results and analysis is to carry out a fuller survey of the two areas. A larger proportion of each area should be sampled, using more quadrats. Learners may also suggest that species could be identified to a better level – for example, they might have classed all limpets as the same species, whereas there could be more than one species present.

Practical investigation 12.3:
Using a transect to investigate distribution and abundance of species

Learning objective: 18.1(d)

Skills focus

The following skills are developed and practised (see the skills grids at the front of this guide)

ACE   Dealing with data: (c)
        Conclusions: (e)

Duration

You may need to allow up to half a day for the collection of data. You could share out the work between different groups, so that each group collects data from part of a transect. However, this is not very satisfying for learners as they will not see any changes in species distribution along the length of it.

Data analysis is likely to take around 45–60 min.

Preparing for the investigation

- It is important to select a suitable area for this investigation. Select a habitat where there is a transition from one area to another. Suitable examples include:

  ◦ from sea level to the top of a rocky shore

  ◦ from a grassy area that gets a lot of sunlight to a grassy area that is more shaded

  ◦ from moist ground to drier ground.

- If you cannot take learners to a large area of ground, consider doing this investigation on a small scale. They could sample along a mini-transect that runs from ground level to a couple of metres up a tree trunk, for example.

Equipment

Each learner or group will need:

- quadrat with sides of 0.50 m (or as required for the selected area)

- a long measuring tape

- string

- pegs to hold string in place.

Safety considerations

- Learners should have read the safety guidance section within the workbook before carrying out this investigation.

- Standard laboratory safety procedures should be followed always.

- Check the area to be studied beforehand, to ensure that it is free of risks such as broken glass or poisonous plants.

- Learners should work in pairs, so that if one has an accident there is always someone close by to help out.

Carrying out the investigation

- Difficulties may be encountered if the transect runs across areas of ground that are difficult to access – for example, across a deep rock cleft in a rocky shore. Safety must be paramount, so check each group's transect position before they start.

  Learners may come across a wider range of species than in their previous investigations, so you will need to help out with identification if necessary. If species cannot be identified by name, then – as before – learners can simply assign a letter to each one.

- If they are working on a rocky shore, learners should begin their survey at low tide, and work from the lowest point of the shore upwards.

Sample results

The data are from a transect running from sea level to the top of a rocky shore. An interrupted belt transect was used, with 0.5 m quadrats placed at 2.0 m intervals. The Braun–Blanquet scale was used to assess the abundance of organisms within each quadrat.

Note that, ideally, learners should find the **height** of each data point above extreme low water springs, so that they can convert distance along the transect to height above sea level. This is worthwhile, but also very time-consuming, so has not been suggested in the practical instructions, and is not included in these data.

Note that the data have been organised with 0 at the bottom of the table, as this is easier for learners to visualise. (As you go down the table, you go down the shore towards the sea.)

The data presented here have been considerably simplified, with only 10 species shown.

159

Distance above water level /m	Laminaria	Himanthalia	Pelvetia	Corallina	Fucus	Patella	Pollicipes	Other barnacles	Mytilus	Verrucaria
16	0	0	0	0	0	0	0	0	0	3
14	0	0	0	0	0	0	0	2	0	1
12	0	0	1	0	2	1	0	4	2	0
10	0	0	0	0	3	1	0	3	1	0
8	0	0	0	1	2	0	0	4	2	0
6	0	0	0	2	1	1	2	2	4	0
4	0	1	0	3	0	1	2	4	2	0
2	1	3	0	3	0	1	1	0	0	0
0	5	0	0	0	0	1	0	0	0	0

Table 12.5

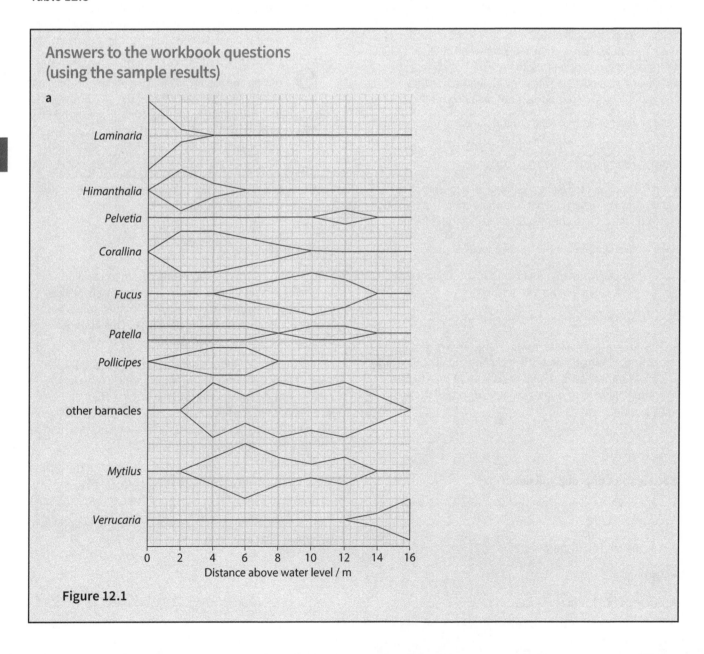

Figure 12.1

b Learners are asked to select two examples. Their answers will depend on their choice from the sample results, or from their own results.

c Answers will depend on the learners' chosen species. For example, they could consider how well the species are able to survive desiccation, with those species found higher up the shore likely to have adaptations that allow them to retain water for long periods. Those living lower down the shore are less likely to have such adaptations, but must be able to compete successfully with other organisms that also need to be under water most of the time.

d For the sample data, an interrupted belt transect was used. A line transect was not suitable, because relatively few organisms would be found touching the line. A continuous belt transect would be possible, but a very large number of quadrats would then have to be analysed, in order to cover the whole distance from the bottom of the shore to 16 m above water level.

Practical investigation 12.4: Planning

Investigating a possible correlation between species distribution and an abiotic factor

Learning objective: 18.1(e)

Skills focus

The following skills are developed and practised (see the skills grids at the front of this guide)

Planning	Defining the problem: (a)
	Methods: (g), (k), (l)
ACE	Dealing with data: (a), (i)
	Evaluation: (i)
	Conclusions: (a), (b), (f)

Duration

The time required for collecting data for this investigation will greatly depend on the habitat within which learners will collect their data. It could take anything between 1 h and half a day.

Learners may be able to use their results from the transect, in Practical investigation 12.3, to generate a hypothesis that explains differences in distribution of one of the species along the transect. You could simply ask learners to reuse these results, which would greatly reduce the time required here. However, in order to use the required statistical tests, the data should have been collected using random sampling. They should place quadrats randomly in an area, and measure both the abundance of their chosen species, and the chosen abiotic factor, within each quadrat.

Data analysis is likely to take about 1 h.

Preparing for the investigation

- Learners will need to be familiar with a method for measuring their chosen abiotic factor.

- They need to know how to use Spearman's rank correlation and/or Pearson's linear correlation. They should understand the type of data that they will need to collect in order to be able to use these statistical tests.

- For Spearman's rank correlation, data must:

  ○ consist of data for two variables

  ○ have been collected randomly

  ○ include at least five pairs of data, but ideally between 10 and 30 pairs

  ○ show a possible correlation on a scatter diagram.

- For Pearson's linear correlation, data must:

  ○ consist of two sets of interval data, both of which show an approximately normal distribution

  ○ include at least five pairs of data, but preferably 10 or more

  ○ show an approximately linear correlation on a scatter diagram.

Equipment

Each learner or group will need:

- a quadrat with sides of 0.50 m (or as required for the selected area)

- a long measuring tape

- a meter for measuring their chosen abiotic factor.

Additional notes and advice

- Relatively inexpensive multifunction meters (to measure light intensity, pH and soil moisture) for use in ecological investigations are available from educational suppliers.

- If learners are investigating time of exposure to air as the abiotic factor on a rocky shore, this can be calculated from tide tables.

Safety considerations

- Learners should have read the safety guidance section within the workbook before carrying out this investigation.

- Standard laboratory safety procedures should be followed always.

- Check the area to be studied beforehand, to ensure that it is free of risks such as broken glass or poisonous plants.

- Learners should work in pairs, so that if one has an accident there is always someone close by to help out.

Carrying out the investigation

- Problems learners may encounter will depend on the choice of habitat, species and abiotic factor.

- Inexpensive meters (e.g. for light or soil moisture) may need care in use in order to obtain useful readings. Follow any instructions provided with the meter carefully.

- It will be important to make all measurements of the abiotic factor in the same way, in the same conditions. For example, if the chosen abiotic factor is light, all readings should be taken with the meter pointing in the same direction in relation to the Sun. Ideally, several readings should be taken in each quadrat at the same time of day, or over a given time period, and a mean value calculated. This will help to compensate for differences in cloud cover or height of the Sun at different times.

  Learners may need reminding that even if they do find a statistically significant correlation, this does not imply causation.

  Learners may need considerable help in organising their results so that they can carry out a suitable statistical test. You could provide them with a structured worksheet to lead them through each step in their chosen test.

  If learners do find a significant correlation between the distribution of the organism and the abiotic factor, they could be asked to plan an experiment to find out if there is a causal relationship between them.

Sample results

Habitat studied: A field with patches of relatively damp and relatively dry ground

Species investigated: *Carex aquatilis* (a species of sedge)

Abiotic factor: soil moisture content

Soil moisture content was measured using a meter that provides readings from 0 (no detectable moisture) to 10 (very wet). Five readings were taken within each quadrat, and a mean calculated.

Quadrats were placed randomly, using pairs of random numbers as coordinates. Each quadrat had sides of 0.5 m, and divided into smaller squares to help with estimation of percentage cover.

Quadrat number	Percentage cover of *C. aquatilis*	Moisture content / a.u.					
		1	2	3	4	5	mean
1	5	4.0	3.2	3.8	4.0	3.7	3.74
2	0	3.0	2.8	2.8	2.5	3.0	2.82
3	24	7.3	7.5	7.3	7.2	7.5	7.36
4	0	2.7	3.0	2.8	2.8	2.9	2.84
5	9	4.0	4.3	4.0	4.5	4.2	4.20
6	15	7.1	7.0	7.2	7.5	7.0	7.16
7	0	2.8	2.7	2.5	2.8	2.6	2.68
8	0	2.4	2.7	2.4	2.5	2.5	2.50
9	2	2.6	2.3	2.4	2.3	2.4	2.40
10	12	7.0	6.9	6.8	7.0	6.9	6.92

Table 12.6

Answers to the workbook questions
(using the sample results)

a

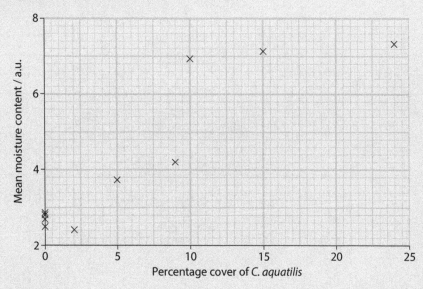

Figure 12.2

b The scatter graph shows that there seems to be a correlation, but that this does not appear to be linear. The most suitable statistical test is therefore Spearman's rank correlation.

Quadrat	Percentage cover of *C. aquatilis*	Rank for percentage cover	Moisture content / a.u.	Rank for moisture content
1	5	5	3.74	5
2	0	(7=) 8.5	2.82	7
3	24	1	7.36	1
4	0	(7=) 8.5	2.84	6
5	9	4	4.20	4
6	15	2	7.16	2
7	0	(7=) 8.5	2.68	8
8	0	(7=) 8.5	2.50	9
9	2	6	2.40	10
10	12	3	6.92	3

Table 12.7

Note that for the tied ranks (there are four values of 0 for percentage cover) each of the tied values is assigned a value of 8.5 (the mean of 7, 8, 9 and 10).

Quadrat	Rank for percentage cover	Rank for moisture content	Difference in rank, D	D^2
1	5	5	0	0
2	8.5	7	1.5	2.25
3	1	1	0	0
4	8.5	6	2.5	6.25
5	4	4	0	0
6	2	2	0	0
7	8.5	8	0.5	0.25
8	8.5	9	0.5	0.25
9	6	10	4	16
10	3	3	0	0

Table 12.8

$\sum D^2 = 25$

$$r_s = 1 - \left(\frac{6 \times \sum D^2}{n^3 - n} \right)$$

$$= 1 - 0.152$$

$$= 0.848$$

c   Looking this up in a probability table (see Practical investigation 8.2) gives a probability of well above the critical value of 0.05 that there is a significant correlation between soil moisture content and the abundance of *C. aquatilis*.

d   These answers will depend on the learners' experience in the field. They may comment on difficulties in placing quadrats, estimating percentage cover or using the meter. For example, the data in the sample results have produced quite large variations in moisture content readings with a single quadrat – were these genuine differences, or do they indicate that the meter is not giving accurate readings? Having identified potential sources of error such as these, learners can then suggest ways of reducing each one.

All learners should be expected to state that increasing the number of samples would be useful. It would also be useful to repeat the investigation in other areas where this species of sedge is found.

Practical investigation 12.5
Estimating the population size of a small, mobile invertebrate

Learning objective: 18.1(d)

Skills focus

The following skills are developed and practised (see the skills grids at the front of this guide):

ACE   Conclusions: (g)

Duration

Allow between 20 and 30 min for collecting and marking the first sample of animals.

Allow another 20–30 min for collecting the second sample.

The calculation and evaluation will take another 10 min.

Preparing for the investigation

- You will need to select a suitable animal to be used, and suitable areas where learners can look for them.

- You also need to select a suitable method of marking them.

Equipment

Each learner or group will need:

- small containers, preferably with lids

- a method of marking the animals (e.g. very small brush and non-toxic paint)

- if required, gloves and/or apparatus for handling the animals (e.g. a pooter or blunt forceps).

Safety considerations

- Learners should have read the safety guidance section within the workbook before carrying out this investigation.

- Standard laboratory safety procedures should be followed always.

- Check the area to be studied beforehand, to ensure that it is free of risks such as broken glass or poisonous plants.

- Learners should work in pairs, so that if one has an accident there is always someone close by to help out.

Carrying out the investigation

- It may be difficult to find enough animals to make the population estimate reliable. Your choice of animals will depend on what is available in the habitats in which learners can work. Woodlice and snails are often present in quite large numbers in school grounds, for example.

- The marked animals must be given time to mix back into the general population. Usually, 24 h is sufficient for this, even with slow-moving animals such as snails.

- If you are unable to do this investigation with real animals, it can be modelled. Take a large container and fill it with sand. Bury a known, large (for example, 300 or more) number of 'animals' (e.g. beans, beads, counters) in the sand. Ask learners to 'capture' about 30 animals and mark them, then mix them back into the sand. They can capture a second sample, and use the formula to calculate their estimate for the total population size, which they can then compare with the actual population size.

Learners may need reminding to release the animals in the same place that they were found. They need to be well-organised to ensure that they capture, mark and release the animals with the least likelihood of harming them.

Learners could be asked to suggest how this technique could be modified for estimating population sizes of much larger animals, for example, elephants.

Sample results

These results are for woodlice captured in a small quadrangle between school buildings.

Number caught and marked in first sample: 32

Number caught in second sample: 71

	Marked animals in second sample	Unmarked animals in second sample
Tally	‖‖ ‖‖ ‖‖‖	‖‖ ‖‖ ‖‖ ‖‖ ‖‖ ‖‖ ‖‖ ‖‖ ‖‖ ‖‖ ‖‖ ‖‖
Number	14	57

Answers to the workbook questions (using the sample results)

a Estimated number in population = (32 × 71) ÷ 14 = 162

b The animals captured in the first sample may not have mixed fully with the rest of the population.

The marked animals may have been more likely to be eaten by predators. This would reduce the number of marked animals in the second sample, and would make the population appear to be larger than it really is.